COMMON STOCKS
FOR COMMON
SENSE INVESTORS

COMMON STOCKS FOR COMMON SENSE INVESTORS

William E. Mitchell
Thomas R. Ireland

JOHN WILEY & SONS
New York • Chichester • Brisbane • Toronto • Singapore

Copyright © 1986 by William E. Mitchell and Thomas R. Ireland
Published by John Wiley & Sons, Inc.

All rights reserved. Published simultaneously in Canada.

Reproduction or translation of any part of this work
beyond that permitted by Sections 107 or 108 of the
1976 United States Copyright Act without the permission
of the copyright owner is unlawful. Requests for
permission or further information should be addressed to
the Permissions Department, John Wiley & Sons, Inc.

This publication is designed to provide accurate and
authoritative information in regard to the subject
matter covered. It is sold with the understanding that
the publisher is not engaged in rendering legal, accounting,
or other professional service. If legal advice or other
expert assistance is required, the services of a competent
professional person should be sought. *From a Declaration
of Principles jointly adopted by a Committee of the
American Bar Association and a Committee of Publishers.*

Library of Congress Cataloging in Publication Data:

Mitchell, William E., 1936–
  Common stocks for common sense investors.

  Includes index.
  1. Stocks. 2. Investments. I. Ireland, Thomas R.,
1942–   II. Title.

HG4661.M56 1986   332.63'22   85-17969
ISBN 0-471-82057-1

Printed in the United States of America

10 9 8 7 6 5 4 3 2

To
Ann Rose and Bill,
loving and supportive parents
WEM

To
Deron and Tera,
my son and daughter
TRI

PREFACE

The first law of investing is: "There's no such thing as a free lunch." But it's a hard law to follow. Although deep down we know we only get what we pay for, it's fun to dream of getting something for nothing. And Lady Luck, in her capricious way, passes out just enough windfall gains to keep our hopes up. After all, someone will win the million dollar lottery. That's why the first law of Wall Street is: "You can make a good living *promising* investors a free lunch." Most brokers and investment advisors promise high rates of return for investors who buy their advice on how to beat the market. With a beat-the-market strategy, temporarily mispriced stocks are bought and sold from uninformed investors who don't realize the true value of the stocks they are trading. In doing this, "smart" investors are supposed to get rich by taking money away from "dumb" investors. (It's not surprising that Wall Street brokers and analysts nearly always recommend trying to beat the market. In-and-out trading generates much larger commissions and advisory fees than buy-and-hold investing.)

Research over the past 25 years has built up overwhelming evidence that trying to beat the market simply doesn't work. Indeed, the result is quite the opposite. Investors who pay unnecessary commissions, advisory fees, and premature capital gains taxes in a futile attempt to beat the market will earn *below* average investment returns. Higher investment returns can only be earned by taking higher risk. This book explains why beat-the-market investing can be hazardous to your financial health and why return–risk tradeoffs exist and must be incorporated as a central feature of any successful financial investment plan.

Although you can't expect a free lunch from common stock investments, you can expect a *fair* lunch. Common stocks offer a very good investment return for the risks taken and represent the most convenient way for most people to invest. You won't get rich quick with stocks, but you can get rich slowly. On a risk-adjusted basis, the investment returns on stocks are as high or higher than real estate (and don't require the specialized knowledge) and are far superior to the so-called tangible investments, such as gold, art, and collectibles.

This book provides a commonsense approach to investing in common stocks. We provide everything you need to know to set up and manage a profitable investment program, including:

how to manage financial risk.

how to construct a diversified portfolio of individual stocks.

how to use mutual funds to improve overall financial results.

how to buy stocks with little or no commissions.

how to choose the best discount broker.

In the appendixes we provide the basic data you need in order for you to carry out your investment plan, including valuable information not available elsewhere on corporate dividend reinvestment plans and commission rates charged by discount brokers. The wherefore's and how to's of successful investing are summarized in four easy-to-understand steps, which we call the total investment portfolio planning (TIPP) investment strategy. With TIPP, your financial management will be as good as the best and better than most.

We wish to thank the scholars and practitioners who have devoted countless hours of research and hard work to the study of financial economics. Without their published work, this book could not have been written. Because this book is intended for a general audience, however, we have limited references to the financial literature in order to avoid interrupting the flow of words and ideas where no practical purpose is served. The Postscript provides a list of books for those who are interested in reading the sources that provide the foundation for this book.

We wish to express special thanks to Jill Ketchum, Stephanie Smith, and Roxanne Viviano for preparing the manuscript.

WILLIAM E. MITCHELL
THOMAS R. IRELAND

January, 1986
St. Louis, MO

CONTENTS

1 AN INTRODUCTION TO COMMON STOCK INVESTING   1

    Real Estate or Common Stocks?   3
    Gold, Art, and Petrified Wood   3
    Investment for All Seasons   5
    Stock Market Gives You Free Investment Advice   6
    Advantage of Being a Small Investor   7
    Should Everyone Buy Common Stocks?   8
    What Is Ahead   9

2 COMMON STOCKS IN THE DYNAMIC DECADES AHEAD   11

    What Is Common Stock?   13
    Who Controls Corporations?   14
    Why Managers Work for You   16

That's Good in Theory, But . . .	18
Stocks in the Coming Dynamic Decades	19
A Change in Attitudes	21
Earning Your Share of Economic Growth	22

3 PAYING TO LOSE 25

Track Record	26
A Unicorn in the Garden	32
Charting for Profit?	34
Profiting from Fundamentals?	36
Bulls, Bears, and Jackasses	38
The Market Will Fluctuate	42
A Financial Plan	45

4 TOUTS, TIPSHEETS, AND TIMING: THE INVESTMENT ADVICE INDUSTRY 49

Surviving on Wall Street	50
Stockbrokers	55
Independent Advisors	63
Investment Newsletters	65
Fraud, Pure and Simple?	72

5 TOTAL INVESTMENT PORTFOLIO PLANNING 77

To Plan or Not to Plan	77
The Meaning of Total Investment Portfolio Planning	79

Basic Logic of Total Investment Portfolio Planning	80
Common Stock Returns and Risk	81
Straight Thinking About Risk and Reward	82
First Principle: Return–Risk Tradeoffs	86
Second Principle: Portfolio Diversification	87
Third Principle: Time Diversification	91
Fourth Principle: Minimizing Costs	95
Appendix: The Financial Asset Menu	96

6 PUTTING IT ALL TOGETHER: TIPP IN ACTION — 107

Managing Systematic Risk	108
Managing Unsystematic Risk	115
Implementing the Investment Plan	119
Finishing Touches	123

7 A PENNY SAVED IS A PENNY EARNING — 129

Dividend Reinvestment Plans	131
No-Load Mutual Funds	136
Mutual Funds or Do-It-Yourself?	143
Discount Brokers	148

8 PUTTING TAXES IN PERSPECTIVE — 157

Tax Planning Under Uncertainty	159
General Framework of Tax Shelters	160
Choosing Tax Shelters That Don't Leak	163

Tax Shelters in Common Stocks	166
Tax-Sheltered Retirement Programs	167
Municipal Bonds	171

9 SUCCESS! 175

Formula for Financial Success	176
Adequate Income	176
Sufficient Savings	177

POSTSCRIPT 181

Appendix A COMPANIES WITH DIVIDEND REINVESTMENT PLANS, CLASSIFIED BY INDUSTRY   185

Appendix B COMMISSION COST DATA FOR INDIVIDUAL DISCOUNT BROKERAGE FIRMS   221

Appendix C SELECTED INTERNATIONAL MUTUAL FUNDS   231

INDEX   235

1

AN INTRODUCTION TO COMMON STOCK INVESTING

For over a decade, books touting new investment gimmicks have been appearing on the nonfiction best-seller list. Fear merchants, capitalizing on the economic uncertainties of the times, play to standing-room-only audiences at "investment seminars" with messages of gloom and doom —coupled with *their* secret systems to avoid catastrophe and become instantly rich. Louis Rukeyser, moderator of the popular PBS program "Wall Street Week," observed that the investment advice industry is adopting the tactics of mail order marketing, where the only objective is to sign up new subscribers.

Gold and real estate have become especially popular investment vehicles for the trip on the road to riches. But purveyors of silver, jojoba beans, children's dolls, comic books, diamonds, stamps, rare coins, and commodity futures also hawk their wares along the way. Books offer "secret" formulas for turning a few dollars into a fortune on the stock market, using financial leverage schemes so you won't have to wait too long for that pot of gold. Investment advisors concoct bizarre tax shelter schemes whose bottom line is often *lower* after tax returns and trouble from the IRS.

Somewhere in all this frenzied activity, prudent investment programs have taken a back seat. The tried-and-true axiom that higher returns *must* imply higher risk has been ignored or forgotten. A few investors have gotten rich chasing these rainbows. In high-risk situations, there are always a few winners against long odds—but very few. Many investors lose their hard-earned savings. Mostly the hucksters are the ones who reap the rewards in this carnival atmosphere. This is nothing new, of course. In every generation con artists pick the pockets of the gullible. Wise investors, as always, continue to invest prudently, gaining no instant riches, but meeting their realistic long-term financial objectives with self-disciplined regularity. The 1970s and early 1980s were a time of abnormal uncertainty in the American economy. Inflation was getting out of control and recessions were occurring more frequently. There were spectacular changes in the prices of real estate, gold, the "collectibles," and the merely unusuals. Common stocks performed poorly in comparison to their track record of the previous 50 years, even with the sharp gains in 1982–1983. As a result, many people came to believe that real estate and tangibles were better investments than common stocks. Even in this unstable time, however, most investors would have done better with common stocks than with other investments.

Common stocks offer an attractive way to invest. They have higher long-run returns than bonds or money market accounts, are more flexible and easier to buy and sell, and require far less expertise than real estate and tangible assets. Even with a small amount of money, anyone can develop an investment program using common stocks that will meet all of the requirements of sound financial investing. And by understanding those requirements, the average investor can earn a rate of return as high as or higher than large financial institutions. One of the attractive features of common stocks is that all of the investment research has already been done for you—if you know how to take advantage of it. That's not true of any other investment that has a comparable return for the amount of risk taken. Everything you need to know to set up an effective investment program using common stocks is contained in this book.

REAL ESTATE OR COMMON STOCKS?

There is a place for real estate in any well-diversified portfolio. Owning one's own home or condominium is usually a good investment, although renting provides a flexibility that is more important for some people. In addition to the tax benefits from deducting real estate taxes and mortgage interest expenses, well-located property provides a good hedge against inflation. But any investment must be considered in the context of one's overall wealth, and no single type of investment should comprise more than 10 percent of an individual's total holdings. Because equity in your own home may represent 10 percent or more of your total net worth, owning additional real estate as an investment (which has been excessively promoted in some popular investment books) may dangerously overconcentrate your investments. Further, because the typical corporation that isn't primarily in the real estate business has 25 percent of its assets invested in real estate, owning common stocks means you are indirectly investing in real estate. So investors who have equity in their homes and own a portfolio of stocks are quite often adequately diversified between real estate and other types of earning assets. Additional diversification into real estate, if necessary, can be obtained with real estate investment trusts (REITs) and limited partnerships (see Chapter 8).

GOLD, ART, AND PETRIFIED WOOD

Although real estate has a place in a well-diversified investment portfolio, tangible assets, which have been heavily touted as investments, do not. The fear of rampant inflation in the 1970s created a classic speculative bubble in tangibles. A painting by J.M.W. Turner, entitled *Juliet and Her Nurse*, sold for $6.4 million. The price index for rare books rose over 16 percent annually, and gold soared to $800 an ounce. Petrified wood was touted as an inflation hedge with the logic that: "Nature can't make it fast enough to meet demand—it's price can only go up." Other experts solemnly intoned the investment features of the sled that was a prop in the movie *Citizen Kane*. Dorothy's slippers from the *Wizard of Oz* were auctioned off for thousands of dollars. Old Masters, Persian rugs, and Mickey Mouse watches each had their brief run during this period.

Why not tangibles? Once the appropriate adjustment is made for the high risk, poor liquidity, and often confiscatory commissions and fees associated with tangible assets, the investment performance of diversified portfolios of common stocks is as good as or better than gold, art, or collectibles and unusuals. This was true even in the volatile 1970s. And common stocks do not involve the work or heart thumping wild fluctuations. Over longer periods of time, investing in nonearning tangible assets has proven to be vastly inferior to traditional investments. Most productive people are involved in their own careers and have little time or training to successfully invest in tangible assets. It is simply counterproductive to take time away from one's principal career to invest in someone else's field of specialization. Collecting art or rare coins can be an enjoyable pastime, but they aren't good investments for anyone but the experts.

Gold Fever

In the 1970s, fear merchants were forecasting the collapse of our political, economic, and financial institutions warning that the only financial survivors would be people who hoarded gold. In the ensuing chaos, we were to experience extreme scarcity of basic life supporting goods, so the fear merchants also advised hoarding food. The food presumably would see us through the "decline and fall," after which gold would become the ultimate form of wealth as the economy struggled to recover. An important question then arose: In a time of such extreme scarcity, how does one keep hungry people from taking one's food away? Buy gold, food, and *guns* counseled the fear merchants. But how does one keep hungry people from shooting first and then taking the food? The fear merchants recommended weapons training.

Assume we experience the collapse and you survive quite nicely with your hoard of food and guns at the ready. Also assume that economic recovery follows the collapse. According to the fear merchants, your gold hoard now soars in value because gold is the only money in the economic system. You'll be able to trade it for lots of valuable goods and services. But as the price of gold starts to rise, it sows the seeds of its own destruction. People will simply create cheaper mediums of exchange, such as beads, wampum, shells, coins, or pieces of paper inscribed with such statements as "This Note is Legal Tender for All Debts, Public and Private" and "In God We Trust."

INVESTMENT FOR ALL SEASONS

Common stocks are the investment for all seasons. They represent the best investment opportunity for the vast majority of individual investors. This book is about how to use that investment for all seasons—and how to use it *in* all seasons. The effort required is not great. All you need is confidence founded in knowledge, rather than in time and energy. Mistakes in common stocks are caused by a lack of knowledge that is easily remedied. You need to know how to diversify and manage risk, and understand why in-and-out trading only benefits Wall Street.

Widely publicized fluctuations in stock prices and wild stories of boom and bust periods have given common stock investing something of a bum rap. There *are* ways to lose significant amounts of money in the stock market. Someone is always coming up with a risky new scheme to "beat the market," which will invariably lead to disappointment or disaster. And the greedier one is, the more one stands to lose. The stock-in-trade of con artists is appeal to greed. Their victims fall for the con because they think they will get something for nothing. In reality, higher investment returns *always* imply more risk and one will rarely get something for nothing. A wise investor looks for a reasonable return for the risk taken and knows that promises of more than that always imply some sort of con game. If an opportunity sounds too good to be true, it is!

The daily, weekly, and monthly fluctuations of stock prices are just that. Fluctuations. They can't hurt you if you ignore them. If they influence your investment planning, however, you may end up "buying high and selling low." As discussed in Chapter 3, with long-run investment planning these fluctuations will be of little concern. Of course, if something like the Great Depression recurs, the market value of your stocks might decline a great deal. But so will the value of real estate, small businesses, and art objects. Because stock prices always fluctuate, the best strategy is to turn this fact to your advantage. If you don't panic, periods of falling stock prices can be viewed as opportunities to buy valuable earning assets at bargain prices. The investment program in this book provides a method of managing stock market fluctuations in a calm, reasoned, *and* profitable way.

There are safer things to do with your money than buying common stocks. Bonds and money market funds, among others, are far safer, but the long-run returns on these safer alternatives are also far lower. If you are willing to assume some additional risk to obtain a higher rate of return, common stocks offer the best way to invest that does not also require a substantial amount of your own valuable time and energy. A sound and profitable common stock investment program requires only a few simple rules, and these are carefully spelled out in this book.

STOCK MARKET GIVES YOU FREE INVESTMENT ADVICE

"But," you ask, "aren't stocks really for people with a lot more money than I have? Am I not at the mercy of wealthy investors and large financial institutions who know more than I do?" Hardly! The stock market actually does your investment analysis for you. Basically, the stock market is a competitive "information market." The role of the stock market is to provide a way to determine the value of information. Investors and financial analysts arrive at a consensus estimate of the per-share price (i.e., value) for each company, based on current information and expectations about its future earnings power. As new information becomes known or expectations change, prices change.

The competitive market price of a stock represents a consensus about the investment worth of a company. If a stock is currently undervalued because of some poorly informed or overly pessimistic investors, others with better information or better analytical skills will buy the stock by offering a higher price. In the process, these better-informed investors bid up the price of the stock toward the consensus estimate of its true value. Conversely, an overvalued stock will experience downward price pressure. There is no evidence, however, that any person or analytical technique can systematically acquire information about mispriced stocks and then earn above-average returns by buying or selling before their prices change to reflect this information (see Chapter 3). (The term *above-average returns* means to earn more dividends and capital gains by buying and selling rather than buying and holding stocks.)

Thus the stock prices quoted in daily newspapers are as close to true values as it is humanly possible to estimate. The most important financial information you need to make good investment decisions is available to you for free! By following a few simple rules, it is almost impossible to go wrong.

ADVANTAGE OF BEING A SMALL INVESTOR

You ask, "I've heard that only wealthy investors and financial institutions can get adequate diversification at a reasonable cost because they deal in large blocks of stock. Won't the commissions on my transactions eat up my financial capital?" This can happen if you let it, but there are easy ways to avoid this problem. Any investor can now obtain the same low commissions as wealthy individuals and institutions, such as mutual funds and bank trust departments, who get volume discounts on very large trades. In fact, we will show you how to avoid commission costs almost completely while you are building up your financial capital.

When it's time to fulfill the goals you were saving and investing for, you'll be ready to use discount brokers who charge very low commission rates. Appendix B provides complete information on the location and commission costs of discount brokers located throughout the United States, and Chapter 7 explains when it is to your advantage to use discount brokers.

"But won't it take a lot of capital to get started?" No, it won't. If you already own some stocks, these will probably be used as the foundation for your overall investment program. Even if you don't own any stock and wish to begin slowly, you can get started for as little as $30 and take as long as you need with small amounts until your earnings allow you to save and invest larger amounts. If you have $30 to invest, you are ready to start now.

"But don't I need to do a lot of reading and research before I get started?" No, you don't. Because stocks are correctly valued, all you need to do is pick stocks offering the right characteristics for your personal investment objectives.

According to the Wall Street crowd, you must have their professional advice to profitably invest in common stock—which they will cheerfully sell to you. This is just another bit of Wall Street folklore, totally unsupported by the evidence. One of the central messages of this book is that individuals can earn a *higher* rate of return by ignoring professional investment advice! This seemingly paradoxical statement is firmly grounded in fact. Contrary to what you may believe or what the experts tell you, it is very easy for individuals to establish and manage their own investment program in common stocks. Most individuals with moderate wealth cannot afford professional management, nor do they need it.

Even with the kind of professional management that is worthwhile (see Chapters 5 and 6), unless your portfolio is very large the additional refinements will not be enough to justify the costs involved. But if you buy the bogus kind of advice (the kind that is usually available), your investment return will be lower—perhaps substantially lower—than if you ignored all of Wall Street's beat-the-market advice.

Mutual funds have been recommended for individuals with moderate means because they provide professional management, efficient diversification, low transaction costs, liquidity, and convenience. In most instances, you can achieve these same desirable objectives *and* earn a higher rate of return than with mutual funds by investing directly in common stocks. There are certain times when a mutual fund is the best investment alternative. Chapter 7 explains how to identify those circumstances and which kinds of mutual funds to buy.

SHOULD EVERYONE BUY COMMON STOCKS?

Common stocks represent a very attractive saving and investment program for most people, but not for everyone. *Common stocks will not make sense if*:

1. You are currently using all surplus funds and perhaps borrowing even more to finance your education, which is an investment in your human capital.
2. You are in the process of starting your own business and need every bit of available cash to increase your chances of succeeding.
3. Your savings will definitely be needed for some important purpose within the next two years. Common stocks are only appropriate for long-term investing. Stocks are quite liquid, but there is always the risk that you will have to sell them just when the market is temporarily depressed. (Other investment alternatives are discussed in the Appendix to Chapter 5.)

Common stocks do make sense when:

1. You must save a portion of your current income for your children's education, future financial security, or retirement income.

2. You have savings that are not needed for at least two years (barring an unexpected emergency).

3. You want to invest most of your creative energy in a career and in leisure time activities. You want a fair investment return on your savings without hard work.

WHAT IS AHEAD

There are nine chapters in this book. These chapters focus on the two key elements that are essential for any successful financial investment program. First, an investor must know what is fact and what is fiction about alternative investment opportunities. This information is presented in the next four chapters. Second, an investor must be able to translate known facts into an effective program that accomplishes his or her objectives. That is the agenda for the last four chapters.

Chapter 2 explains how market forces provide corporate managers with strong incentives to produce good results for their stockholders, relieving you of the burden of closely supervising your common stock investments. This chapter also explains why investment returns on common stocks will probably be especially impressive over the next several decades. Chapter 3 explains the myths and emotional traps that can prevent you from achieving your financial goals and how to insulate yourself from them. Chapter 4 explains why a lot of investment advice is self-serving, inaccurate, and not worth the money.

Chapter 5 presents our investment strategy in detail: total investment portfolio planning (TIPP). This strategy includes risk management, efficient portfolio diversification, time diversification of purchases and sales of assets, and elimination of unnecessary transaction expenses. Chapter 6 explains how to apply the principles of risk management and diversification in a step-by-step program to build a profitable portfolio of stocks. Chapter 7 explains how to obtain economical transaction services with dividend reinvestment plans, mutual funds, and discount brokers. Chapter 8 considers the effects of IRAs, Keoghs, and other tax shelters on investment planning. Finally, Chapter 9 presents the true "secret" for financial success.

2

COMMON STOCKS IN THE DYNAMIC DECADES AHEAD

A great deal of effort is made by Wall Street[1] "experts" to convince you that common stock investing is a complicated game, with rules so complex that you must buy their advice. Otherwise, they warn, you'll naively miss a number of crucial plays, and your wealth will melt away. That may be true of high-stakes poker, but it's not true of investing in common stocks. The stock market isn't a game. It isn't very complicated. You don't have to spend an inordinate amount of time and resources to become a successful investor. And you most certainly don't need the advice of experts—advice that's generally useless and always expensive.

To be a successful investor, however, you must understand the true nature of common stock. *Stocks represent investments in the productive assets of corporations*, not tickets in a Wall Street lottery. Too

---

[1]*Wall Street*, as we use the term, means the entire financial investment community. This includes brokers, security analysts, private advisors, pension fund managers, national investment services, and newsletters, wherever they're located—Wall Street, Main Street, New York, Cincinnati, or Dubuque.

often, people forget the simple fact that a stock certificate represents ownership in a real company, managed by competent and conscientious men and women, producing and selling useful goods and services. A clear understanding of the true nature of common stocks makes it easier to see the underlying simplicity of the stock market, the relationship between common stocks and corporate earnings, and the difference between genuine and bogus investment advice.

The objective of financial investment management developed in this book is to increase your *total* wealth. In order to do this, you must take two major facts into account. First, beat-the-market investing, which has become the conventional wisdom largely through the promotional efforts of Wall Street, will *reduce* the rate of return on your financial assets. Why? Because the information Wall Street sells you will *not* increase investment returns above what you would have received with a buy-and-hold strategy. But, in the process of using that information in an attempt to beat the market, you will incur unnecessary commissions, advisory fees, and taxes that will reduce your net investment return. Thus you will be a financial underperformer.

Second, time is a scarce resource. When it is wasted on futile stock market games, it is impossible to fully utilize your human capital, which is your most important earning asset. Human capital is that combination of physical and mental qualities that makes you a productive person. In terms of earning power, the average U.S. citizen's human capital is worth more than all other personal assets combined—home, business, automobiles, life insurance reserves, and financial assets. Yet, the impact of financial management activities on the productivity of this important asset is widely ignored. If we take the broader viewpoint that you are managing both your human capital and your financial capital, then the important question becomes: "Will I be better off by allocating *more* time to managing my financial assets rather than my human capital assets?" The answer is almost always *no*.

In this chapter, we explain why common stocks are the investment for all seasons and will be especially profitable in the coming decades, why "indirect" investment through stocks is better for most people than direct investment, and why your financial management strategy should be designed so that most of your work effort is devoted to using and improving your human capital.

WHAT IS COMMON STOCK?

A share of common stock is a claim representing fractional ownership of a corporation. Legally, it is a claim that entitles the owner to a share in future earnings of the company, as well as voting rights on a one share–one vote basis in selecting the board of directors and determining other basic issues affecting the corporation. The legal definition, however, falls far short of adequately describing common stock. An operational description of a corporation provides a more fruitful way of understanding the true nature of stock ownership. A corporation consists of a *network of contracts* between six distinct groups of people who are associated with the company: employees, outside suppliers, creditors, managers, board of directors, and stockholders. Each group specializes in performing a specific service that contributes to the overall effort of the company. The members of each group are paid for their services from the revenues earned by selling the company's products to its customers.

These contracts represent agreements that specify what is expected of everyone and how revenues will be distributed to each person. For example, in exchange for wage and salary payments, the corporation contracts with employees to obtain the workforce necessary to produce goods and services. Outside suppliers make contractual agreements to deliver raw materials, parts, and other services to the corporation at specified prices. Creditors lend the company money to finance capital expenditures in exchange for a contractual agreement that calls for periodic interest payments and repaying the principal.

Managers act as a special class of employees. Their job is to arrange for and coordinate the various inputs in the production process. They negotiate, renegotiate, and monitor all of the contracts made between the corporation and its employees (including managers themselves as employees), outside suppliers, and creditors. The board of directors is the connecting link between managers and stockholders. The board contracts with the principal managers to carry out the corporation's activities *on behalf of* the stockholders. The principal managers, in turn, are responsible for lower-level management activities. In the contract between the board of directors and stockholders, the board's functions are to establish overall corporate policy, appoint the principal managers, and ensure that managers make decisions that benefit the stockholders.

Stockholders also have a contractual arrangement with the corporation, but the nature of the contract is different. Whereas employees, managers, creditors, outside suppliers, and board members are promised specific amounts of money in exchange for services rendered, stockholders' compensation is not specific, but depends on what is left from revenues after all other contractual costs are paid. These residual revenues are called *net earnings*.

The stockholders bear risk because they put up money to buy capital assets and guarantee, to some extent, performance of the contracts made on their behalf by the corporate managers. What they own is *the rights to net earnings*. They gain if net earnings grow and lose if they decline. Except in the case of bankruptcy, stockholders are the only group in this network of contracts that assumes risk in the corporation.[2] As compensation for assuming risk, net earnings are either paid directly to stockholders in the form of dividends or reinvested in the company. Earnings that are reinvested increase the *expected ability* of the company to pay future dividends, and the value of these future dividends is reflected in the price of the stock. Because the future is uncertain, however, stock prices can only reflect the stock market's best estimate of the company's ability to pay future dividends—an estimate that changes as new information becomes available. Stock prices fluctuate as investors change their expectations of the future prospects of overall economic activity and the specific circumstances of individual firms.

Technically, stockholders also own the market value of the firm's physical assets (such as plant and equipment, patents, and licenses), but this is often more apparent than real. They must share ownership rights to physical assets with creditors. Furthermore, if a corporation goes bankrupt, the resale value of buildings and equipment is often quite low because these assets are usually designed for the specific needs of the company and are not particularly valuable in other uses.

WHO CONTROLS CORPORATIONS?

When you buy stock, you buy a piece of the company's action, but without having to worry about the details. The market value of your

---

[2]Board members and managers, however, may be personally liable for financial risk of the corporation in the case of dishonesty or willful mismanagement.

investment is determined in large part by the quality of the contracts negotiated by the managers. You, as a stockholder, have *indirectly* contracted with managers, through the board of directors, to handle the day-to-day details of running the company. This is one of the important advantages of common stock ownership. You specialize in doing what you do best—earning a living as a butcher, a baker, a candlestick maker. With your savings, you hire professional managers to do what they do best—negotiate and monitor good contracts for the corporation so you can earn a fair rate of return on your investment capital.

This is known as a principal–agent contract. The principal hires an agent to perform a service for pay. Both parties gain in the trade. The principal receives a service at a lower cost than if he or she had to produce it himself or herself, and the agent is able to concentrate on producing and selling a service for which he or she has a special expertise or talent. Thus both parties are allocating their resources most efficiently. Principal–agent contracts are very common in our society: for example, patient–doctor, client–lawyer, insured–insurer, taxpayer–government, *and* stockholder–manager.

In all principal–agent contracts, one of the major concerns of the principal is whether the agent will perform the service satisfactorily. Because there is no *direct* control exerted by stockholders over managers, an important question arises for you as a stockholder. Are professional corporate managers working for you or for themselves? It might seem on the surface that once a group of managers becomes entrenched in a corporation, they can do whatever they want. When they obtain control, the manager group could select a board of directors sympathetic to its own interest and proceed, say, to milk the corporation's assets with exorbitant salaries and bonuses, fat retirement plans, ironclad job security, and lavish entertainment and vacation expense accounts. In short, they would work as little as possible and pay themselves as much as possible, taking care to milk the cow without killing it.

Do managers have this kind of control? If so, do investment returns on stocks suffer? Stockholders appear to lack *direct* control over managers. Stock ownership in most large corporations is so widely distributed that no one stockholder or group of stockholders has any real influence on corporate decision making. The board of directors is supposed to exercise control over managers on behalf of the stockholders. But due to the size and complexity of large corporations, the board must delegate considerable control to the managers. It is simply impossible for the board to carefully monitor all of the activities of corporate managers. Furthermore, the top managers are often either members of the board or have a considerable amount of influence on who is elected, thereby further weakening control exercised by the board.

This lack of *direct* control by stockholders over managers led to a common belief, first suggested by Thorstein Veblen in 1921[3] and widely publicized by Adolf Berle and Gardiner Means in 1932,[4] that managers were, in effect, the real owners of corporations and that corporate policy was established and carried out to serve the interests of managers rather than the interests of stockholders. Fortunately, things don't really work that way. If they did, there would be real differences in the profits of owner-controlled companies in comparison to manager-controlled companies. Those controlled by owners would act in the interests of owners, whereas those controlled by managers would act in the interests of managers. The result would be lower profits and higher management compensation in the manager-controlled companies.

In fact, studies have shown that there is no difference in profits or management compensation in the two types of companies. In all respects, manager behavior appears the same, regardless of the organizational structure. The reason the pessimistic viewpoint of Berle and Means is wrong lies in the nature of the corporation as a network of contracts. The competitive marketplace where these contracts must be negotiated provides an incentive system that rewards good managerial performance and punishes (or replaces) the larcenous, the incompetent, and the lazy. The self-interest of managers, which is to maximize their own income and well-being, must be achieved by maximizing the profits of the corporation, which *is* in the self-interest of stockholders. The lack of *direct* controls by stockholders over managers is replaced by *indirect* controls established by the marketplace.

WHY MANAGERS WORK FOR YOU

There are a number of reasons why managers will work hard for you, the stockholder, even if you're not constantly looking over their shoulders. The managers of a corporation realize that their economic welfare

---

[3]Thorstein Veblen, *The Engineers and the Price System* (New York: B. W. Huebsch, 1921).
[4]Adolf Berle and Gardiner Means, *The Modern Corporation and Private Property* (New York: Macmillan, 1932).

is dependent, in large part, on the success of the company they work for. A company can be viewed as a team of individuals that is in competition with other teams (companies), and the overall team effort affects each individual member of the team. Being successful at the "business game" means better salaries and fringe benefits and continued employment for everyone on the team. It also creates a competitive labor market within the company that helps ensure that the stockholder has the best available management. Lower-level managers work hard to obtain higher-level positions. Managers monitor one another because poor performance by some will affect the incomes of everyone. Managers who do not perform well are encouraged to change their behavior, or they are replaced.

Managers also face competition in the capital market. The stock market penalizes a company that performs poorly by bidding down its stock price, which encourages rival management teams to use the assets of their companies to make an "unfriendly" takeover or merger bid. A hostile takeover (or threat of one) can be very beneficial for stockholders. Because a rival can purchase the poorly performing company at a depressed price and presumably improve its performance, it can expect to increase earnings for its own stockholders as well as for the stockholders of the acquired company. Existing stockholders of the poorly managed company will be more than happy to have a better management team. The would-be milkers or poor managers would soon be looking for new jobs.

The labor market for managers outside the company provides another powerful incentive that helps stockholders obtain good managers to operate the company. An effective prior managerial record is essential for landing a good new management job. A bad reputation in a prior position is a liability in future job applications. For that reason, would-be milkers whose team "lost the game" would not only be out of their present jobs, but would also find it difficult to negotiate new contracts with other teams at anything near their previous salaries. Conversely, managers who are doing an exceptionally good job can use the managerial labor market to bargain for better pay, either by landing a job with a new company or using an offer from a competitive team to renegotiate their present contracts. Managers, in short, succeed in achieving their own goals by doing as well as possible to produce high profits, not by playing some short-sighted milking game.

Finally, managers often have a personal financial interest in the profitability of the companies they manage. Stock options, which is a form of profit sharing, are often part of the compensation package for top management. Dividend and capital gains income from the stock top-level managers own in the company they work for represents a relatively large percentage of their wealth and overall compensation.

THAT'S GOOD IN THEORY, BUT . . .

Does this all work perfectly? Hardly! Managers don't *always* act in the best interests of stockholders. Although there are powerful and pervasive market forces working to indirectly control manager behavior that is contrary to stockholders' interests, the larcenous, the incompetent, and the lazy will always look for ways to get around the monitoring systems. Because market controls don't work instantaneously or perfectly, they will sometimes be unsuccessful, which lowers corporate profits and investment returns for stockholders.[5]

The important consideration, however, is not the fact that a particular monitoring system is imperfect, but what we could expect from an alternative system of controls. In that light, there is a consensus that the controls we have are far better than any feasible alternative. To understand why, let's consider two possibilities.

First, suppose a group of stockholders felt that the indirect controls of the marketplace were not working and managers were clearly diverting large amounts of corporate resources to their own purposes. Stockholders could substantially reduce this undesirable behavior by reorganizing the board of directors into a powerful police force with a large budget and staff. Yet this doesn't happen in the U.S. economy. Why? Because experience suggests that such a policing system would not be economical: The additional benefits in the form of more responsive management would not be worth the additional costs involved in maintaining the policing system. For this reason, there is widespread agreement that the present system of minimal direct controls provided by the board of directors and the numerous indirect controls exerted by the marketplace produce a better net return for stockholders than a system involving a large, active internal police force.

[5]The "golden parachutes" and "greenmail" of the early 1980s are examples of instances where the control systems did not prevent some managers from acting in their own narrow interests at the expense of stockholders. But counter measures soon developed to repair the leaks in the system of controls over management's power.

A second alternative is for stockholders to become owner-managers of their companies. This would eliminate potential conflicts of interest created by the present principal-agent arrangement, which separates ownership from direct control. An owner-manager doesn't delegate basic control over the operations of the corporation, so he or she doesn't have to worry about whether indirect controls will work. This solution, however, would be inferior to the principal-agent system for several reasons. First, it's impractical. Only investors with large amounts of money could choose this approach.

Second, it assumes that investors know how to manage and are willing to take the time to do it. But people with funds to invest aren't necessarily good managers. They may be artisans, scientists, carpenters, salespeople, office workers, teachers, or doctors. As such, they may not have the talent, and unless they are willing to jettison their present careers, they certainly don't have the time to devote to the specialized task of managing a business corporation.

Third, owner-managers must be willing to accept a *lower* rate of investment return per unit of risk taken than those who invest in a diversified portfolio of stocks. An owner-manager who has to take a personal interest in day-to-day operations obviously couldn't invest in more than one or two different companies. This would severely reduce the owner-manager's ability to achieve adequate diversification. Owner-managers would be taking too much risk[6] for the potential rewards of the investments.

STOCKS IN THE COMING DYNAMIC DECADES

Common stocks are the investment for all seasons because the U.S. economy is basically healthy; it will survive and prosper, not just in the next few years, but in the foreseeable future as well. The economy will always experience periodic problems with inflation and recession, adjustment and indecision, but the experience of the last 200 years suggests that its basic momentum is to grow.

Real per-capita output in the United States has roughly doubled in each of the five generations since 1800. This trend will continue and quite likely accelerate in the next several decades because the economy is currently in the midst of a revitalization and technological revolution

---

[6]This is unsystematic risk (see Chapters 5 and 6).

that is expected to produce very rapid economic growth. This situation is in sharp contrast to the slow economic growth, recurrent recessions, and high rates of inflation experienced in the past two decades. There is simply no basis for the pronouncements of the fear merchants who have predicted the collapse of the U.S. monetary and economic system.

The economic "stagflation" of the last 20 years was triggered and nurtured, in part, by such gloom-and-doom notions as the approaching limits to economic growth, an inevitable population explosion with catastrophic consequences, an environment choking on pollution, and the paralyzing fear of widespread and uncontrollable economic, political, and military instability in the world. Coupled with this negative mentality, we were suffering through a particularly disruptive political and social malaise that produced an aura of indecision and low morale in our economy. The twin fears of a rapid depletion of resources and a population explosion had led some forecasters to predict that world output would collapse and population would plunge out of control within 100 years, causing a fatal destabilization of the political fabric of the world's societies—a sort of secular version of the Biblical end of the world!

The indications are everywhere that we are rejecting these negative and erroneous ideas. As researchers began to examine those forecasts[7] more closely, it was evident that their predictions were going to be far off the mark, principally because the gloom-and-doom studies failed to account for how efficiently free market forces allocate resources. Economic theory predicts that when a product falls in short supply, there will be a dual reaction: its price will rise relative to other products, causing us to use less of it, *and* the higher price will encourage us to produce more of it. In the mid-1970s, for example, these disaster studies forecast that we would virtually exhaust our reserves of oil by the turn of the century. This was the infamous "energy crisis." (Remember how serious *that* seemed at the time!) By 1981, however, the world was awash in oil, and its price was tumbling.

What happened? Just what economic theory would predict. In response to the dramatic Organization of Petroleum Exporting Countries

---

[7]The two most prominent studies were: Donella H. Meadows and Others, *The Limits to Growth* (New York: Universe Books, 1972). Council on Environmental Quality, *The Global 2000 Report to the President of the U.S., Entering the 21st Century* (New York: Pergamon Press, 1980). A more reasoned and balanced discussion is provided in Julian L. Simon and Herman Kahn, eds., *The Resourceful Earth: A Response to Global 2000* (New York: Basil Blackwell, 1984).

(OPEC) oil price increase in 1974, we began to (1) simply use less of it, (2) switch to lower-priced fossil fuel substitutes, such as natural gas and coal, (3) convert to energy-efficient houses, cars, and machinery, and (4) step up oil exploration and production. In addition, we set in motion the development of other sources of energy to supplement fossil fuels, ranging from fission and fusion to geothermal, ocean-gradient, and solar. In fact, the only crisis in the energy crisis turned out to be the absurd government regulations that drastically slowed the market adjustment process. For the foreseeable future, there will be large increases in both conventional and unconventional sources of energy that will be available at moderate prices. There will be no energy shortage to limit economic growth!

Coupled with this change in energy conditions is the high-tech revolution, including the rapid development of robotics and computers. These high-tech tools will significantly increase the efficiency with which we can use energy and all other resources. The bottom line is that external conditions are positioned for rapid economic growth, which will reverse the previous two decades of doldrums.

A CHANGE IN ATTITUDES

Internal conditions are also changing for the better. We are beginning to reemphasize the values of thrift, hard work, and pride that produced our highly productive, dynamic, and creative economy in the first place. We are developing more sensible labor–management relations, rationalizing the regulatory structure of our federal and state governments, and turning back to a greater use of the efficient free enterprise price system to allocate resources.

There is tentative evidence of bipartisan support in Washington, D.C. for a return to federal fiscal sensibility. Government policy making is concentrating more on the *long-run* objectives of encouraging a sound, stable, economic system rather than using the *shortsighted* macroeconomic policies of Keynesian demand management, which has contributed so much to the destructive economic instability experienced in the past two decades. We're not out of the woods yet, but the future certainly appears most promising.

In an atmosphere of rapid economic expansion, growing confidence, and rising morale, we will be able to translate the new technologies into a substantial increase in our standard of living. These new technologies will touch on nearly every facet of our lives, including food, medicine, energy, transportation, communication, and automation of homes and jobs. Higher output will also enable us to allocate the necessary resources to substantially reduce poverty in the United States, address our serious health and pollution problems, and effectively guard against the ever-present political and military instability around the world that threatens our well-being.

EARNING YOUR SHARE OF ECONOMIC GROWTH

There are two ways you can participate in this bright future. The first way, of course, is to invest in common stocks. The second—and most important—way is to invest in your own human capital. Human capital provides the *income*, which is the source of *savings*, which are directly related to the success of your objective to accumulate *financial* capital. Barring inheritance, you have *no* other choice. There are simply no shortcuts to acquiring more wealth, no secret method to parlay a few dollars into a fortune. Rather, you must earn more, and save and invest more of what you earn. The prospects are very good, however, for earning a high rate of return on your human capital.

The United States is moving rapidly toward an economic system that will be heavily dependent on the communication skills and knowledge of human capital. As we develop new ways to perform dull, repetitive, and "sweaty" jobs with computers, robotics, and other technological innovations, and as our economy becomes more services oriented, there will be a continual (and ultimately dramatic) shift from manual work to mental work. The computer, which is very useful for keeping track of information and people, reduces the need for the old vertical or hierarchical (boss–worker) style of management. As decision making becomes more horizontal, it allows—indeed requires—greater participation in decision making by everyone in the organization. But this also means that there will be a greater reliance on knowledge and communication skills.

Real incomes will be rising at a more rapid rate than during the stagflation and malaise of the previous two decades, but the higher pay will be going to those with the skills, education, training, and credentials necessary to manage and service the high-tech, services-oriented economy. Conversely, people who do not allocate sufficient time and resources to a continual process of learning will earn ever-smaller shares of our productive economy. The financial management approach offered in this book is based on the fact that managing human capital and financial capital are interrelated and that most of your scarce time should be devoted to investing in human capital.

3

PAYING TO LOSE

A FABLE ABOUT WALL STREET

Once upon a time there were two kinds of people in the world. The first group was very skillful in gathering and interpreting information that helped them forecast future stock prices. Then, by locating stocks that were currently mispriced relative to eventual worth, they were able to earn trading profits by buying low and selling high.

These skillful people, who were called supertraders, included both individuals who used their own money to trade for profit and professional financial managers who were hired by others to trade for profit for them. As the talents of the financial managers became widely recognized, however, their salaries were bid up higher and higher by mutual funds, pension funds, personal trusts, and others who wanted these supertraders on their team. Consequently, most of the trading profits earned by professional managers were absorbed by their salaries and bonuses, rather than accruing as additional income for the owners of the money being managed. The individual and professional supertraders began to become quite wealthy.

The other group of people just couldn't seem to get the hang of it. Every time they tried to trade stocks, they lost money because the supertraders had better information and better skills in interpreting that information.

> The supertraders would buy underpriced stocks from them and sell overpriced stocks to them. After a while, the supertraders had won all of their money and the losers had to get jobs as concert pianists, bricklayers, physicists, and movie stars.
>
> But in the group of remaining supertraders, there were some who were smarter than others. Through astute trading, they gradually acquired all of the money of the other supertraders who were not quite as smart. After the losers ran out of money, they quit trading stocks and became school teachers, mathematicians, truck drivers, and movie stars.
>
> By this time, the remaining supertraders had become enormously wealthy. But something else had happened. The supertraders had reached a standoff. None of them could gain at the others' expense. Partly, this was because the survivors were all more or less equally skillful. But also, because of the supertraders' combined analytical skills, current stock prices were no longer mispriced. The collective knowledge of stock market traders was greater than that of any individual supertrader. Now stock prices only changed in unpredictable ways when new, unexpected information became known. The supertraders had inadvertently invented what was later to be called an efficient stock market, where current stock prices reflected all knowable information.

There are documented cases every year of individual investors and professional managers who have earned sizable profits from trading stocks. Are these modern day supertraders who, through skill and hard work, amass fortunes by fleecing innocent lambs? Remember that the extra profits of supertraders must be earned at the expense of investors too dumb to recognize that the stocks they are trading are mispriced relative to their actual investment value. Are investors as dumb as in the fable? Or are these success stories due to luck alone? After all, there are also documented cases of people winning millions of dollars in lotteries, but no one attributes this fact to skill. Are there really supertraders today, or have the combined efforts of countless investors searching for mispriced stocks indeed created an efficient market that eliminates the possibility of earning super profits in any way except by luck alone? *This is the single most important issue in financial investing.*

TRACK RECORD

It is widely believed on Wall Street that stocks frequently become mispriced because investors in general have incomplete information and faulty analytic skills. On this basis, it is believed that individuals who are smart and work hard can find stocks that are mispriced, enabling them or their clients to make above-normal profits by buying those stocks that are underpriced and selling those that are overpriced. This beat-the-market approach is supposed to yield higher investment returns than an alternative strategy of simply buying and holding stocks. A large percentage of the investment advice industry is based on selling you information for the purpose of beating the market in just this way. Can this really work? Or is there an efficient market that makes this effort futile, expensive, and dangerous to investors who engage in it? The answer will determine your whole outlook on the investment process.

After hundreds of thousands of hours of scientific study by thousands of independent researchers, not a hundred, or ten, or even one clear-cut case has been found where an investment technique or the prowess of a stock market analyst has consistently beaten the market. Not one! In all of these studies, there were always a few analysts who were successful at one time or another, but invariably their good results gave way to poor results later on. The success rate turned out to be about what you would expect at the Las Vegas roulette tables—every number comes up once in a while. The laws of probability can predict how often, but there is no way of telling when. It's the same with investing. In any given year, the laws of pure chance state that half of all investors will have investment returns higher and half will have returns lower than the market average. Twenty-five percent should beat the market two years in a row, and 12 percent should have superior performances for three straight years. Out of 1000 investors, eight would be expected to beat the market seven years running, just on the basis of pure luck. The number of people who have earned large profits from trading stocks is about the same as the number of people who have hit it big in state lotteries. A supertrader must be able to do better than that.

Most of the scientific studies have focused on the investment performance of financial managers during the last 25 years. The idea was that if anyone could beat the market, it would be professional financial managers who have access to a great deal of information and the training and analytical skills to use that information to locate mispriced stocks—if they exist. Each of these studies compares the investment returns of professionally managed funds to a buy-and-hold (i.e., unmanaged) investment strategy, as measured by a broad market average, such as the Standard and Poor's 500 (S&P 500) or the New York Stock Exchange Index. What follows is a small sample of the results:

1. In a study using a sample of 57 mutual funds covering the years 1953–1962, there was no evidence that any of them could successfully time purchases and sales to stock market fluctuations.

2. During 1961–1970, out of 180 mutual funds studied, none had investment returns higher than the S&P 500 for all 10 years or even nine out of 10 years. One mutual fund beat the market in eight out of 10 years, which is just what the laws of probability would predict on the basis of pure chance. *Someone* had to get lucky.

3. For the years 1960–1968, the average return on a sample of 136 mutual funds was 10.7 percent, compared to 12.4 percent for the average of all stocks on the New York Stock Exchange.

4. In a study covering the years 1968–1977, the yield on the S&P 500 was 3.6 percent, compared to 3.2 percent for a large sample of mutual funds. In the same study, the stock portfolios of investment counselors had an average yield of 2.3 percent, and insurance companies and bank trust department funds only earned 2.0 percent. A separate study covering the 1970s also found that bank trust departments sharply underperformed on the market averages; bank-managed portfolios had an investment return of 4.2 percent, versus 6.1 percent for the S&P 500. In a third study, 93 out of 112 bank and insurance portfolios underperformed in comparison to the S&P 500 in the 1970s.

5. During the period 1965–1980, 78 percent of the 571 largest pension fund stock portfolios performed below the S&P 500. The average investment return for all pension funds was 5.5 percent, versus 6.8 percent for the market averages.

6. The staff of *Financial World*, a monthly financial magazine, tracked the investment recommendations of the top 100 security analysts. These men and women, who often earn salaries of $200,000 and up, were ranked the best in a poll taken by the trade magazine *Institutional Investor*. The overall conclusion: The superstars were overrated and overpaid. In a more intensive study of 132 recommendations made by 20 of the superstar analysts who worked for six of the largest brokerage firms, the average investment return for the period June 1979 through June 1980 was 7.3 percent, which was sharply below the 14.1 percent for the stock market average.

7. *Institutional Investor* magazine conducted an annual beauty contest, in which each analyst could pick one favorite stock for the next year. The results were *so* bad they dropped the contest after several years to save the superstars any further embarrassment.

8. Analysts who sell advice through investment newsletters, managers of college endowment funds, and discretionary accounts at brokerage firms experienced the same poor results.

9. Consistency of performance is just as bad. If a manager is rated near the top in a particular year, the chances are that his performance will be *worse* than average the following year. In repeated tests, past successes and failures had nothing to do with future results.

10. Apparently, the failure to beat the market is not a recent phenomenon. In a 1933 study, a sample of 20 insurance companies underperformed the market by 1.2 percentage points; 16 financial services lagged the market by 1.4 percentage points; and 25 financial publications yielded 4.0 percentage points below a buy-and-hold investment strategy.

Time after time, in these and numerous other studies, all but a few stock market professionals failed to beat the market and, indeed, most failed to even match the market averages because they wasted commissions, advisory fees, and operating expenses in their quests for high performance. In fact, the idea that it would be difficult, if not impossible, to beat the market was first proposed by Louis Bachelier in 1900.[1] The self-proclaimed supertraders obviously aren't earning extra profits by trading with "ignorant" nonprofessional investors. This evidence contradicts the inflated and misleading claims made by the financial analysts themselves in their advertising (see Chapter 4).

The one point repeatedly demonstrated in these studies is that investment results are proportional to risk. Financial managers who invest in average-risk stocks have average returns before accounting for management expenses. Higher-risk portfolios yield higher returns, and a low-

---

[1] Louis Bachelier, *Theorie de la Speculation* (Paris: Gauthier-Villars, 1900). Translated and reprinted in Paul H. Cootner, ed., *The Random Character of Stock Market Prices* (Cambridge: MIT Press, 1964).

risk strategy results in proportionately lower investment returns. (The concept and measurement of financial risk are discussed in Chapter 5.)

Inside Dope or Just Dope?

For the most part, the professional managers who have been studied so carefully were only able to use public information in their search for mispriced stocks. If, however, investors or analysts could have access to "inside" information, it is likely that they could earn above-average investment returns. By definition, inside information is valuable because it is new information—it relates to facts that will affect the earnings prospects of a company and that have not yet been publicly disclosed and thus are not reflected in the current price of the stock. An investor with true inside information can buy or sell before the stock price changes to reflect the new information. But there are some serious problems associated with using inside information. It's illegal, difficult to interpret, and often wrong or useless.

The SEC vigorously prosecutes anyone caught trading on the basis of inside information. Of course, the SEC doesn't catch everyone who uses inside information, but the threat of detection and penalty provides a significant deterrent, especially for professional financial managers and corporate officials, whose careers may be jeopardized by such illegal activity. Due to public disclosure laws and the watchful eye of the SEC, corporate executives are generally diligent in the timely publication of facts that may affect the market's evaluation of a company's earnings prospects. Still the lure of riches constantly tempts some to try. They devise ingenious schemes to obtain inside information and conceal trading activity. Some unknown number of these trades are profitable and go undetected, but it is believed that they represent a minute fraction of overall stock market activity.

But even people who don't mind breaking the law and are in a position to obtain inside information are not home free. It's not enough to be the first to know of an important new contract, a major breakthrough in product development, or a shake-up in top management. How that information will affect future earnings and, more importantly, how that information will be interpreted by other investors must be evaluated correctly. And that's very hard to do. Even "corporate insiders"—directors, executives, and majority stockholders—have great difficulty in determining the intrinsic value of new information about their firms.

Corporate insiders are free to trade in the stock of their own companies as long as profits from stock transactions are not short term (i.e., less than six months) and the trading is not related to essential undisclosed information. However, their transactions must be promptly reported to the SEC, and this information is published two months later in the *Official Summary of Securities Transactions and Holdings*.[2] Studies using information in the *Official Summary* have shown that corporate insiders are just as confused as the rest of us. They do not consistently beat the market by trading in their company's stock. They often buy when they should sell or sell too soon. Even with their presumably superior knowledge, corporate insiders, on the average, earn little more on their investments than if they had followed a buy-and-hold investment strategy.[3]

And even people who don't mind breaking the law *and* have a super-trader's skill still will have a problem because much of what passes for inside information on Wall Street is worthless. Often the advance information simply turns out to be incorrect. The new discovery may not be as dramatic as originally supposed, or the crop failure not as complete as initially reported, and so forth. In other instances, the effect of the advance information is offset by a separate unexpected event with implications in the opposite direction. Finally, although corporate insiders sometimes have genuinely valuable information about their own companies that is not known by the general public, rarely will a securities analyst or an average investor find out about it before the price of the stock changes to reflect the news. Although such information may have been quite valuable at one time, by that time it is useless.

An "Efficient" Market

If there are some people who really do know how to use public information to consistently beat the market, they are keeping it a secret. And

---

[2]United States Securities and Exchange Commission, *Official Summary of Securities Transactions and Holdings* (Washington, D.C.: U.S. Government Printing Office), SE 1.9.

[3]In most cases, it may be difficult to prove that corporate insiders are trading on privileged information, but because their overall trading profits are so small and they appear to be wrong nearly as often as they are right, the SEC rarely pays attention to most of them. The regulatory authorities concentrate on the relatively few cases where corporate insiders have clearly abused their privileged positions.

well they should! Once they made their valuable system public, it would no longer work. Success attracts a crowd, and a crowd would spoil the success. As investors began to buy the undervalued stocks and sell the overvalued ones that were located by the new system, prices would change very quickly to reflect the value of the system's new information, rendering it worthless for future trading to improve profits.

When a market is very thorough in gathering and evaluating information, it is called an *efficient market*. In an efficient market, a large number of investors and professional analysts are constantly collecting and carefully evaluating all available public information to determine the investment value of each stock. As a result, current stock prices become consensus estimates of the intrinsic value of the stocks in the market. The empirical evidence discussed earlier in this chapter clearly supports the idea that the U.S. securities markets are efficient. Without exception, in these and other studies rates of return on unmanaged buy-and-hold portfolios have exceeded yields on managed funds where managers tried to outguess the market consensus. Because current stock prices are best estimates of future earnings prospects in efficient markets, in-and-out trading cannot obtain a higher rate of return, but the unnecessary transaction costs expended in the effort will produce inferior results.

An efficient market is sometimes referred to as a *fair game* because it is impossible for supertraders to obtain special knowledge or formulas that would enable them to earn a high rate of return at the expense of other investors. This means that investors can earn a fair rate of return for the risks taken by buying and holding shares in the productive assets of corporations. It also means that investors who ignore the concept and evidence of an efficient securities market and resort to futile and costly efforts to beat the market will end up *paying to lose*. They will earn *less* than a fair return because they will be lining the pockets of Wall Street gurus with unnecessary commissions and advisory fees and stuffing Uncle Sam's coffers with unnecessary tax payments.

A UNICORN IN THE GARDEN

James Stone[4] once characterized the task of locating mispriced stocks as more difficult than just looking for a needle in a haystack—it is more like

---

[4]James Stone, *One Way for Wall Street* (Boston: Little, Brown, 1975).

trying to find a unicorn in the garden. With a beat-the-market strategy, an investor (or the investor's advisor) must locate mispriced stocks, buy those that are underpriced, sell those that are overpriced, and do all of this before the majority of other investors recognize that those stocks are mispriced. To beat the market, not only must one be smarter than the other investors, but one must also be smarter than the *combined* intelligence of *all* other investors. The stock market is like a huge vacuum cleaner, attracting and evaluating countless bits of information from a wide variety of sources that relate to determining corporate earnings prospects. Analysts and investors rarely have identical opinions about future prospects, but the stock prices that emerge reflect a consensus, or weighted average, of what investors believe are the earnings capacities of each company.

This market consensus method of determining the value (price) of any given stock works better than any other known system precisely because it uses more information and processes that information more effectively than any other system. The market consensus method makes pricing mistakes, but the openness of markets and the competition of ideas coming from numerous sources allows the price of a stock to continuously adjust to a wide and rapid distribution of information, so errors are kept to a minimum.

What does it take to beat an efficient market? The supertrader must be able to know when other investors are making an error in judgment, meaning that a current stock price does not accurately reflect the future earnings prospects of that corporation. Unless the supertrader is infallible, he or she must also be able to detect market valuation errors often enough to offset those times when money will be lost because the market was right and the trader wrong. On top of that, the market errors must be large enough to yield a return high enough to more than compensate for the additional commissions and taxes that will be incurred by in-and-out trading. With all of these conditions, it is no small wonder that beat-the-market strategies have failed.

Nevertheless, would-be supertraders continue to look for unicorns in the garden. There are two primary approaches to beating the market: technical analysis and fundamental analysis. A technical analyst looks at charts of past stock prices for patterns that will provide clues about the path of future prices, focusing on either individual stocks or overall stock market prices. A fundamental analyst believes that known economic and financial facts hold important clues about future events and that stock prices often fail to properly reflect relevant information about earnings prospects. Although technical analysts, or chartists, and fundamental analysts approach the task of finding mispriced stocks in different ways, both believe they can forecast future stock prices better than the market consensus. Because all investors are confronted at one time or another with the nostrums of these two approaches, it is important to understand what they are and why they don't work.

CHARTING FOR PROFIT?

A technical analyst believes that information related to earnings prospects determines stock prices but once new information becomes public, it's too late to be of any use. The price of the stock will already reflect or discount the news. The technical analyst believes that price patterns are formed by slowly spreading information about earnings prospects. As the demand-supply balance changes, this creates a trend in prices that continues until the information becomes widely known. The world according to the chartist works this way: A few people obtain important information about a company that's not generally known. The stock price begins to change as they buy or sell. Then, as the knowledge spreads to more and more investors, the stock price begins to trace out an identifiable pattern, such as a *flag*, a *breakout gap*, or a *head and shoulders*. As information spreads and the price changes, psychological factors, such as a bandwagon effect or the greed-fear cycle (discussed later in this chapter), often contribute to the price pattern. Finally, the price reaches a level that fully reflects the value of the new information. (The same techniques are applied to forecasting overall stock market prices.)

In the quest for trading profits, chartists must do three things. First, they must find a pattern of past stock prices that signals that new information is beginning to be impounded into the stock price. Second, they must identify the pattern when it is only partially completed. Third, based on their knowledge of what the remaining part of the pattern will look like, they must be able to forecast the future price of the stock.

Technical analysis may seem a plausible approach to forecasting because price charts often appear to have definite patterns, but this is an optical illusion. Charts that record a random event, such as heads or tails from successively flipping a coin, look remarkably like the most cherished price patterns that chartists claim can foretell future prices. On close inspection, the chart patterns of technical analysis produce forecasting results no better than would be expected with random guesses. The reason is quite simple. If the stock of General Maynard Corporation, for example, is trading in a normal daily range of $50–$50$\frac{1}{2}$ on June 15, this price level reflects the market or consensus estimate of earnings prospects for the company, based on knowable information on that day. Only new, *unexpected* information about earnings prospects will change the price of the stock. Because new information is a surprise and a surprise is something that cannot be anticipated, the pattern traced out by any given set of past price changes will be unique and completely unrelated to future prices.

Moreover, technical analysis relies on a predictable pattern of investment information that slowly but inexorably becomes known to an ever-larger number of investors. But as new information becomes known, stock prices usually change rapidly to reflect the value of that information. Economic, financial, and business news is constantly being released by companies, financial analysts, portfolio managers, economists, and the government. News about earnings reports, lawsuits, test-market results, and mergers is quickly made available to investors through wire services (such as UPI and Dow Jones), newspapers, radio, television, registered representatives, and the informal gossip network of the business community. Other important information is continuously published by magazines, investment advisory services, trade journals, and books. As a result, prices change long before the vast majority of investors have a chance to gain a trading edge. Few, if any, investors will be nimble enough to buy or sell the stock before its move is completed.

The idea that past prices cannot be used to predict future prices is an application of the mathematical theory called *random walk*. As applied to stock market pricing, however, the term is often misunderstood. It doesn't imply that stock prices are determined in a random or irrational manner. Random walk is perfectly consistent with the fact that changes in stock prices are caused by changes in earnings prospects. Stocks of companies with good earnings prospects will be priced higher than those with poor prospects, so that the expected investment return will be the same for all stocks in the same risk class. There is nothing random about that. Nor is there anything random in the fact that new information about earnings prospects will cause the price of a stock to change. Looked at in retrospect, price movements make perfect sense and are anything but random. What *is* random is the arrival of new information—something that past price patterns cannot predict.

PROFITING FROM FUNDAMENTALS?

The basis for both technical and fundamental analysis is the well-known relationship between a company's earnings and its stock price. As explained, the technical analyst reasons that past changes in the price of a stock reflect undisclosed information about a company's earnings prospects, which will ultimately cause changes in the price of its stock. Thus the technical analyst uses past stock prices to forecast future stock prices. The fundamental analyst, however, tries to forecast stock prices indirectly by forecasting future earnings. The objective is to determine whether the present price of a stock accurately reflects its earnings prospects. Fundamentalists believe the market consensus pricing mechanism is often temporarily wrong and that they can make better estimates of the true value of stocks. They reason that eventually the market will discover its valuation error and the stock price will adjust to reflect its true value, so the trick is to buy or sell before the price adjusts. This approach has widespread appeal because it appears to be so logical, but it doesn't work any better than technical analysis.

The Caribou Visit

A fundamental analyst tries to estimate how economic, financial, and business conditions will affect a firm's profitability. The forecast depends on such information as past sales and earnings trends, product development, management changes, basic knowledge of the economy and of how economic conditions will affect the company, and the impact of government regulations and tax laws. The fundamentalist may also do an in-depth study of the industry, interview corporate executives, and make on-site visits. The assumption is that these facts will form an observable pattern or trend that is associated with future events that will determine future stock prices. It *sounds* sensible, but is it?

Forecasts are only extrapolations of past trends and are only accurate if past trends persist. If a company experiences no surprises, its earnings forecasts will turn out to be correct, but unimportant, because the stock price will reflect this information. Given the efficiency of the market, it is only when consensus earnings forecasts are wrong that supertraders can earn profits by locating mispriced stocks. But such forecasts usually miss predicting changes in the rate of earnings growth and, worse, fail to anticipate a complete reversal of earnings. As a result, forecasts are right when it doesn't matter and wrong when it does.

The reason for this is simple. When engineers were designing the Alaska pipeline, for example, they allowed for every contingency, or so they thought. But when the project was at an advanced planning stage, someone pointed out that the pipeline would block the annual migration of the caribou. As a result, the pipeline required costly design changes, which significantly lowered the earnings prospects for several energy companies. The future is full of surprises, and in the absence of psychic power, there is no way to anticipate the truly unknowable. As Anthony Hitschler has observed,[5] the "caribou" eventually visit every forecast.

Corporate earnings are affected by many factors that management has little control over. Fluctuations in gross national product and aggregate employment affect the firm's sales. Consumer tastes change. Tariffs are imposed or lifted. The cost of raw materials increases or decreases. Strikes occur. Interest rates rise or fall. Technological developments or new mineral discoveries often happen by chance. These and many other factors that can radically change the prospects of a firm or an industry cannot be anticipated in a forecast. Further, the typical company has a varied and changing line of products that are sold in multiple markets and often in several countries. As a result, past earnings growth provides very little useful information about future earnings potential.

The empirical evidence in the numerous studies referred to here clearly indicates that analysts can't forecast earnings any better than anyone who simply does an extrapolation of past earnings trends. This is easy to do, but provides no information that would enable investors to locate mispriced stocks. This is not because analysts are incompetent, but because forecasting is a hazardous business. In spite of great advancements in scientific knowledge and the wonders of computers, the future is still unknown. No matter how hard we work, how sophisticated our tools, or how good our intentions, forecasting stock prices

---

[5]Anthony Hitschler, "To Know What We Don't Know or the Caribou Weren't in the Estimates," *Financial Analysts Journal*, January–February, 1980.

BULLS, BEARS, AND JACKASSES

> A bull thinks stock prices are going up.
> A bear thinks stock prices are going down.
> A jackass listens to bulls and bears.

It's the summer of 1979, and Charlie Smith is reviewing his investments. A year and a half ago he bought his first stock, 100 shares of Ford Motor Company for $28 a share. The stock has been paying a steady dividend, but it's still selling at 28. The rest of his money is in a safe, but low-yielding, passbook savings account. After doing some research and reading reports from several Wall Street brokerage firms, Charlie concludes that Ford will do about as well as the market averages in the foreseeable future. In Wall Street parlance, it's a "hold." Although that isn't a particularly exciting prospect, Charlie decides to keep his Ford stock, but to use his savings to play the stock market and increase his overall investment return.

After further research, he decides to invest in Compugraphic Corporation. The company seems to have a bright future. He is especially impressed with their plan to develop equipment for the graphic arts industry that could be adapted to a computerized office system. Charlie thinks the stock is undervalued by the market, so he buys 100 shares at $38\frac{3}{4}$.

Over the next few months, Charlie makes a careful study of the world energy situation. He thinks that, due to the development of alternative fuel sources, the future prospects for the coal industry are very poor. In particular, he thinks North American Coal is way overpriced relative to its prospective earnings, so he sells short 100 shares at 32. (Selling short just reverses the usual process. Instead of buying a stock first and selling it later, one borrows the stock and sells it first and then repays the loan by buying it later on.)

As a result of these transactions, Charlie's portfolio in the late fall of 1979 looks like this:

	100 shares	Ford Motor Company
	100 shares	Compugraphic Corporation
short	100 shares	North American Coal

It's now January 1980. Compugraphic is selling at $29\frac{1}{2}$. Charlie thinks it's a terrific bargain now, so he buys another 100 shares. His Ford stock has slipped to $22\frac{5}{8}$, but since he wasn't overly enthusiastic about its prospects to begin with, he just continues to hold the 100 shares.

North American Coal is Charlie's big problem at the moment. Soon after he sold short at 32, it began to rise rapidly! It is now selling at $47\frac{5}{8}$. His broker has sent him a margin call, requesting (actually, demanding) more money as security against the loan of the stock. Charlie is beginning to have doubts about his decision on North American Coal. Perhaps he had overlooked something in his research. In the last few weeks, several brokerage firms have issued research reports that suggest the prospects for the coal industry are improving. One of them changed its investment recommendation from sell to hold. Charlie is scared that the stock will go up even higher. He begins to realize that if one buys a stock, one can only lose what one paid for it, but if one sells short, potential losses are unlimited. He has also read somewhere of a stock market trading rule that says, "Never meet a margin call." It had something to do with cutting one's losses when one has obviously made a mistake. So, he covers his short position by buying 100 shares of North American Coal at $47\frac{5}{8}$. His total loss, including commissions,[6] is over $1600.

At this point, his portfolio includes:

    100 shares   Ford Motor Company
    200 shares   Compugraphic Corporation

It's now spring of 1980. Compugraphic is down to $23\frac{5}{8}$. Charlie is a little worried, but finally concludes that the market still hadn't recognized the true value of this dynamic company, so he buys another 100 shares. Ford has sunk to $20\frac{5}{8}$. Charlie wishes he had sold it at 28 last summer, but it is too late now, so he grimly holds on. He resolves that in the future he will always promptly sell any stock that he doesn't expect to outperform the market.

His portfolio in spring of 1980 is:

    100 shares   Ford Motor Company
    300 shares   Compugraphic Corporation

---

[6]Charlie deals with a discount broker who charges a flat $30 commission per 100 shares traded. See Chapter 7.

But his stocks keep falling! By early summer in 1980, Compugraphic is at 19, and it looks like it is never going to stop falling. Charlie reads an article in a financial magazine in which an investment analyst says the depressed economic conditions around the world will have a very severe impact on companies in the precision instrument industry. The analyst predicts that Compugraphic's earnings will fall at least 50 percent in 1980 and the company might show a loss in 1981, which could result in a dividend cut. At the same time, Ford has slipped to $19\frac{1}{2}$. Some people are saying that the Japanese will take over world auto production and Ford will be reduced to a spare parts supplier.

Charlie begins thinking that perhaps the market was right and he was wrong. His losses in these two stocks are piling up and, at the present rate, all of his savings will soon be gone. In a panic, he sells his 300 shares of Compugraphic at 19 and his 100 shares of Ford at $19\frac{1}{4}$ for a total loss, including commissions, of about $4600.

To his dismay, North American Coal began to drop soon after he closed out the short position at $47\frac{5}{8}$. By now it is down to 34. Charlie realizes that he lost his nerve and bailed out too soon. In fact, he thinks, he *should* have sold more stock short at $47\frac{5}{8}$, rather than covering the short position at a loss. He is tempted to buy in at 34 because the stock looks cheap relative to its price just several months ago. But he also remembers that when he first sold short, he thought the stock was overpriced at 32. By now, he is thoroughly confused. He has lost over $6200 in just one year, and he doesn't even have a clear idea why.

Greed–Fear Cycle

Obviously, Charlie needs help. He was buying high and selling low, which is a guaranteed ticket to the poorhouse. Charlie started out very bullish on Compugraphic. His optimism reduced the concern for risk, which was why he easily explained away the temporary setbacks after his initial purchase. Indeed, he viewed the lower prices as opportunities to really make a killing. But as Compugraphic's price continued to fall, his mood turned pessimistic. He became overly concerned about risk. A heightened sense of optimism and pessimism is sometimes referred to as the *greed–fear cycle*. As the prices of Compugraphic and Ford tumbled, Charlie began to fear that they would continue to fall. Fear led to panic, and he sold out at a large loss. He had bought high and sold low. With short sales, the same result occurs, but with price increases rather than price declines. Charlie closed out his short position in North American Coal when he began to believe that its price would never stop going up, thus buying high and selling low.

It's not just the so-called amateur investors who are susceptible to extreme optimism and pessimism in financial investing. A number of studies have shown that professional investment analysts, managers, and counselors also fall victim to the emotions of the greed–fear cycle. As prices soar in the euphoria of a bull market, there is panic buying because many are afraid to miss the big move. As prices sink into the deepest gloom of a bear market, the same people are apt to panic again and sell those stocks previously bought or recommended at lofty prices. Actually, the transactions described in our Charlie Smith story were the precise buy, hold, and sell recommendations (stocks, dates, and prices) made by three of the superstar analysts in the *Financial World* study discussed earlier. These supposedly rational, unemotional professionals made all of the classic mistakes that individual investors had hired them to avoid! The point is this: Every investor, professional and amateur alike, must take precautions to avoid overreacting to boom and gloom. Failure to do so may be very detrimental to one's financial health.

Suppose that, instead of trying to beat the market, Charlie had used a buy-and-hold investment strategy during the same time period, June 1979 through June 1980. And suppose that, instead of trying to time his purchases and sales to catch stock price fluctuations, he spread his purchases evenly over time to avoid the possibility of investing all of his money at a market peak. To keep this example on a parallel with the previous example, let's suppose he bought 50 shares of stock at every point in the story when the stock price was mentioned.[7] With this investment approach, his portfolio in June 1980 would have been:

		Average Price
200 shares	Ford Motor Company	$22\frac{5}{8}$
200 shares	Compugraphic Corporation	$27\frac{3}{4}$
150 shares	North American Coal	$37\frac{7}{8}$

[7]This particular assumption is used simply to illustrate a point. The proper techniques of financial planning, including stock selection and time diversification of purchases, are discussed more fully in Chapters 5 and 6.

Four years later, in addition to dividend payments, his portfolio would have appreciated in value by about 35 percent.

Thus if Charlie had followed a simple buy-and-hold strategy, coupled with spreading out his purchases over time, he would have enjoyed a 35 percent gain instead of huge losses. For financial success, it is absolutely essential to avoid the big mistakes caused by the emotional elements of financial investing, especially the greed–fear cycle. And not only does a buy-and-hold strategy coupled with periodic purchases outperform trading strategies, but it also provides psychological insulation against the emotional trap of the greed–fear cycle.

THE MARKET WILL FLUCTUATE

The current price of a stock reflects the market consensus about prospective earnings of the company and thus its ability to pay dividends, which is the ultimate investment return for stockholders. The market tries to look far into the future. It is estimated that more than 70 percent of the price of an average stock is determined by dividend prospects beyond the next five years. As the expected earnings and dividend paying power of a company changes, its stock price will change. But the *long-run* prospects of most corporations don't change rapidly or by large amounts, so one might expect stock prices to change only gradually. But that's not true. For example, Ford's price began falling sharply when it became apparent that the company would experience a large loss in 1980. Ford eventually had large losses in 1980, 1981, and 1982. But by 1983, the company's earnings were back to pre-1980 levels. Compugraphic also had a few poor years before bouncing back, but its stock price plummeted in the meantime.

If the market had its eye firmly fixed on long-run prospects, why did these stock prices react so sharply to a temporary condition? At one point in 1981, for example, investors were estimating that the market value of the entire Ford Motor Company was worth 60 percent less than its average valuation in 1979. Compugraphic Corporation had been marked down by 75 percent over the same period of time. Is it reasonable to believe that the actual long-run earnings prospects of these two companies had changed so drastically in such a short period of time?

In retrospect, stock prices always fluctuate in the short run by more than they seemingly should, given their subsequent long-run earnings performance. Clearly, short-run price fluctuations are influenced, sometimes greatly, by factors other than long-run earnings prospects. Why do stock prices fluctuate so widely? No one really knows. Theories purporting to forecast price changes come and go, but the fluctuations remain an enigma. Newspapers and the evening television news faithfully report the daily meandering of the Dow Jones Industrial Average, and analysts are regularly asked why the market was up or down that day. If the Dow was up, for example, they simply look around for a piece of good news that would plausibly explain the price increase. The fact that they ignored all of the bad news of the day doesn't seem to bother them or their audience.

It is probably incorrect to view the market pricing process as a super-efficient automaton finely calibrating the price of a given stock to reflect every ounce of information and coming to the conclusion that it's worth exactly $35 per share. Given the uncertainty of forecasting the murky future, the market more likely believes the stock is worth, say, between $32 and $38 per share. Any price within these boundaries is considered a good estimate of the intrinsic value of the stock. As long as there is no new information to change the market's estimation of long-run prospects, the stock price can fluctuate freely within these boundaries, buffeted by day-to-day events that defy prediction. There could be a rumor, later proven false, or a national news item that is momentarily unsettling. A major stockholder could be selling a large block of stock in order to buy a business for her son-in-law, who can't seem to find steady employment.

Significant new information may change investors' expectations of future earnings. But it often arrives in bits and pieces; there is usually some initial uncertainty and confusion about its reliability; and investors frequently have conflicting views about its relative importance. The price adjustment to new information is analogous to a marble in a bowl. The final resting place (new price after adjustment) is the bottom of the bowl, but after the initial push (new information), the marble continually overshoots its mark as it rolls up and down the sides of the bowl. But the overshooting diminishes until the marble finally stops at the bottom. The fact that the market is trying to forecast events in a distant and uncertain future, using an intermittent flow of new information —some good, some bad—of varying degrees of clarity and importance, helps explain why short-run price fluctuations are always greater and more frequent than would be expected on the basis of long-run earnings prospects. It also helps explain why it is impossible to predict the daily, weekly, or monthly ups and downs of stock prices.

Contrarian Charybdis

Some people believe the stock market is ruled by excessive emotionalism and crowd psychology, which causes investors to buy too much stock at market peaks and sell too much at market lows. In this view, the market is basically irrational, dominated by greed, fear, and even hysteria. To these people, called *Contrarians*, the greed-fear cycle is not simply market fluctuations that trap people like Charlie; rather, it's the Charlies of the world who *cause* these fluctuations by their excessive emotionalism. Their ideal models are the Holland tulip speculation in the 1600s, the South Sea Bubble in the 1700s, the Florida land boom in the 1920s, the stock market boom and bust during 1924-1932, and the gold frenzy in the 1970s. To a Contrarian, however, the classic speculative bubbles are just like ordinary stock market fluctuations, only writ larger. The driving force is always believed to be the crowd syndrome. A Contrarian[8] believes he or she can beat the market by interpreting these psychological swings. Because Contrarians assume that most investors overreact, they advocate doing the exact opposite of whatever is popular.

In Greek mythology, a successful sailor had to steer carefully between the twin threats of Scylla and Charybdis. If the emotionalism of the greed-fear cycle is the Scylla of successful investing, the Contrarian approach is the Charybdis. A Contrarian is just a conventional speculator turned upside down. Although Contrarians believe they are above the crass emotions of the crowd, they are really just as controlled by the actions of the crowd and the fluctuations the crowd is supposed to be creating. They must make the same judgments about the dominant mood of investors. Is the price move a speculative bubble, or does someone really know something? Is the crowd overly optimistic? Darkly pessimistic? Is the market approaching a peak or poised for a strong upward surge, fueled by speculative fever?

---

[8]Broadly defined, a *contrarian* is any investor who thinks the market price is wrong for whatever reason—that is, his or her judgment is *contrary* to popular belief. Contrarians with a capital C are the gurus who think that market prices are wrong specifically because of the emotional excesses of investors.

If it is impossible to forecast future stock prices, it should be equally impossible to know when the market is forecasting incorrectly. Optimism and pessimism are human emotions that undoubtedly affect investor decisions. It is one thing to know that psychological factors can affect stock prices. It is quite another thing to know when this is occurring and by how much. Rarely can one identify a dominant mood, which is simply to say that for every buyer there is a seller who apparently has a different opinion. Contrarian pundits seldom agree among themselves, but this shouldn't be surprising. If Contrarians began to agree, they would become the financial orthodoxy, and then only Anticontrarians could be successful. Anticontrarians would have to analyze the ability of the Contrarians to analyze the emotional temperature of investors, and then . . . .

A FINANCIAL PLAN

The name of the game on Wall Street is buy and sell. The conventional wisdom, nurtured by generations of professional advisors, is that an "active" strategy of buying low and selling high is the correct way to invest. Active investing *sounds* positive and successful. Wall Street scoffs at buy-and-hold as "passive" investing, which sounds negative and vaguely unsuccessful. But it's not negative to say you can't beat the stock market—unless, of course, you find it impossible to admit there are no geese who lay golden eggs. There are geese who lay regular eggs, and you can indeed earn a good investment return by owning shares in a company that raises geese. And, contrary to popular belief and Wall Street hype, a buy-and-hold strategy will yield a *higher* investment return in the long run than active trading. Wall Street's "active" investing will reduce your return because their advice won't help you beat an efficient stock market, but you've still got to pay commissions, advisory fees, and unnecessary taxes incurred from in-and-out trading. How *much* less you earn will depend on how much money is wasted on these futile attempts to beat the market.

A buy-and-hold investment strategy is passive only in the sense that the investor doesn't engage in actively buying and selling stocks. As explained in Chapter 2, when investors buy stock, they enter into a principal–agent contract, assigning the job of *actively* managing their investments to corporate executives. With a buy-and-hold approach, the investor depends on the special expertise of corporate executives to make the right decisions regarding product development, manufacturing, marketing, personnel, capital expansion, and finance. The system of indirect controls provided by competition in various markets encourages executives to manage the corporation's resources for the benefit of stockholders.

Because the world is an uncertain place, however, investors diversify among a number of stocks to reduce the risk of loss from the decisions of any one management team. The principal–agent contract also allows investors to devote the maximum amount of time to developing their own expertise, which provides a better overall return on their "portfolios" of human and financial capital.

You don't have to understand why stock prices fluctuate in the short run any more than you need to know how an internal combustion engine works to drive a car. By using a buy-and-hold approach and spreading purchases (and sales) over time, you can safely ignore the fluctuations. As shown in Figure 3.1, short-run fluctuations tend to smooth out over time. Even the turbulent stock market boom and bust of 1924–1932 becomes just a temporary deviation from the long-run trend. Over the past half century, for example, the total investment return (dividends plus capital gains) on average-risk stocks was about 9 percent compounded annually. The return on higher-risk stocks, mostly new and smaller companies, was 1–2 percentage points higher. This compares to an average return of about 4 percent on corporate bonds and $2\frac{1}{2}$ percent on U.S. Treasury bills. (The average inflation rate over this period was about $2\frac{1}{2}$ percent.)

The logic and evidence of the efficient markets hypothesis, which has been developed in the last three decades, is now too compelling for investors to ignore. Most investment advisors, of course, are openly hostile to the concept of an efficient stock market because it directly threatens their economic well-being. Chapter 4 examines why the investment advice industry must sell a beat-the-market approach to investing and why it thrives in the face of consistently bad results. Then, in the remainder of the book, we will develop a financial plan based on the efficient markets hypothesis. The plan is founded on four well-documented facts:

1. Because the stock market pricing process is highly efficient, traditional security analysis isn't necessary or desirable. Since returns

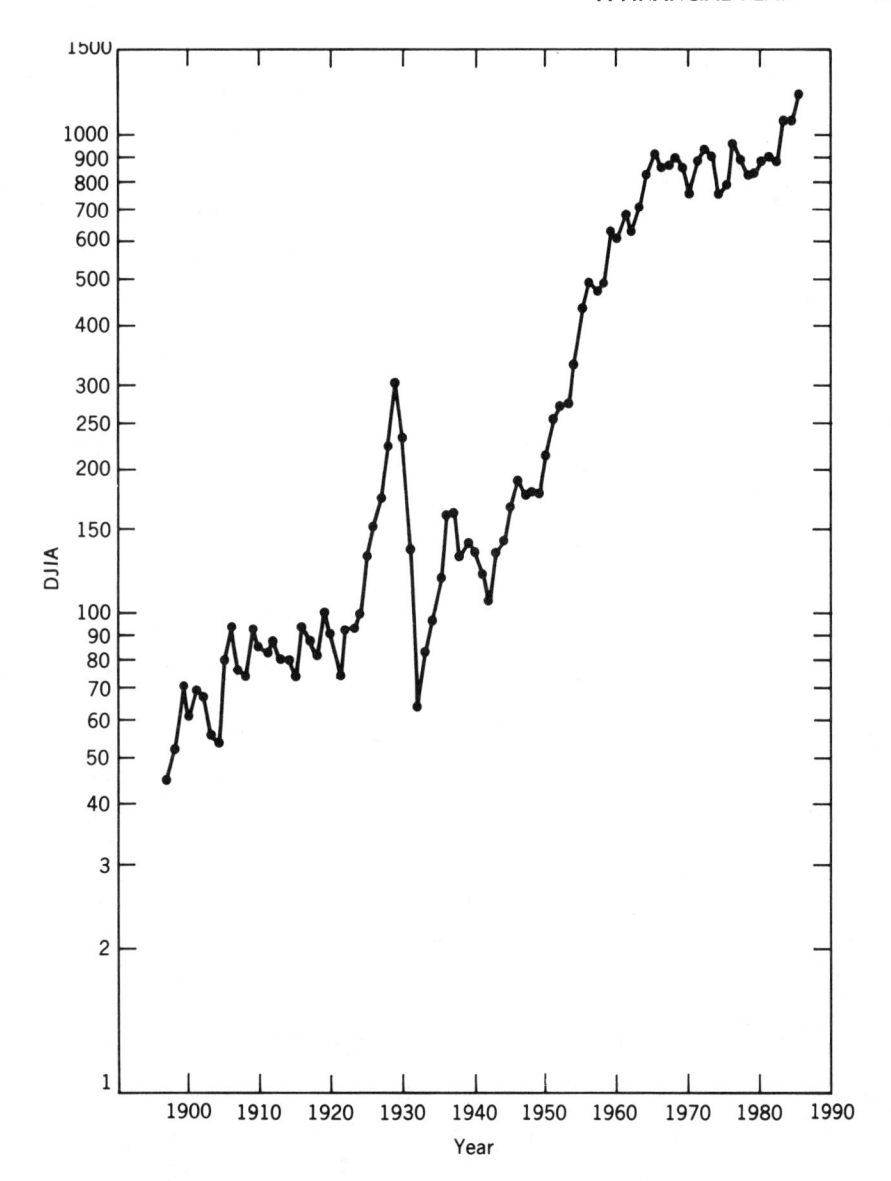

FIGURE 3.1 Dow-Jones industrial averages, 1897–1985

are proportional to the riskiness of investments, the management of risk becomes a central feature of financial investment planning.

2. Active management of investments is accomplished through the principal–agent contract between corporate executives and stockholders.

3. Short-run price fluctuations are ignored by using a buy-and-hold investment strategy and spreading purchases and sales over time.
4. Commissions, advisory fees, and taxes, which lower investment returns, are minimized by a buy-and-hold strategy and by using institutions that sell financial services at least cost.

4

TOUTS, TIPSHEETS, AND TIMING: THE INVESTMENT ADVICE INDUSTRY

Candor is rare on Wall Street, which makes it all the more delightful when it does appear. In an interview published in *Bondweek*, an executive at Citibank, the megabank in New York, commented on the large losses recently suffered by his bank because of its poor forecasts of interest rates: "We thought this kind of market would separate the men from the boys—only we didn't realize we might be one of the boys." Instead of making an admission of this sort, most Wall Street pundits would simply have ignored such a mistake or devised an ingenious rationalization to cover it. They earn their livings by claiming to know in advance how the struggle for corporate profits will turn out—who the winners and losers will be, which stocks are being mispriced by the public, and when the economy will surge or sputter. Yet, as we saw in Chapter 3, they don't know how to do these things, and it appears that they never will. They can't forecast corporate earnings any better than a naive extrapolation of past data can. They can't forecast changes in overall financial and economic conditions. And they can't systematically identify mispriced stocks.

SURVIVING ON WALL STREET

Why does the investment advice industry continue to grow and prosper in the face of well-documented, overwhelming evidence that it isn't providing value for price? For a number of reasons, the investment advice industry will survive and prosper. None of them bode well for the investor.

Investors find it virtually impossible to sort out the good from the bad from the awful when buying investment advice. Most markets function to provide good information about relative qualities and prices so that buyers can make rational choices among competing goods and services. However, the vast majority of investors have very little objective information about the relative quality of different advisory services, making it impossible for the market to reward superior investment services and eliminate the incompetent. Information about the actual performance of beat-the-market advice is not readily available. And given the nature of that information, Wall Street has every incentive not to publicize it.

Instead, investors are confronted with a wide array of investment advisory services, all clamoring for attention. What they hear is a chorus of advertising claims trumpeting successful past performances and promises of more in the future. What they don't hear about is the even longer list of past failures, which advisors conceal or rationalize away.

However, because the future is always uncertain, investors naturally seek advice in an attempt to reduce that uncertainty, especially when they feel bewildered by the seeming technical complexities of securities markets. Sometimes it appears that investors let the soothsayers do the guessing, even when they sense that it's simply a guess.

It Sounds So Plausible

People are disposed to believe that information offered for sale by Wall Street is worth the price. We regularly hire experts to give us advice—

from accountants and auto mechanics to Dr. Spock and Julia Child. And generally the advice is worth the money. Thus the idea that professional investment advice will not yield higher investment returns seems to contradict common sense. It seems so reasonable to assume that time, effort, and money spent on research will produce above-average results. Wall Street analysts are intelligent, well educated, articulate, hard working, and just as honest as the next person. Surely, then, if one hires the best and the brightest, and pays them well, one should be able to earn higher investment returns than uninformed and unadvised investors.

The reason common sense is wrong in this instance lies in the nature of an efficient market. Because so many people are thinking, studying, and searching for mispriced stocks, the market consensus is the best estimate of the true value of common stocks. Consequently, you cannot expect to earn above-average returns in the long run. For short periods of time, luck produces winners and losers—those who outperform or underperform the market average. But in the long run, things begin to equal out. Winners lose and losers win. In any typical 10-year period, about 85 percent of the Wall Street experts underperform the market and 15 percent outperform it. (There are more losers than winners because of transaction costs.) The 15 percent who earn above-average returns is just the amount you would expect on the basis of pure luck. And the evidence clearly shows that, as more years pass, these winners will join the ranks of the 85 percent who are losers—and some of the previous losers will get lucky and take their place in the 15 percent winners group for awhile.

But far more than 15 percent of the experts will *claim* winning records! If commissions, advisory fees, and unnecessary taxes are (conveniently) ignored, the laws of chance give each expert a 1-in-2 chance of outperforming the market averages during any short period of time (see Chapter 3). Then the expert can "fine tune" his or her record to provide even better results by carefully selecting for publication the most favorable time period from past results. This is the only record you will see. When you can't see the whole picture, things are rarely what they seem.

Information Costs Are High

Advisors often claim that the highly competitive nature of the investment advice industry eliminates analysts who provide bad information.

Consequently, the fact that investment advisory firms survive and people continue to pay for their services is offered as proof that the firms are providing value for price. What really happens is that advisors survive because the majority of investors have a difficult time properly evaluating the worth of their services. It is too costly in terms of time, resources, and special analytical skills for most individuals to learn enough to properly evaluate an investment advisory service. To determine whether the service is worth its price, an investor needs to ask: Can a given advisory service recommend investments that, on balance, yield a higher risk-adjusted, after-cost rate of return on a basis that cannot be attributed to luck alone? To properly answer that question, the investor needs:

1. A long record of data showing all of the unambiguous recommendations of the firm
2. A good research design that adjusts for risk and avoids measurement bias
3. An alternative buy-and-hold investment record for the same period of time for comparisons
4. The necessary computational skills and computer facilities

That represents more time and resources than most people are willing to invest in evaluating advisory services. Most investors either take the advertising claims at face value or depend on low-cost anecdotal evidence, such as advice from a friend that: "I bought some stock that was recommended by Jeffrey Chris at Hobson Securities and it has done very well." After all, we choose medical doctors, lawyers, and dentists on personal recommendations. Why not investment advisors?

But if investors wish to read about the scientific studies that have measured the performance of the investment advice industry (such as those presented in Chapter 3), where would they go? The most likely places are newspapers and magazines. Unfortunately, financial journalists are in the business of reporting news, not evaluating it. Their principal task is to fill up space for each edition, so they uncritically report financial news as it occurs. A journalist may come across the publication of a new scientific study of mutual funds that concludes that fund managers underperformed the market averages on a risk-adjusted basis for the last 20 years. This information would be dutifully reported, including the conclusion that no mutual fund in the study was consistently able to obtain an above-average performance. But the next day, the same journalist is apt to write a story about the Goforbroke Mutual Fund, which outperformed the market averages by 30 percent *last year*. The fund manager is interviewed, and the readers are regaled with stories about how she beat the market. In blissful ignorance of the article on the previous day, nothing will be said about risk or the short-term nature of Goforbroke's results.

The promotional practices of Wall Street, often reminiscent of toothpaste and deodorant advertisements, makes it even more difficult for investors to determine the value of investment advisory services. Brokerage firms and independent advisors regularly provide "studies" purporting to show their investment acumen. These self-studies, of course, are part of their advertising efforts to generate commissions and fees. Human nature being what it is, however, self-studies end up being self-serving. That's why independent CPA firms are hired to check the books of corporations and conduct inventories, and government regulators pull surprise audits on banks. It isn't that basically honest people always deliberately alter data or outright lie and cheat, but there are subtle ways to arrive at favorable results when self-interest is involved.

There is a natural tendency to loudly trumpet successful advice, while quietly forgetting the bloopers. The investment results from past advice are gleened from carefully tailored time periods. And invariably in self-studies, investment returns are not adjusted for risk and are not compared to returns that could have been expected from a buy-and-hold strategy. The studies cited in Chapter 3, on the other hand, were conducted by people who had no proprietary interest in producing any particular outcome. In effect, those studies are the "outside auditors" and they have concluded that Wall Street advice does not produce above-average investment returns. But which set of studies is the average investor apt to hear about? The ones someone has a self-interest in promoting, of course.

The Wish Is Parent to the Thought

Not only are investors predisposed to believing they receive value for price and find it very costly to prove otherwise, but many investors also have an intense *desire* to believe there are ways to beat the market.

Often, because we fervently want to believe something to be true, we think it is true. Earning an income is hard work. Saving enough of it to reach long-run financial goals always means giving up things we would like to have now. A beat-the-market approach offers the chance to substantially reduce the sacrifice—and perhaps even become rich without any real effort. It's hard to completely reject the possibility that such an opportunity exists. After all, how much is a dream worth?

If we receive information that challenges something we truly believe, there is a tendency to "assimilate," or change the way we understand the information, to make it conform to our cherished beliefs. Here again, the unwary investor will have help from Wall Street. Obviously, investment advisors are aware of the efficient markets hypothesis and know that at least some of their clients have heard of its predictions and implications for financial planning. It's important for advisors to reassure their clients that efficient markets is just a silly bit of academic nonsense. A favorite way to assimilate the evidence about efficient markets is to draw unrealistic conclusions from its basic propositions:

1. *Random walk* means that stock prices are not related to earnings, but rather are determined by irrational and emotional investors.
2. *Efficient markets* mean that investors know every bit of information about every stock in the market.
3. The stock market is like a science-fiction computer, instantly analyzing and understanding all information related to earnings prospects.
4. The stock market never makes a mistake, so stocks should be picked with a dartboard.

Investors and advisors who convince themselves that any of these outlandish statements are true can easily reject the efficient markets hypothesis and continue trying to beat the market.

This process of assimilation of information about efficient markets is also aided and abetted by the fact that scientific studies show only that there is a preponderance of evidence that Wall Street advice hasn't worked in the past. The future always remains unknown. Thus the latest trading strategy concocted has not yet been proven worthless. For some people, hope springs eternal. They cling to the fact that it can never be proven, on the basis of past experience, that something will or will not happen in the future. There is always the possibility of finding a pot of gold at the end of the next rainbow or a Rosetta Stone in the next computer run. In effect, what some investors say is that, in spite of the evidence to the contrary, they want to believe the market can be beaten. It's a case of hope winning over experience.

Thus in spite of their dismal track record, the people in the investment advice industry have a lot going for them. It isn't surprising that the industry is thriving, and there's no reason to believe it won't continue to prosper and grow. We'll now look at the industry in detail, beginning with stockbrokers.

STOCKBROKERS

Although securities trading in the United States dates back to the late eighteenth century,[1] the practice of selling investment advice along with brokerage services has rather recent origins and has become a big business only in the last three decades. This type of business has come to be known as full service brokerage. (Discount brokers, who offer just title transfer services, are covered in Chapter 7.) By the latter half of the nineteenth century, business and financial news was being published regularly in daily newspapers and in specialized journals, such as *Poor's Manual* and the *Commercial and Financial Chronicle*. The publications on financial investment advice, however, only began to appear toward the end of the century. The *Wall Street Journal* started as a newsletter in 1889, providing financial prices, business news, Wall Street gossip, and Charles Dow's ideas about how to invest in stocks. Books dealing with how to invest began to appear, and in 1907, a magazine called *The Ticker* began publishing articles on how to understand the stock market and invest in stocks.

Around the turn of the century, two things gradually began to change. First, the emphasis shifted from advice on "how to" look for good investments to specific advice on "what to" buy and sell. The second change, which was eventually to have a significant impact on the make-up of the securities industry, was the development of newsletters and research reports by brokerage firms as sales tools. Some of the earliest

---

[1]Stock trading began in Amsterdam, The Netherlands, in 1602 when the first known stock certificates were issued for the newly chartered Dutch East India company.

investment recommendations were printed on single sheets of thin paper that were sold at newsstands and by mail subscription. They were called *flimsies*.[2] (Presumably no pun was intended.) C. W. Barron began publishing a flimsy in 1887. By 1900, some individual customers' men (as stock brokers were called then) began writing their own flimsies as a way to attract new customers and promote more trading.

In 1912, Jones and Baker became the first brokerage firm to publish an investment advice newsletter as a promotional device to increase commission income. Their newsletter, the *Jones and Baker Curb News*, was distributed free to customers. It was successful, and within a few years most brokerage firms were providing some kind of investment advice as a way to promote their business. However, the investment advisory part of the brokerage industry receded in importance after the stock market crash of 1929.

After World War II, Merrill Lynch led the way in reviving and expanding the investment advisory part of the brokerage business. Following the earlier approach used with the *Jones and Baker Curb News*, Merrill Lynch research reports were given away free to obtain new sales leads and generate more trading volume—with resounding success. Other brokerage firms quickly followed suit. This established the basic conflict of interest in the modern full service stock brokerage business.

Conflict of Interest

As brokerage firms began offering free advice about which stocks to buy and sell, a fundamental change took place in the character of their business. With brokers searching for prospective investors, rather than the other way around, the brokerage firm began to resemble a manufacturer. Investment analysts are the salaried workers who assemble the product. They write plausible stories about investment opportunities. Customers' men, now called *registered representatives* or *account executives*, are the salespeople who perform the distribution function. They are paid a commission for selling the investment stories created by the analysts. The brokerage firm itself provides management expertise,

---

[2]Many of these were put out by "bucket shops," which were places where speculators could bet on whether stock prices would rise or fall. Although this was considered a low-class business, it nevertheless flourished. Bucket shops died out after the 1929 market collapse, but the same practice was recently reinvented, spruced up, and renamed as the options market. Now it is very fashionable!

pays the rent and utilities, and supplies desks, paper, and clerks in exchange for a cut of the commissions earned by the analysts and registered reps.

The primary motivation for producing research stories is to generate trading volume. Therein lies a fundamental (indeed, fatal) flaw. The commission-driven sales approach creates a basic conflict of interest between the objectives of the investor and those of the brokerage firm. Because compensation for the research product depends on getting investors to buy *and* sell, the attention of everyone in the brokerage firm is focused on ways to create more trading. The research department writes attractive stories that encourage short-term investing. Management supplies advertising material designed to enhance the reputation of the research product and reinforce the idea that short-term trading is both necessary and profitable (see Exhibit 4.1). The registered reps

EXHIBIT 4.1. Slogan Wars on Wall Street

"When E. F. Hutton talks, people listen." In its television commercials, someone whispers "Well, my broker is E. F. Hutton, and E. F. Hutton says...." This promptly halts parades, weddings, and baseball games as people stop to listen. The whisper conveys the message that E. F. Hutton offers its clients valuable, secret information. We know it's valuable because the clients in the advertisements always appear very prosperous.

You can also watch the Merrill Lynch bull carefully threading its way through a china shop, which obviously means you need Merrill Lynch's advice to pick successful investments. (Merrill Lynch <u>is</u> "A breed apart.") Sometimes the bull runs across an open prairie, looking very powerful, accompanied by the message that "Merrill Lynch is bullish on America." But on one occasion, the bull was in a cave, looking out at the rain!

"You look like you just heard from Dean Witter!" The investor is ecstatic, presumably from having just learned about the fantastic profits she has earned because of Dean Witter's advice. "Thank you, Paine Webber" undoubtedly means the same thing. Blyth Eastman Dillon thinks you should count <u>them</u> among your assets. John Houseman reassures us that "Smith Barney makes money the old-fashioned way . . . they <u>earn</u> it!" Shearson/American Express declares that their approach is "Minds over money." Inexplicably, Prudential-Bache exhorts investors to "Bring us your future."

work under the intense pressure of straight commissions to move the product—their incentive to sell the concept of short-term trading is the greatest of all.

Because brokerage firms earn when you trade, not when you succeed, it would be a lucky coincidence if investors received appropriate investment advice. To be sure, most persons in the brokerage business do not callously direct investors in wrong directions just to create trading volume, but the whole strategy of the brokerage business must be toward generating trading volume. Strangely enough, there is no compelling reason why the brokerage business had to be arranged this way. The customers' men of old could just as easily have been salaried order takers so that when brokerage firms began selling investment advice, it could have been priced just like any other product. Indeed, the flimsies started out that way. But because the compensation structure was historically based on commissions and wasn't changed, the approach pioneered by Jones and Baker produced the strong incentive for brokerage firms to design their products in such a way as to generate maximum trading volume.

Designed to Sell

Wall Street is no different from Fifth Avenue. Fifth Avenue sells clothes and expensive baubles. Wall Street sells investment advice. And as the advertising people on Madison Avenue know very well, it pays to push fashion. Fashion changes with the shifting winds, so there's always new merchandise to sell. Skirt hems rise and fall. Lapels widen and shrink. There's always a new style, a new color, a new accessory. Wall Street also sells fashion. The creative pens of investment analysts turn out a steady stream of new stories: CB radio manufacturers; nursing homes; the "nifty-fifty"; personal computer companies; cosmetic companies; and 'tronics (any name with). There are concept stocks, glamour stocks, conglomerates, special situations, and exotic tax dodges. And once a particular set of investment ideas is thoroughly sold, out of fashion, or beginning to fail, new ones are devised and new stories are written.

Because almost everyone is a potential buyer of stocks, most research stories recommend buying stocks. Analysts rarely make recommendations to sell particular stocks because the sales pitch could only be made to the relatively few people who own that stock. (Short sales, in which someone sells a stock without actually owning it on a buy-it-back-later basis, are not commonly recommended.) Registered reps must find customers with funds to invest who will buy the new investment ideas. But what about the customers who are fully invested in yesterday's fashions? Because the analysts concentrate on writing buy-recommendation stories, it is up to the registered reps to persuade customers to switch to the new merchandise. They do this by using a "comparative value" story. Stockbrokers are always comparing the value of one stock to another.

Suppose you bought stock in Ace Trucking Company last year and its price has appreciated by 20 percent. Although you've done quite well, your registered rep calls to tell you about a new stock, Soaring Sonics, which his research department is strongly recommending. It's relatively easy for him to develop a story where it makes sense to "upgrade" your portfolio, switching from Ace Trucking, which has "had its play," to Soaring Sonics, which is poised for a sharp increase in the near future. And if you buy that story, he earns two commissions.

Another way to wean investors away from a pesky long-run buy-and-hold investment strategy, which generates few commissions, is to convince them that these are complicated and troubled times, so that short-run investment *timing* is all important. Investors who buy this argument can be persuaded that successful investing requires frequent buying and selling to catch market swings. The variations on this theme are virtually limitless. Examples include:

"Never marry a stock." A basic tenet of Wall Street is that one should never "marry a stock"—that, with changing conditions, one must always be ready to sell something and buy something else.

"Cut your losses and let your profits run." With this Wall Street trading rule, the investor makes a lot of short-term buy-and-sell transactions as he or she gropes around for a profitable trade.

"The world is becoming increasingly complex, and stock market influences are more difficult to define" (from a *Merrill Lynch Investment News* bulletin).[3] Presumably, if you trade with Merrill Lynch, you're provided with the correct interpretation.

"To survive you must be alert and nimble . . . willing to adjust to

---

[3] "Research Comment 1741," *Merrill Lynch Investment News*, October 16, 1978.

sudden shifts in conditions and get out of things quickly if they don't behave properly" (from an advertisement for a popular investment newsletter). The advisor proceeds to tell you he is *very* alert and will sell you information so you too can be alert, nimble, and know when "things" are not behaving properly.

"Continuous supervision" is what Standard and Poor's claims is required for successful investing. By regularly reading its publication, *The Outlook,* you'll be fully advised on economic and financial trends so you can keep changing, keep succeeding, and, above all, keep subscribing.

Technical analysis is a particularly useful sales tool in promoting an investment timing strategy because it is based on catching short-term price movements.[4] Moreover, it is a more versatile sales tool than fundamental analysis. When an especially ominous "upside resistance level" or "head-and-shoulders top" appears in the charts or the stock market averages, for example, the technical analyst may recommend selling all stocks. The registered rep can then make this sales pitch to a broad range of investors because the sell recommendation is not restricted to specific stocks.

Baby Needs Shoes

The people in the full service brokerage business who experience the most severe conflict of interest are the registered reps. Every morning these men and women must say to themselves: "Baby needs shoes." The words may differ, but the intent is the same. How am I going to reach my commission quota today? Although the tactics may vary, the strategy is the same as the strategy in most sales jobs. The registered rep must contact the largest possible number of people each working day and try to get them to make a purchase or sale.

Make no mistake—a registered rep is a salesperson first and foremost. His or her salary does not depend on giving objective investment advice; rather, the rep is compensated in direct proportion to the amount of commission income generated for the brokerage firm. Merrill Lynch, for example, is quite clear about this sales focus in the job description brochure given to prospective account executives (i.e., registered reps):

[4]Recall the discussion of the chart readers in Chapter 3.

> We select our candidates on the basis of ability and past performance. Generally, we look for a history of successful employment especially in related sales areas or other responsible positions as closely related to sales as possible. Since the position of account executive is basically one of sales, we also look for applicants who communicate well and who have the ability to deal easily with others.... To develop clients, the account executive uses prospecting methods such as telephone solicitations, mailings, personal contacts, lectures and seminars.... The career of an account executive can be very rewarding financially.

The whole idea is to get investors to move from one stock to another. It's a numbers game. The more people a registered rep contacts, the more orders (tickets) can be written. While registered reps are getting you to buy and sell, however, they must contend with one important constraint. They cannot churn customers. *Churn* is a four-letter word on Wall Street. It means to advise one's customers to make an unnecessarily large number of transactions for no other purpose than to earn commissions. However, what is unnecessarily large is hopelessly vague and can be proven only in extreme circumstances—and not always then. The legal definition of churning depends on both intent *and* results. If the intent is to churn, but by luck the churning happens to result in reasonable profits, that's astute investing, not churning!

The comparative value stories spun by registered reps are an especially effective sales tool because they are created subconsciously through the process of assimilation. Fred Schwed tells it best:

> But I doubt if there are many, or any, Wall Streeters who sit down and say to themselves cooly, "Now let's see. What cock-and-bull story shall I invent and tell them today?" I don't think you can supply any guarantee of accuracy when looking into the heart and mind of someone else. But I feel, from years of personal observation, that the usual thought process is far more innocent. The broker influences the customer with his knowledge of the future, but only after he has convinced himself. The worst that should be said of him is that he wants to convince himself badly and that he therefore succeeds in convincing himself—generally badly.[5]

The registered rep gets a lot of help from the investor. In a confidence game, it's not who one is, but who the victim thinks one is that matters.

---

[5]Fred Schwed, Jr., *Where Are the Customers' Yachts?* (New York: Simon and Schuster, 1940). Copyright © 1940 by Fred Schwed, Jr. Renewed © 1967 by Harriet Wolf Schwed. Reprinted by permission of Simon & Schuster, New York.

Victims assist in their own downfalls. They want to believe in the rep because they think they're going to get something for nothing. The con artist simply tells victims what they want to hear.

There is constant pressure on registered reps from management to produce more tickets because commissions support everyone in the brokerage firm. This has been especially true in recent years because overhead costs in the brokerage business are rising sharply as they expand their menu of financial services. In 1983 large brokerage firms wanted each of their registered reps to generate, on average, $300,000 per year in gross commissions. This is double the target level in 1980. From this amount, the registered rep earns between $100,000 and $135,000 per year—which is what Merrill Lynch meant when its job description brochure stated that "the career of an account executive can be very rewarding financially." Management makes it quite clear that a registered rep who doesn't meet the quota will be replaced.

Registered reps want their customers to do well. That makes the job easier! But they know, as do all investment advisors, that there will be a considerable turnover of accounts. When a rep's advice works out, all is well. But inevitably, there will be bad recommendations, and customers will move on to brokers promising better results. This condition provides an incentive to earn as much commission income as possible before the customer leaves. It also means that reps' recommendations will be biased toward short-term investments.

Registered reps also deal with account turnover by diversifying their recommendations. If a rep recommends the same stock to every customer and it turns out badly, the rep could lose a large number of accounts all at once. To minimize this risk, a rep recommends a particular stock or investment idea to only part of the customer list. The rep keeps track of the recommendations made to each account. The investors who bought the winners will be happy and very receptive to the rep's next comparative value recommendation. Indeed, some registered reps reason that these investors *owe* them a couple of extra commissions as a bonus for recommending a winner. The people who did not take the rep's advice on the winners will be firmly reminded of that fact, making them good prospects for the next recommendation.

Investors who bought the losers are much more difficult to handle. A really talented registered rep will convince some of these investors that "you can't win 'em all" and get them to switch to a new stock (with great potential, of course). Sometimes a customer can be persuaded to accept part of the responsibility for the bad recommendation on the grounds that the customer agreed with the original idea. Used in moderation, these tactics at least slow down attrition. Many disgruntled losers will still transfer their accounts. But all is not lost! Registered reps at the firm across the street will experience the same attrition. As long as all of the registered reps keep prospecting, each will pick up his or her share of these unhappy investors. So in effect, brokers simply swap customers.

This pool of customers gradually shrinks, however, as some people retire, expire, run out of money, or quit the game in disgust. So the registered rep must continue to prospect for first-time investors. Did you ever meet a broker at a party/wedding/golf match/laundromat who didn't eventually turn the conversation to the stock market?

INDEPENDENT ADVISORS

Clearly there is a fundamental conflict of interest in the commission-driven approach of full service brokerage firms. But conflicts of interest also exist for other investment advisors. There are incentives, varying from slight to serious, for an independent advisor to recommend particular investments or strategies that will yield higher fees but are inappropriate for the objectives of the investor. As with the preceding discussion of stockbrokers, the issue here is not whether the advice is bad because one cannot beat the market, but whether the advice is bad because it's biased by a conflict of interest due to the nature of the compensation procedure.

Fee-Only Service

Some advisors offer a fee-only service where investment information is purchased on an hourly rate or flat-fee basis, regardless of whether or not the investor follows the advice. In this case, the advisor sells only advice. This type of service involves the least conflict of interest and, assuming the advisor is competent and honest, it represents the best way to purchase investment advice. It's also the least used.

But there is still a potential conflict of interest with fee-only advisory services. A periodic review is necessary for all investment programs to determine whether a program is still meeting the investor's long-term financial objectives. If the review is a routine assessment of the return-risk characteristics of a portfolio constructed according to the best principles of finance and if the advisory fee reasonably reflects the cost of the review, the investor will probably receive good value for the price. (This review process is described in Chapter 6.) Unless circumstances change drastically, however, a review of this type is only needed about every five years. A fee-only advisor may recommend an inappropriate short term investment strategy that requires frequent and costly reviews. Thus an investor dealing with an independent advisor must be able to distinguish between genuine and bogus advice (see Chapter 5).

Fee-Plus-Commission Service

Many independent advisors charge on a fee-plus-commission basis. In this case, the investor pays a fee for developing a financial plan, but the advisor also provides brokerage services. The investor, however, is under no obligation to implement the plan through the advisor. The recommendations merely give the advisor "fishing rights" in the investor's wallet. But the potential for a serious conflict of interest is the same as with registered reps in brokerage firms. Here is an actual case: Mrs. Smith, recently widowed, wanted to invest $60,000, the proceeds from her husband's life insurance policy. Other than her house, which was paid for, she had no other investments. She contacted an independent investment advisor. His major recommendation was a $40,000 limited partnership share in a new shopping center; but she had to hurry because the deal would be closed in three days.

What's wrong with this advice? Everything! The diversification requirement, a basic tenet of finance, was ignored. Mrs. Smith should never put more than 10 percent of her funds in any single investment. The return–risk requirements of the investor, another basic tenet of finance, was ignored. This investment had far too much risk for Mrs. Smith's objectives and circumstances. (The advisor didn't know that because he didn't ask.) But there just happened to be a 13 percent commission for selling the investment, which might have had something to do with the recommendation. The advisor would have received, perhaps, 50 percent of that. Imagine, one recommendation, one fee of $2600! Fortunately, Mrs. Smith had the presence of mind to ignore the pressure tactic of a close deadline and checked with her lawyer. He told her he didn't know much about finance, but it certainly didn't sound right to him. He advised her to avoid the investment and the advisor, which she did. This is a worst-case example. It doesn't happen all the time, but it does happen.

Major brokerage firms are expanding into fee-plus-commission advisory services, adding razzle-dazzle computerized analysis to increase the credibility of the financial plans they offer. This makes it easier later on to sell the securities to implement the plan. The procedure works something like this: First, the customer fills out a form listing income, assets, liabilities, tax status, dependents, goals, and risk tolerance. Then, following an interview or two where additional information is collected, the customer's life history is fed into a computer, and out pops a personalized financial plan. Fees range from $150 to $1500—and up.

At first glance, this appears to be a fee-only service, but the financial plan is actually just a marketing device. The real payoff comes when the brokerage firm gets the customer to make the transactions to carry out the recommendations made in the plan. That's the job of the registered rep, who is undergoing another title change. In this capacity, the rep is called a *financial consultant*, befitting the new job, which is to sell everything from stocks and tax planning services to insurance and real estate.

It's quite improbable that the financial plan would recommend you do nothing, which clearly would not be in the interest of its promoter. There are always a number of alternatives that would roughly accomplish a given set of investment objectives, so it's quite easy to come up with reasons to sell some of what the customer already owns and buy something else. And there's no end to the financial products being sold by these new financial supermarkets: stocks, bonds, mutual funds, commodities, annuities, unit investment trusts, film financing partnerships, real estate, life insurance, homeowners' insurance, IRAs, and money market funds. The registered rep—financial consultant—also has enough latitude to select items that produce the greatest amount of commissions. Tax shelter fees, for example, are generally 5–8 percent, and real estate deals have commissions ranging up to 13 percent. Of this, the financial consultant typically gets 40–50 percent, which helps explain why these items are pushed very hard.

INVESTMENT NEWSLETTERS

"I close my eyes and look way up into the eye of my mind. If I see the image of a ship sinking, I know the market is going down. But if I see a train gathering speed, for instance, I know it's going up." No, that's not Madame Victoria holding forth at her Friday evening seance. It's Joseph

DeLouise preparing the material for an edition of his stock market newsletter, *Prophet-Sharing*. DeLouise is a profit prophet. Arch Crawford publishes *Crawford Perspectives*, which provides forecasts of the stock market based on the position of the planets. Stan Weinstein writes the *Professional Tape Reader*. Weinstein believes that the stock market is a giant psychological casino, and he tries to identify major moves as they are developing.

All three of these men are SEC-registered investment advisors.[6] They are part of a cottage industry that includes hundreds of newsletters, subscribed to by over 250,000 people, that forecast everything from stock prices and interest rates to the price of gold and soybeans. In 1981 DeLouise reportedly had 300 subscribers at $250 per year. That's $75,000 annually—for a business run out of his apartment. In the same year, the *Professional Tape Reader* had about 9000 subscribers at $175 each. That's $1.5 million before paper clips, postage, and advertising.

The most prominent investment newsletter writer in recent times has been Joe Granville. Dubbed the "Market Maven" by the *Washington Post*, Granville admits to a gross income of $4–6 million a year from his epistle, *The Granville Market Letter*, and ancillary services. Joe uses technical analysis to forecast movements in the stock market. In-and-out trading recommendations are based on such timing devices as a "net field trend" indicator, "upside nonconfirmations," and price–volume configurations. Granville's creed is that "the market always tells you where it is going." And he claims to know how to interpret the road signs.

What's the attraction? Why do hundreds of thousands of subscribers pay over $50 million a year for investment newsletters? It's quite simple. Buyers and sellers alike see dollar signs. Because there would be enormous profits for anyone who actually could outsmart the market, subscribers keep conning themselves into believing they may get something for nothing. The dazzling dream of riches blinds them to the fact that no one would really sell genuine information on how to beat the market for a mere $200 or even $2 million when they could use it to trade stocks

---

[6]To become a registered advisor with the SEC, one must fill out a form saying that one has not violated any securities laws lately, does not have a police record or a history of fraud, and promises to disclose whether one owns any of the securities one recommends. Investment advisors are not approved by the SEC or accredited by any certifying or licensing agency. Investment advisors are held accountable for the quality of their advice only by their clients (or their clients' lawyers). This arrangement is based on the premise that no one should attempt to license people who are simply giving opinions because this would violate the First Amendment protection of freedom of speech.

and amass a far larger fortune with far less effort than is involved in putting out a monthly newsletter.

Investment newsletter writers are the modern-day alchemists. They turn *words* into gold.[7] Huge rewards await the fortunate letter writer who hits on an attractive approach, is reasonably lucky, and has a gift for "creative writing" (which means obscuring the fact that his or her advice won't enable you to beat the market). A newsletter writer must justify the subscription fee by convincing investors that the information is timely, valuable, and needed on a continuous basis. This is made easier by relying on the facts discussed earlier, namely: People are predisposed to believing that advice increases investment returns; it is difficult to obtain information to disprove this conviction; and greed makes some investors highly vulnerable to the incantations of financial gurus. A newsletter writer is always making predictions about future changes and inserting teasers about important information that will be in the next edition. After all, who wants to pay for advice that says the next six months will be pretty dull?

Brokers often traffic in newsletter advice because it's heavily biased toward in-and-out trading. Major firms like Prudential-Bache, E. F. Hutton, Dean Witter, and Merrill Lynch sponsored Granville's seminars when he was at the peak of his popularity. Financial journalists lend respectability to the newsletters by dutifully reporting on the ones that are currently "hot." Although we smile gratuitously at the local palm reader, if the prophet wears a business suit, uses financial terminology, and advertises in, say, *Barron's*, he can often earn a tidy sum by risking little more than his words and occasionally some egg on his face when the gods are unkind to him.

Jesse Livermore, Meet Joe Granville

Every era has its seers—people who can seemingly forecast the future. Wall Street oracles have learned that it is less risky and more profitable to sell their advice than to take it themselves. But it wasn't always this way. Back in the days before the SEC spoiled all the fun with its stuffy regulations, speculation and attempts to manipulate stock prices were great sport. In those days of yore, one of the prominent stockmarketeers was a man named Jesse Livermore. Livermore generally traded with his own money. By his own account,[8] his trading was based on such funda-

---

[7]A tip of the hat to Adam Abelson, the wordsmith at *Barron's*.

[8]Jesse Livermore, *How to Trade in Stocks* (New York: Duell, Sloan and Pearce, 1940).

mental information as expected business conditions and how they would affect the profitability of various companies and industries, coupled with his own brand of chart reading and his intuition about future movements of stock prices. He claimed he didn't try to manipulate or force stock prices, but let the public, the investment pools, and the big insiders make their moves. Then, by correctly interpreting their motives, he traded with them.

Through some combination of knowledge, luck, and the instincts of a riverboat gambler, Livermore was able to amass large profits from stock market trading. He became something of a celebrity who was watched, talked about, and interviewed for newspaper stories. He acquired the usual trappings of wealth—a large home, travel, and parties with prominent people. Occasionally, he would lose his touch and be all but wiped out. He earned—and lost—three or four fortunes in his lifetime. At the bottom of one of these swings in luck, he committed suicide in a public washroom. His estate was valued at $10,000.

Alas, Livermore lived before his time. Had he been born 30 years later, he too would have learned the Golden Rule of Wall Street: Sell your advice; don't *ever* take it yourself. With *The Livermore Market Letter*, Livermore could have earned a good living and provided a secure financial future for his family. Instead, he suffered an ignominious end.

In some ways, Granville is like Livermore. The business of both is (or was) forecasting stock prices, and they both became celebrities. Granville made the front page of the *Wall Street Journal* and the *New York Times*, and appeared on television shows like *Good Morning America*, and *Nightline*. He was invited to play in Pro-Am golf tournaments, and he has played before standing-room-only audiences in investment seminars across the country. But that's where the similarity ends. Livermore's objective was to win money by buying low and selling high. Because he was risking his own money, the measurement of his success or failure was simplicity itself: Did his bank account grow or shrink because of his trades? Today's financial astrologers are different. Granville and the other stock market pundits don't have to be right to be winners, they just have to *appear* to be right.

The Sap Flows Freely

Granville came to prominence as a financial guru who predicted every stock market turn from 1975–1980. This appears to be a remarkable record, but it's hardly unique. The world abounds with stock market analysts who claim unusual powers to forecast economic and financial events. And sure enough, if you sift through their published records, you can usually find evidence of uncanny accuracy and fantastic profits for anyone willing to pay the subscription price and follow the advice. But how can this be? Chapter 3 emphatically stated that the future is truly unpredictable. Is it possible that a few people really *do* know how to forecast the future and are willing to sell this information?

Closer inspection of newsletters and other forecasting reports, however, reveals a confidence game—a con that has worked for generations of investment advisors who have discovered that if one carefully taps the Tree of Greed, the avaricious sap flows freely. Smart prophets (those who survive) realize that forecasting is a very chancy business and they are going to make a lot of errors. To cope with this highly uncertain situation, they depend on several rules:

Maintain a consistent style

Make the forecast fit the facts

Continuously prospect for fresh, new customers

These rules are used, to a greater or lesser degree, by everyone in the investment advice business, but they are employed in a particularly audacious and flagrant manner by the newsletter writers.

Most advisors develop a unique style or investment strategy, such as concentrating on hot or fashionable stocks, small emerging companies, or high-technology industries. Others rely on market timing, trading precious metals, or divining with ouija boards. At any point in time, the changing fortunes of the market will always be favoring at least one of these investment approaches. Even a broken clock is right twice a day! Analysts who stick to their own special approaches can expect their recommendations to occasionally earn above-average investment returns. And when Lady Luck grants them their spot in the sun, they exercise full bragging rights. This helps replenish the customer or subscription list that became depleted during the lean years.

Analysts (or investors) who keep changing their style, however, run the risk of losing their "turn" for the occasional winner. From the late 1960s to the late 1970s, for example, the University of Pennsylvania endowment fund kept switching managers and investment objectives. And, as luck would have it, they always seemed to be adopting last year's fashion. For the 10-year period ending in 1978, the market value of the University's portfolio increased by 6 percent, whereas the average for all university endowment funds with roughly the same risk level increased by 45 percent. By continually changing directions, the University of Pennsylvania lost millions of dollars they would have earned if they had simply made no changes at all. A broken clock is right twice a day—*unless* one moves the hands!

The prophet's job is to make forecasts about future facts. As time passes, of course, the future becomes the present, and the facts become known. Naturally, prophets would like to advertise a track record that looks better than the one bestowed by Lady Luck. Because they can't change unassailable facts, whenever necessary they "change" their forecasts to fit the facts. Their objective is to present a record[9] of prophetic forecasts that can be used to get current subscribers to renew and new ones to sign up. The variations on this con are only limited by the imagination of its perpetrators. This is the realm of creative writing.

Creative prophets always seem able to discuss an event that just happened—one they predicted would *never* happen—and make it sound as if they had really predicted it. Once analysts of this sort have a chance to reinterpret what they actually said, rarely does it turn out that they have made a bad forecast. The truly gifted seer, moreover, can get investors to blame themselves for not taking the advice that was so "clearly" given to them. In that case, we have the paradox of an investor losing money and still renewing his or her subscription.

The basic approach to forecasting is simply to forecast—often. Make a number of reasonably definite, but not necessarily consistent forecasts. Wait for one of them to come true, then discharge bombastic pronouncements about yet another "successful" prediction, while quietly letting the others fade away. Usually, the forecasts are vague[10] enough so that when the actual events unfold, the oracle can turn sows-ear recommendations into silk purses.

The type of forecast that has provided a good living for generations of stock market seers goes something like this:

---

[9]In the past, these records were completely unaudited. The *Hulbert Financial Digest* recently began publishing the track records of advisory services, which has elicited screams of anguish (and some lawsuits) from some of these analysts.

[10]We do not intend to tar every advisory service with this accusation. Some analysts provide clear and unambiguous recommendations. According to all the evidence, however, their investment results aren't any better.

> We are in a long bull market. It is quite likely that stock prices will continue to rise. The market should reach 1500 on the Dow in this run. But the probabilities are getting greater that the market may soon experience a very sharp correction. We will monitor day-to-day movements.

Let's diagnose this statement line by line: "We are in a long bull market." Stock prices rise, on balance, 78 percent of the time. After the fluctuations are smoothed out, we have been in a bull market at least since the turn of the century (see Figure 3.1). So the prediction that prices will "continue to rise" is not particularly useful information.

"The market should reach 1500 on the Dow in this run." This is a time-honored forecasting ploy: Give 'em a date or give 'em a number, but don't give 'em both at the same time. This approach allows the forecaster considerable latitude to fine-tune a prediction to fit the facts. Predict that the market will reach 1500, but not when—or predict that the market will be up over the next two years, but not by how much.

"But the probabilities are getting greater . . . ." Is that an increase from one chance in ten to two chances in ten or to nine chances in ten? It would make a lot of difference to the investor!

"The market may experience a very sharp correction." The prophet didn't say it *will* experience a correction, only that it *may*. If it doesn't, the prophet has correctly predicted that the bull market will continue. If it does, it's another accurate forecast of a market turn. It's just a matter of waiting to see which should be emphasized in subsequent newsletters. In this case, the forecaster has held onto the greatest amount of flexibility—this statement hasn't provided either a date *or* a number.

And just how sharp is a "sharp correction?" That is open for creative interpretation after the fact. If the market happens to have a 75-point pullback before continuing its upward trend, the prophet can decide it was sharp enough to fulfill the prediction, even though there would be little or no profit to investors from trading on the basis of such a small fluctuation. But if the market declines by 400 points, the forecast will look somewhat suspect because there *are* limits to how far one can stretch the word *sharp*, and *correction* does seem rather out of place under those circumstances. But as the market sinks ever lower, *sharp* can be gradually transformed into *severe* in subsequent newsletters. Soon it will appear that the prediction always was "severe," which better fits the facts. The word *correction* will disappear altogether. Voilá! Another accurate forecast. This con could be called *forecasting back-*

wards, whereby the con artist makes a collage of various and sundry past predictions to fit today's facts. This takes the uncertainty out of forecasting, which is the major occupational hazard for stock market seers.

"We will monitor the day-to-day movements." Interpretation: Renew your subscription!

Forecasters know that occasionally a recommendation or two will turn out so badly they can't talk their way out of it. When this happens, they boldly admit their mistake (since it's impossible to hide the fact anyway) and announce that they have made the necessary adjustment in their technique or discovered a fantastic new approach that will line the subscriber's pockets with gold (in the future, of course). This may help retain at least some of the current subscribers, but many will desert, so the prophets continuously prospect for fresh, new customers. Sooner or later, a prophet's luck will change for the better, and new subscribers, not burned by past bad recommendations, will be convinced they have found the true prophet.

FRAUD, PURE AND SIMPLE?

It has been said that Wall Street is a street with a river at one end and a graveyard at the other—to which Fred Schwed added: and a kindergarten in the middle![11] Most of the grown-ups who play in the Wall Street kindergarten are involved in an innocuous little con game. The analysts and stockbrokers are selling dreams, and investors are the enthusiastic buyers. Few people doubt that most Wall Streeters have good intentions, although, as Milton Friedman observed, good intentions is an overrated virtue.[12] Nevertheless, most of these people would never consider actually lying or cheating in business or personal transactions.

But there is a lot of fraud committed on Wall Street because that's where the money is. Advertisements promising fantastic investment returns are placed by crooks, and some investors respond because they are misled by the fact that the advertisements appear in highly respectable places, like the *New York Times*, the *Wall Street Journal*, and

[11]Schwed, *Customers' Yachts*, p. 3.

[12]Milton Friedman, "Doing Good," in *An Economist's Protest* (Glen Ridge, New Jersey: Thomas Horton, 1972). See also: Milton and Rose Friedman, *Free to Choose* (New York: Harcourt, Brace, Jovanovich, 1980), Milton and Rose Friedman, *Tyranny of the Status Quo* (San Diego: Harcourt, Brace, Jovanovich, 1984).

FRAUD, PURE AND SIMPLE?

Barron's. They reason that if it appears in the *Journal*, the deal has to be legitimate. Although these publications try to screen out such advertisements, convicted swindlers and persons known to have violated securities laws in the past do get by the safeguards and bilk the unwary and trusting out of millions of dollars each year.

However, fraud is never pure, and rarely simple. Somewhere between the kindergarten and the crooks is a troublesome gray area where promotional tactics range from slightly deceitful to outrageously larcenous. Consider the following advertisement, which arrived by mail under the letterhead of one of the top 10 brokerage firms in America. It offered to supply information on an investment that:

1. Had a 50 percent-per-year return that was
2. Highly liquid and
3. Very safe—and
4. One third of the profits were tax exempt.

Does this sound too good to be true? Why would anyone be willing to share such a fantastic deal with you? Even if you paid a 50-percent income tax each year on all taxable profits, a modest initial investment of $20,000 in this deal would grow to $640,000 in just over 10 years. You'd be a millionaire in 13 years. There's no doubt this brokerage firm can "prove" its claim by pointing to a short period of time in the past when this investment opportunity earned a 50 percent return. But the tooth fairy notwithstanding, this is not a fair way to depict the returns one can expect from a highly liquid and safe investment. In fact, that's a wildly exaggerated claim for the returns on a very risky investment. Is it just a little white lie when a well-known member of the New York Stock Exchange makes a claim like this?

Consider another example. This was a slick advertising package that arrived from a smaller, but still well known brokerage firm brandishing such credentials as a member of the New York Stock Exchange and clearing through Merrill Lynch. Their pitch was very smooth:

> We specialize in creating investment programs to meet the varied demands and requirements of a discriminating clientele. The philosophy of our strategies is to define the clients' investment objectives and then translate these objectives into a working dialogue that results in an appropriate allocation and direction of investment capital.

What were they selling? A managed options trading program. They included the inevitable "track record of a typical account" for the five-month period June 1, 1980 through October 20, 1980, showing 100 percent returns. Why that particular time period? You can guess! They unobtrusively slipped in a disclaimer that the SEC insists on about risk and past performance not insuring future results, but the message was clear. They can win *big* for you. Why would anyone mess around with the previous investment that only promised a 50 percent return when one can earn 100 percent every five months? That way, one could cut down on that bothersome waiting and retire a millionaire in four years.

Other examples, which escalate their claims even higher to attract attention in the highly competitive market for investment advice, arrive almost daily in our mailbox—and perhaps in yours too:

"The World's First Insured Investor Program—*You Can't Lose!*" With this deal, you invest $10,000, and the advisor guarantees a minimum return of $50,000 or you get all your money back.

Government oil lease advisor,
Coral Gables, Florida

"Over $35,000 profits from my mechanical trading system for the S&P 500." The advisor will sell you a formula that takes less than 1 minute a day (no computers, no charts, and presumably no thinking). He claims $35,975 profits in about six months.

Investment advisor,
Kalispell, Montana

A letter to investment advisors offers a program of trading in government securities. The minimum investment is $4500, and the offer claims potential returns of 100–300 percent within 30 days. The letter suggests that investment advisors sell this deal to their customers; in return, they will receive a very good commission.

Securities firm,
Cleveland, Ohio

A book that teaches you how to trade in stock options. "Profits of 1000% are not unusual. Profits of 500% available every day. . . ."

Mail order publishing company,
Huntington Beach, California

Finally, there's the gold medal winner:

> "The _____ system, in just over four years trading only (1) contract each of 11 commodities, had a total profit after all commissions of $1,097,156—no doubling up, no pyramiding." And all of this is accomplished within a few minutes per day in a completely mechanical way—no judgment (thinking) necessary.
>
> A research "Institute"
Charlotte, North Carolina

The seller tells us he is independently wealthy (which is presumably why he is willing to sell us this valuable information). The seller promises to limit sales to 200 units, which includes a hand-held computer, and you must "promise" not to trade more than five contracts of any commodity per month. Notice that the claim of $1 million profits was earned by trading only one contract for each commodity. With five contracts, you could have earned $5 million, so a five-contract limit certainly seems reasonable to us. The price? Only $3000, which is cheap, considering how much money you're going to make. It's curious, however, that if the advertiser does sell 200 units, this will gross $600,000, which he could presumably make in several months by trading with the system himself!

Are the claims made by the giant Wall Street brokerage firms, the independent advisors, the newsletter writers, and the mail order flimflams harmless enthusiasm, mildly deceitful, or fraudulent? Investors must decide that for themselves. But regardless of intent, scientific evidence has shown that investment returns of this magnitude are clearly unobtainable unless the investor is very, very lucky.

5

TOTAL INVESTMENT PORTFOLIO PLANNING

Once you realize that the only significant result that comes from Wall Street's beat-the-market advice is commissions and fees for the financial community, the focus of your investment strategy will shift drastically. Instead of buying and selling stocks in a futile attempt to outperform the stock market, you will shift the focus of your activities to selecting stocks that meet your personal risk preferences and meet the minimum standards for good portfolio management. And once you start thinking in these much more realistic terms, you will find the process of actually choosing the right stocks quite easy.

TO PLAN OR NOT TO PLAN

The most serious mistake an investor can make is not having an overall, consistent investment strategy based on sound principles of finance. A central plan provides a set of well-defined standards and the discipline to select investments that will help an investor meet his or her own financial objectives. Without a central plan, investors are vulnerable to the emotional pitfalls of the greed–fear cycle and easy prey for Wall Street gurus hawking the latest fads and special angles. Successful investors learn to make their own decisions, based on their long-term objectives, rather than responding willy-nilly to the beguiling stories of every salesperson who comes along.

There are just four basic principles you need to understand. The first three relate to what is called *risk management*, and the fourth is just a matter of obtaining good information on the where, the when, and the how of buying cost-effective financial services. Good investment planning flows quite naturally from these four principles. They are:

1. *An appropriate return–risk combination must be selected.* Only charlatans try to sell high return–low risk investments. They don't exist. You must determine for yourself how much risk you are willing to bear, realizing that reaching for higher returns is risky.

2. *Investments must be diversified.* The return–risk tradeoff applies to only *necessary* kinds of risk. There is no payoff for the risk of putting all of your financial eggs in one basket. You can easily avoid this unnecessary risk, however, with portfolio diversification, which spreads your financial eggs among 12 or more baskets.

3. *Investment purchases must be time-diversified.* The first rule of stock market prices is that they fluctuate. (Some say that's the *only* rule!) If you invest your life savings into stocks all at one time, you might be unlucky and pick a temporary market high, and you might not get back to even for years. Time diversification is the technique for protecting yourself against that trap by spreading your purchases (and sales) over time. Time diversification also helps insulate you from the emotions of the greed–fear cycle.

4. *Transaction costs must be minimized.* It is absurd to pay for services you don't need or to pay higher prices than necessary for services you do need. Both errors are made by investors with distressing regularity. Why? Partly because of the prohibitive cost of acquiring information. For most people, it is too costly to take large chunks of time away from their careers, avocations, and social lives to study financial markets and institutions. And Wall Street has a direct financial incentive to make things that are really quite simple appear mysterious and intricate. People who are confused or uninformed are easily sold advice they don't need!

THE MEANING OF
TOTAL INVESTMENT PORTFOLIO PLANNING

The term *portfolio* is used in finance to mean an investor's list of assets. *Portfolio management*, then, means having an investment plan and using it as one buys and sells securities. Our approach to investment planning requires that *each* change in your portfolio must satisfy *all* four of the principles we have just listed. Each transaction that changes your list of holdings must be consistent with the target level of risk you have chosen for your overall portfolio. Each change must conform to the principles of portfolio diversification and must provide adequate time diversification. Finally, each change must be accomplished with minimum transaction costs.

We call this approach Total Investment Portfolio Planning (TIPP). It is not a secret wealth formula. There is no mystery or magic involved. The four principles of TIPP are based on the results of careful scientific research carried out by many people in the field of finance. Much of this research has been published in just the last two decades. These principles of investment management are now used by many large institutions that handle multimillion dollar portfolios for pension funds, insurance companies, and bank trust funds.

Most of this new knowledge about effective investment planning, however, is written in highly technical language and is buried in professional journals. Much of it depends on collecting tons of data, and using elaborate computer programs and very sophisticated techniques for achieving technical perfection in portfolio management. For most investors, trying to achieve the principles of TIPP with this degree of perfection is far more costly than it's worth. That's where we come in. There are some shortcuts you can take to achieve *approximately* the same result without the expense.

Unfortunately, one shortcut that isn't readily available to the average investor is hiring an investment advisor who uses the principles of TIPP. Most advisors who deal with individual investors are still selling the old-time religion of beat the market. They will be busy helping you *under*perform, rather than concentrating on setting up an efficient portfolio plan for you. And even if you could find an advisor who uses all of the TIPP principles of finance, it would be time consuming for him or her to tailor a program to meet your personal financial objectives. As a result, the advisory fees would cost considerably more than it would be worth in terms of your improved performance.

When your financial assets exceed, say, a half million dollars, it may become worthwhile to pay a professional advisor for refinements in your portfolio. When you reach that point, the knowledge provided in this book will enable you to select the right kind of investment advisor and judge the quality of service by TIPP standards. Until then, what we present here is a step-by-step program allowing you to capture most of the benefits of the TIPP principles of finance.

BASIC LOGIC OF TOTAL INVESTMENT PORTFOLIO PLANNING

Your investment approach should be based on the two fundamental ideas presented earlier. The first is the principal–agent relationship discussed in Chapter 2. As a stockholder, you are the principal, and corporate managers act as your agents. When you purchase stock in a company, you rely on competitive markets to ensure that the corporate management team conducts the activities of your company on your behalf to the best of its ability. Because of competitive markets, corporate managers generally succeed only when you succeed. Most of your efforts are devoted to developing your own human capital, not trying to outguess corporate management strategies.

The second fundamental investment management idea is the efficient markets principle discussed in Chapters 3 and 4. Rather than trying to make your own valuations or listening to the beat the market chorus of Wall Street, you depend on the market pricing process to accurately value the corporate stocks you own. You don't play stock market games. And, with TIPP, your financial investment plans proceed in an atmosphere of order, rationality, and calmness. No frantic scheming; no nail-biting anxiety.

The principal–agent relationship and the efficient markets principle mean that you're not going to try to beat the market because it's futile and will only reduce your investment rate of return. What you *are* going to do is take advantage of these two fundamental ideas by applying the four TIPP principles. You must determine the amount of return and risk that is appropriate for your own investment objectives and temperament. You must minimize unnecessary risk by diversifying among a number of stocks—that is, among different corporate management teams. You must insulate yourself from the emotions of the greed–fear cycle, and because you may inadvertently pick a bad time for buying stocks, you must eliminate unnecessary timing risk by not investing all of your money at one time. Finally, you must minimize the commissions, advisory fees, and taxes you pay.

COMMON STOCK RETURNS AND RISK

The investment return on a common stock is measured over the period of time you own the stock. This is called the *holding period return* (HPR). Investment return comes in two forms. First, the corporation may pay a cash dividend (D). Second, due to a change in expected profitability of the corporation, the market price of the stock may change. The difference between the price you paid for the stock (P) and the price at the end of the holding period (P') is the capital appreciation or depreciation of your investment. The HPR is calculated as the total return during the holding period (D + P' - P) divided by the initial price or cost of the investment:

$$HPR = \frac{D + P' - P}{P}$$

For example, if you buy a stock for $20 and sell it one year later for $21 (after adjusting for commissions), and it pays a cash dividend of $1 during the year you owned it, your holding period yield would be 10 percent:

$$HPR = \frac{\$1 + \$21 - \$20}{\$20} = \frac{\$2}{\$20} = 10\%$$

At the beginning of the year, you know the stock price (P) is $20, but you can't be sure of the dividend payment (D) or the stock price at the end of the year (P'). This uncertainty of return is what creates investment risk. It is the *possibility* that you will experience an investment loss because of a dividend cut or a price decline on one or more of your stocks. *In finance, risk is the same thing as uncertainty*. If an investment has more than one possible return during your holding period—that is, the HPR cannot be guaranteed—the investment involves some degree of risk.

All investments have some risk of loss. Some have more risk than others. Dividend payments and stock prices are determined by the future earnings of a company. If business is poor and dividends are cut, you will suffer a loss of wealth. Moreover, with poor earnings prospects, the stock price may decline. Of course, if you don't have to sell right away and the stock price subsequently recovers, this latter event will not result in an actual loss of wealth. But there may be unforeseen reasons why you must sell when the stock price is depressed. If so, you *will* experience a real loss of wealth. This possibility or uncertainty of loss from selling at an inopportune time constitutes risk. You also run the risk that the earnings capacity and stock price of your company will decline permanently. Thus both fluctuations in dividend payments and stock prices produce financial risk. And the wider the swings in returns, the greater the risk.

The concept of using variability of returns as a measure of risk is illustrated in Figure 5.1 by two stocks, Duke Power and Asarco. If you bought Asarco before mid-1979, you could have realized a nice capital gain by the end of 1982. But if you bought in 1980 and had to sell in 1982, you would have a sizable loss. Dividend payments of Asarco, shown at the bottom of the figure, were also highly variable. If you bought in 1980, expecting a dividend payment of $1.85 per share, you were in for a rude shock when the dividend was subsequently cut to $.50 in 1982!

Because its returns are so variable, Asarco is considered a risky stock. Depending on when you bought and sold, your *gains* could be very large, or your *losses* could be very large. In contrast, Duke Power is a much less risky investment. Dividend payments grew at a remarkably steady rate—no nasty surprises there! And your risk of capital loss from price fluctuations, even in the worst-case scenario, was comparatively modest.

STRAIGHT THINKING ABOUT RISK AND REWARD

Duke Power is a less risky or safer investment than Asarco *because* its dividend payments and stock price are more predictable. This stability, or safety of return, is a valuable and worthwhile objective. Because most investors prefer lower risk in their investments, stocks with more risk are regarded as lower quality than those with less risk. Given this

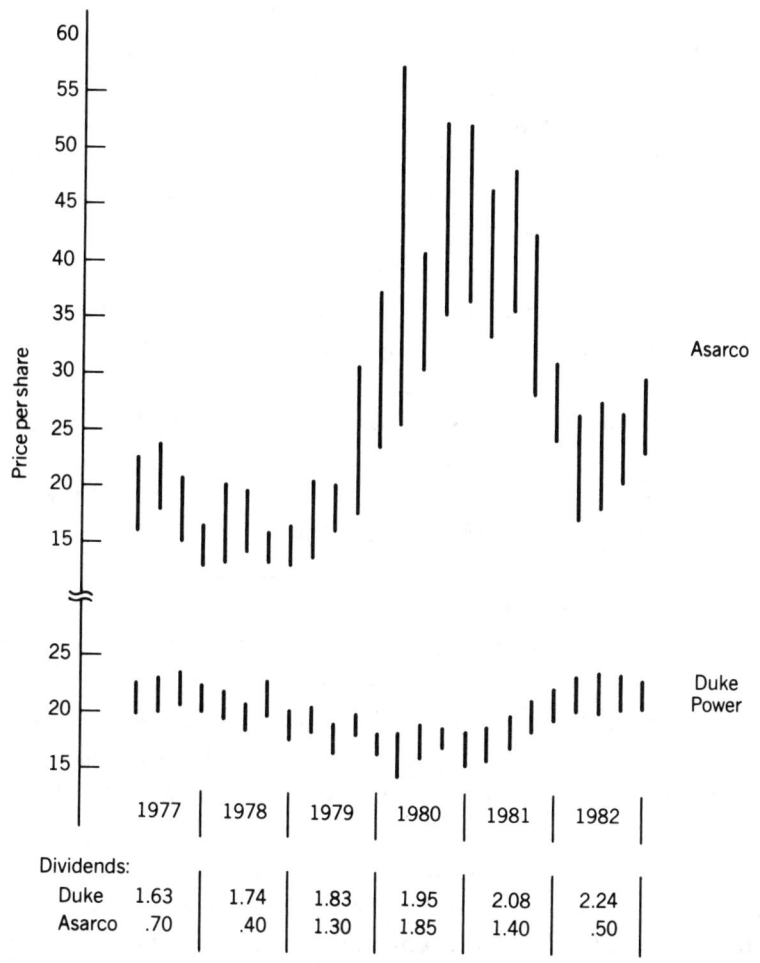

FIGURE 5.1 Quarterly high and low prices and dividends, Duke Power and Asarco

lower quality (greater risk) characteristic, higher-risk stocks should sell at lower prices than lower-risk stocks that have the same *expected* rates of returns.

The expected rate of return is the *average* return the investor anticipates at the beginning of the holding period. Let's say that, on the basis of past experience, investors anticipate that the price of Stock A will be between $30 and $70 one year from now, while Stock B will be worth anywhere from $40 to $60 by then. Let's also assume that when dividends are taken into account, the expected price of both Stocks A and B is $50 one year from now. (To keep the example simple, we are using the midpoint of the range of possible outcomes, $50 in each case, as the expected price.) But the *range* of possible outcomes, or risk, is much greater for Stock A than for Stock B. Consequently, investors would not pay as high a price for Stock A as for Stock B, leaving a somewhat higher expected HPR for Stock A. (A lower price now means a larger difference between the price today and the price expected a year from now, and thus a higher HPR.)

And indeed, this is exactly what happens in the stock market. Extensive research has confirmed that stocks with a history of volatile returns do sell at lower prices as compensation for assuming this risk. Conversely, investors are willing to pay a higher price (accept a lower return) for blue chip stocks like IBM, General Foods, and Exxon. The stock market pricing mechanism takes care of the adjustments. If, for example, a stock has an HPR that is too low relative to what investors think is necessary to compensate them for the expected risk, there will be a lack of investor demand for the stock, and its price will fall until it is proportional to the expected risk.

The return–risk tradeoff proposition, however, is widely misunderstood. You may earn higher returns when you take more risk, but there is also a chance that you may earn lower returns. The preceding example, which compared the performance of Duke Power and Asarco, makes it quite clear that a higher-risk stock may underperform a lower-risk one for short periods of time. If you bought both stocks in 1978, Asarco would have outperformed Duke Power by the end of 1982. But Duke Power would have been the clear winner if your initial investment was made in 1980. Even in a comparison of diversified portfolios of low-risk and high-risk stocks, which would not just depend on the performance of a few stocks, the same result could happen in the short run.

There is a conventional belief, however, that if one "gives it enough time," a diversified portfolio of high-risk stocks will always outperform a lower-risk portfolio. *This is simply not true*. If high-risk stocks *always* have higher returns in the long run, this is the same as saying they have *guaranteed* higher HPRs—guaranteed in the sense that all you have to do is hold on long enough to obtain the higher yield. But if this were the case, the higher HPRs would not persist. Institutional investors with long holding periods, such as trust funds, pension funds, and insurance companies, would switch to these so-called high-risk stocks. After all, the returns would be higher, and there would be no additional risk to these institutions. Many individual investors would do the same thing.

They would be able to earn guaranteed higher returns by developing strategies to lengthen their effective holding periods so they wouldn't be forced to sell during time periods when stock prices were temporarily depressed. As a result of this switch in investor preferences, the demand for stocks with highly volatile returns would increase and their prices would be bid up until their HPRs fell to levels comparable to low-volatility stocks. In other words, investors would correctly perceive that these were not truly high-risk stocks, but merely high-volatility stocks.

Because stock returns are not guaranteed, we should expect (and, in fact, observe) that stocks with highly volatile returns will sell at lower prices to provide the compensating higher return. But there is no guarantee that high-risk stocks will outperform low-risk stocks, even in the long run, *because expectations are not always realized*. The return–risk tradeoff proposition simply states that the odds are better than 50–50 that, when stock market prices rise, high-risk stocks will have higher realized returns. But the odds are also something less than 50–50 (but greater than zero) that a high-risk portfolio will underperform a low-risk one.

Let's say you select a large sample of stocks and divide them into two well-diversified portfolios, where one has only low-return volatility stocks and the other only high-return volatility stocks. You will find that the latter portfolio initially has lower average prices per dollar of expected returns. Assume that you followed the fortunes of these two portfolios for five years, and contrary to expectations, low-risk stocks turned out to have higher returns. You might conclude that the test period was too short. If you extended the holding period to 10 years, the odds will *increase* that the high-risk strategy will produce superior performance. But even if overall stock market prices rise during this time period, there is still some possibility that the low-risk portfolio will have higher returns. Each time you extend the holding period, the odds will increase in favor of high returns for high risk, but you will never reach the point where the probability is 100 percent that high risk ensures high returns.

Because risk management is a central component of good portfolio management, this distinction between *expected* and *realized* returns is very important. The point is this: If you choose a high-risk investment strategy, you should be prepared to accept the consequences that you may underperform over your holding period. What you can usually expect with a high-risk strategy is higher-than-average returns in periods when the stock market is strong and lower-than-average returns when the stock market is weak. What is uncertain is whether the stock market will, on balance, be stronger or weaker over your holding period. If you underestimate the potential for loss, you may inadvertently choose stocks that are too risky for your preferences and circumstances. There are steps you can take to improve your chances of success, and we will discuss these, but you'll never find a sure-fire golden guarantee in financial investing. This shouldn't surprise you, though. When was the last time you were guaranteed anything?

FIRST PRINCIPLE: RETURN–RISK TRADEOFFS

A fundamental principle of finance is that most people do not like risk. Some are unwilling to take risks under any circumstances. They seek out the safest investments. Others dislike risk but are willing to assume some if they have a chance to earn more income. Still others shoot for a high level of return and are willing to take high risks to obtain it. In spite of the different results, all of these investors are return–risk traders. They will only take more risk if offered a reward for doing so in the form of a higher expected rate of return. A few people may *prefer* risk because they like the thrill of gambling, but they represent a small minority in financial market transactions, and they have little effect on financial asset prices.

Even most gamblers are return–risk traders. They may enjoy gambling as a pastime, but they don't mix their gambling funds with their investment funds. They might buy a lottery ticket, spend a Saturday at the racetrack, a week in Las Vegas, or trade stock options and commodity futures contracts. But they are risk averters with their investment funds. They may be willing to take more risk in their investments, but only if the possible return is commensurate with the cost of the uncertainty they find distasteful. The fact that most people diversify rather than plunge with all-or-nothing investments is evidence that they are risk averse—that is, return–risk traders.

The first step in financial planning is to determine the return–risk tradeoff that suits your temperament, circumstances, and objectives. This is sometimes described as looking for your "sleeping point." If you're apt to lose sleep over a particular investment, its potentially higher return may not be worth the risk. But then you may be willing to lose some sleep over an investment if it gives you a chance to eat better. The appendix to this chapter describes and compares the important attributes of marketable securities. This comparison should help identify the type of securities that are best suited to your objectives. In addition to the basic sleep-better or eat-better tradeoff, the appendix also discusses such investment attributes as the stability of current income (dividend or interest payments) and the degree of inflation protection offered by alternative securities.

SECOND PRINCIPLE: PORTFOLIO DIVERSIFICATION

Once you have determined your appropriate risk level, the next step is to build a portfolio that provides the greatest return for that level of risk. If you aren't sure yet what that risk level is, you may want to consider several "what if" portfolios with different return–risk combinations. But whether you are sure or just considering alternatives, your objective is to select a portfolio of investments that will give you the highest possible return for the amount of risk taken. Such a portfolio is called an *efficient portfolio* in finance. To understand exactly what that means, you must understand three distinctions within the concept of risk: (1) portfolio risk, (2) systematic risk, and (3) unsystematic risk.

Portfolio Risk

Because your objective is *portfolio* management, you will be concerned most about the risk of your entire portfolio of investments, not the risk of the individual stocks you select. Although you can't change the return–risk tradeoff characteristics of individual stocks you buy, you can reduce the riskiness of your portfolio by diversifying your investments, which will "balance out" *some* of the risk you would otherwise have to bear. While all stock returns are variable (risky), not all stock return fluctuations are perfectly synchronized, so that the upswings of some balance out the downswings of others. To the extent this type of offsetting effect occurs, the amount of risk in the portfolio as a whole is reduced. Although diversification reduces risk, it does not reduce your expected return from the portfolio because the expected HPRs of the individual stocks are not affected. Thus by diversifying, you reduce the amount of portfolio risk without giving up *any* amount of return. In other words, diversification gives you the ability to increase your expected return without increasing risk.

As an example, consider two corporations. The first, Exotic Trips, Ltd., provides unusual (and expensive!) vacations at a place it owns in the Caribbean called Fantastic Island. When the economy is doing well, people spend more on entertainment and travel, so the profits of Exotic Trips are high and its dividends and stock price increase. As a result, whenever economic conditions are good, the investment return on the stock of Exotic Trips is 19 percent. But during recessions, people cut back on entertainment, causing profits of Exotic Trips to decline and dividends to be cut, thus also reducing its stock price. Whenever the economy is struggling, the investment return on this stock is 3 percent. Under these circumstances, Exotic Trips would be considered a risky stock because its investment returns fluctuate from 3 to 19 percent.

The second company, Dark Clouds, Inc., is just the opposite. Its business thrives during recessions because it provides advisory services to help reorganize companies that are in financial trouble. So when the economy is weak, Dark Clouds' profits are high, and its investment return is 17 percent. When the economy is prosperous, however, very few companies need its services, so profits fall, and the investment return on this stock declines to 1 percent. Dark Clouds is an equally risky stock because its investment return fluctuates from 1 to 17 percent.

The investment returns of these two stocks are summarized in Table 5.1. If you invest $1000 in each company, your total portfolio return will be $200, or 10 percent ($200/$2000 = 10%) during *both* good and

TABLE 5.1 Investment Returns of Exotic Trips, Ltd. and Dark Clouds, Inc.

	Amount Invested	Good Economy	Poor Economy	Variation of Return[b]	Level
Exotic Trips	$1000	$190 19%	$ 30 3%	3–19%	High
Dark Clouds	1000	10 1	170 17	1–17	High
Total portfolio	$2000	$200 10%[a]	$200 10%[a]	0%	None

[a] Average portfolio return: $200/$2000 = 10%.

[b] A more precise way to measure the risk of a stock or a portfolio is to calculate the variance of the distribution of possible returns. Variance is the average of the squared deviations from the mean of a distribution.

poor economic conditions. The balancing-out effect of diversification completely eliminates fluctuations in the overall portfolio returns. Although both Exotic Trips and Dark Clouds are individually risky stocks, the *combined* risk of the two stocks—that is, the *portfolio risk*—turns out to be zero.

Systematic Risk

In this example, the investment return on Exotic Trips moves up and down with the overall stock market, whereas Dark Clouds' return fluctuates exactly opposite. But very few stocks perform exactly like Dark Clouds. Generally, there is a strong tendency for the earnings of most companies to be at least somewhat dependent on the business cycle. As a result, when national economic conditions change, dividend prospects, earnings expectations, and the degree of investor optimism or pessimism cause simultaneous changes in the investment returns of all stocks. These synchronized changes in the investment returns of all stocks in the market create what is called *systematic risk* because all stocks are affected systematically by a common element—unexpected changes in economic conditions. Systematic risk is sometimes referred to as *undiversifiable* risk because if stock returns move up and down together, one cannot get the balancing-out effect that reduces portfolio risk.

Unsystematic Risk

The profits of all companies aren't affected to the same extent when the economy goes up and down. There are often *other* uncertainties or surprises in store for investors. Conditions in some industries always vary somewhat from those in others. When the economy is expanding, people spend more freely on entertainment, clothing, cars, and furniture. When employment and income fall, however, spending on these items is curtailed. Because companies in these industries experience wider-than-average swings in sales and profits, the investment returns on these stocks also tend to be more variable. In contrast, amounts spent on food, tobacco, and electricity are fairly constant regardless of economic conditions. Consequently, the earnings and investment returns of these companies fall less than average during recessions and, of course, rise less than average during periods of economic expansion.

In addition to the fact that the general condition of the economy affects some businesses much more than others, many other specific factors may affect industries or particular firms in such a way as to cause variability in their expected returns and, hence, risk level. Changes in tax laws, inflation rates, and government regulations affect some industries more than others, as, for that matter, does the weather. There are also circumstances that affect only specific companies. Introducing a new product, winning a large contract, suffering a crippling strike, or losing key sales or management people to a competitor can have a large impact on a company, causing considerable variability in its HPR.

Whenever the investment returns on a stock are not perfectly correlated with other stocks in the market, these fluctuations are called *unsystematic risk*. The unsystematic effect on some stocks is so strong that the returns move in the opposite direction (as in our example of Dark Clouds). Most of the time, however, the returns of all stocks move up or down together (systematic risk), but the patterns are not exactly the same (unsystematic risk). Thus most stocks have both systematic and unsystematic risk. Whenever you combine stocks with patterns that are not exactly the same, you reduce the overall risk of your portfolio through the balancing-out effect. Unsystematic risk is considered unnecessary risk because it can be eliminated with proper diversification.

An efficient portfolio is one where all of the unsystematic (unnecessary) risk has been eliminated through the balancing-out effect. But as the size of your portfolio increases, the risk-reducing effect of each new stock added to the portfolio becomes smaller and smaller. After you have selected 12–15 stocks that aren't closely related, it's difficult to find more stocks whose returns aren't highly correlated with the ones already in the portfolio. Why? Simply because most stocks have some systematic risk. A carefully chosen portfolio of 15 stocks will eliminate about 91 percent of all unsystematic risk. To eliminate the remaining 9 percent, however, would require a portfolio of 500–1000 stocks, so the additional reduction in risk would be too costly in terms of transaction and bookkeeping expenses for individual investors.

Measuring Systematic Risk

A perfectly diversified or technically efficient portfolio, then, eliminates all unsystematic risk. What remains is systematic risk. Systematic risk for a particular stock can be measured by how much its investment return fluctuates relative to the average returns of all stocks. The most widely used measure of systematic risk is called *beta*, which is a volatility index. The beta index that measures the fluctuations of the overall stock market is set at 1.00. A stock with an estimated beta of 1.20, for example, is expected to fluctuate as much as the market *plus* 20 percent more. Thus if average market returns rise by 40 percent, the return on a stock with a beta of 1.20 will tend to go up by 48 percent. This additional 8 percent increase is 20 percent more than the 40 percent stock market increase. Likewise, if average market returns fall by 40 percent, returns on this stock are expected to fall by 48 percent. This stock is rated as above-average risk.

A stock with a beta of 1.00 will experience investment returns that fluctuate the same as the market average, which represents average risk. The investment return on a stock with a beta of, say, 0.70 will fluctuate by 30 percent *less* than average. When market returns rise by 40 percent, the returns on this stock will tend to increase by only 28 percent. Conversely, its returns will fall by only 28 percent when average stock market returns fall by 40 percent. This result, of course, represents less risk to the investor.

If you have a well-diversified portfolio, in which unsystematic risk has been *almost* eliminated (12–15 stocks properly chosen), the risk of your portfolio will be close to the weighted average of the beta values of the stocks in your portfolio. If you have three stocks in equal amounts, with betas of 1.10, 1.20, and 1.30, the average beta of this portfolio is 1.20. Ignoring for the moment that three stocks is not enough diversification to protect you against unsystematic risk—we'll say that the investment return of this portfolio will be 20 percent riskier than average —and *your expected return will also be higher than average.*

THIRD PRINCIPLE: TIME DIVERSIFICATION

The third component of TIPP is time diversification. There are two basic reasons for time diversification—the first is an extension of the logic of portfolio diversification, and the second is emotional, related to the greed–fear cycle. We will consider these in turn.

Prescription for Financial Motion Sickness

As noted in Chapter 3, current stock prices reflect investors' best estimates of future earnings of those stocks. Scientific evidence has clearly shown that efficient markets value stocks as accurately as is humanly possible. Still, mistakes are a fact of life. As new information becomes known and mistakes are corrected, earnings estimates, and consequently, stock prices, change. From time to time, these fluctuations are accentuated by the emotional forces of extreme optimism or pessimism. Thus over short periods of time, stock prices can be very volatile. This is illustrated in Table 5.2. During the period 1951-1981, there was one year when stock prices rose by 52 percent (row 1, column 1). Over some shorter periods of time, prices were even more volatile. For example, from August 1982 to June 1983, stock prices rose by about 65 percent. In the single worst year, stocks declined by 26 percent (row 1, column 2). Fluctuations were also considerable in most other single years.

TABLE 5.2 Common Stock Volatility, 1951-1981

		(1) Highest	(2) Lowest	(3) Average
(1)	1-year periods	52%	-26%	11%
(2)	5-year periods	20	-2	9
(3)	10-year periods	16	1	9
(4)	15-year periods	14	4	8
(5)	20-year periods	12	6	8
(6)	25-year periods	10	8	9

Note: Data rounded off to nearest whole number.
Source: Vanguard Index Trust, *Quarterly Report*, March 1, 1983.

There is nothing you can do to avoid these occasional wild gyrations in the value of your stocks, but you can neutralize the risk this creates when you make purchases or sales of stock. How? By recognizing that these fluctuations cancel out over longer periods of time and tailoring your financial planning accordingly. For example, in the most volatile five-year period (five years back-to-back) during 1959-1981, stock returns fluctuated between minus 2 percent and plus 20 percent (row 2,

THIRD PRINCIPLE: TIME DIVERSIFICATION   93

columns 1, 2). If you arrange your purchases and sales of stock to accommodate a five-year holding period, your financial risk (measured by volatility) is considerably reduced. As the holding period is lengthened beyond five years, stock price fluctuations decline sharply. For holding periods of 25 years, the average annual return was about 9 percent and only fluctuated between 8 and 10 percent (row 6). These are fluctuations that most investors can live with.

The data in Table 5.2 clearly show that, over longer periods of time, the ups and downs of stock prices tend to offset each other. An investment strategy based on this fact can neutralize the potentially debilitating effects of financial motion sickness. The medicine prescribed to deal with this volatility is time diversification, whereby you spread out your purchases and sales over time. Because stocks can jump around wildly from year to year, it just doesn't make sense to pour your life savings into the market at any one time. No one can consistently predict these ups and downs, so you will want to avoid the risk that your long-run investment returns will be below average because you unluckily bought or sold stocks at a momentary high or low. This is simply another application of the principle of risk aversion. The cost of below-average returns is too high when compared to the benefit of above-average returns if you were lucky and caught the swings just right. Diversifying your purchases and sales over time helps you to achieve the TIPP objective of a fair return for the risks you take.

There is another important objective of time diversification. Once you have purchased a portfolio of stocks, you must hold it for a long enough period of time to improve your chances of earning the expected long-run rate of return. A well-diversified portfolio of 10, 20, or even 500 stocks that are held for only short periods of time will be vulnerable to the same risk of unluckily catching an interim high or low in the constantly fluctuating stock market. Increasing the holding period of a stock portfolio *reduces* the risk that you will earn below-average investment returns just as efficiently as increasing the number of stocks held reduces risk.

William Lloyd and Richard Haney[1] estimated that an investor could obtain more risk reduction by holding any *one* stock 12 months than by holding 100 stocks of a well-diversified portfolio for only six months.

---

[1] William P. Lloyd and Richard L. Haney, Jr., "Time Diversification: Surest Route to Lower Risk," *The Journal of Portfolio Management,* Spring, 1980.

Their study indicates that the investor is able to significantly reduce risk each time the holding period is lengthened, whereas the amount of risk reduction earned by adding more stocks to a portfolio held for a long period of time is negligible beyond about 12–15 stocks. In other words, once you have a portfolio of 12–15 stocks, you can get much more risk reduction through increasing the holding period of these stocks than through increasing the number of stocks in the portfolio. In addition, by increasing the holding period, you save transaction costs, which increases your investment returns.

What! Me Worry?

Many investors get caught up in the emotions of short-term stock market fluctuations. They forget about the fundamental investment values offered by the corporations they own shares in. Make no mistake! *The greed–fear cycle is very real*. It afflicts amateur and professional investor alike. Although there is often an irresistible urge to run with the crowd, overreacting to these transitory events is very harmful to your financial health. You must devise an investment strategy that produces calm in this otherwise turbulent environment. When stock prices fall, you must be able to persevere with your original investment plan because you have confidence in the long-run future of the economy and confidence that stock prices will eventually reflect this. When stock prices are rising, you must avoid the temptation to plunge.

The best way to avoid the madness of the crowd is to develop a formula for investing and the confidence to use it. Then you are in control of your investment program rather than being controlled by the day-to-day gyrations of the stock market. With time diversification, you do not worry about whether the stock market is up or down. You do not try to time your purchases and sales to catch the peaks and valleys of stock market cycles. Your emotional insulation lies in the routine required by your time diversification program.

Your routine for investing will depend on your investment objectives and the pattern of your income stream. If you are saving and investing with some future goal in mind, you want to add to your investment portfolio on a periodic basis and reinvest dividends. If the funds you plan to save and invest are earned on a regular (say, monthly) basis, then a monthly investment routine is best. If your funds become available irregularly, say from lump sum bonuses, commissions, or seasonal income, then the best plan is to invest these monies immediately when you receive them. In the latter case, your investment timing rule is this: Invest funds when they become available, regardless of the temperature of the market. Although your purchases will be irregular in this case, the chance that they will occur systematically at the high points of stock market cycles is remote. Finally, if you receive a large amount of money all at once, say from the sale of a large asset or an inheritance, put the money temporarily in a money market fund and then invest equal amounts per month, spread over a year or two.

The same logic applies to sales. If you plan to sell some stock because you want to use the money for a down payment on a house or to begin a business of your own, try to plan ahead and sell stock over a period of months. Of course, emergencies may arise that would force the sale of a large amount of stock all at once. This is the only time you must bear the full risk of stock market fluctuations.

FOURTH PRINCIPLE: MINIMIZING COSTS

Risk management must be carried out in a cost effective manner. Transaction costs, including commissions, advisory fees, and taxes, can sharply reduce investment returns. To keep these costs to an absolute minimum, you must do two things: Avoid all unnecessary transactions and conduct those transactions that *are* necessary as inexpensively as possible.

The principal message of Chapter 3 was that current market prices for common stocks are the best available estimate of their investment potentials. Beat-the-market schemes and hunting for "bargains" involve you in a futile effort to outguess the market consensus and also subject you to the emotional dangers of the greed-fear cycle. Our focus here is on the fact that trading decisions made in this vain effort will inevitably reduce your investment returns. Each trading decision involves paying two commissions, one to sell a stock presumed to be overpriced and another to buy a stock thought to be underpriced. And to this double commission must be added advisory fees and taxes that would not have been incurred if you had stayed with the original stock. This is part of what we meant in Chapter 3 by "paying to lose." Dollars wasted on unnecessary transaction costs are funds that are gone forever from your

96 TOTAL INVESTMENT PORTFOLIO PLANNING

investment capital, ensuring that you will be a financial underperformer.

You must also be careful not to overpay for the financial services you do need. The TIPP approach to financial management minimizes the payment of commissions, advisory fees, and taxes through use of a buy-and-hold strategy. But there are still transactions that must be made—initial purchases of stock, continuing reinvestment of dividends, and periodic sales of stock when investment objectives have been reached. There are also circumstances when you need to buy legitimate investment advice (as discussed earlier), and of course, taxes are as inevitable as . . . well, Christmas ties. Chapter 7 shows how commissions can be kept to a minimum *with only a modest effort*. Chapter 8 shows how taxes can be reduced without resorting to any of the questionable tax dodges peddled by Wall Street. Your time and peace of mind are too important to play "let's see what we can put over on the IRS."

APPENDIX: THE FINANCIAL ASSET MENU

Table 5.3 lists the major types of marketable financial securities and the tradeoffs that must be considered with each of them. The top half of the table (the first three rows) deals with debt securities, which are *loans* made to the issuers of the securities, and the bottom half lists different types of common stock, that is, *ownership* of rights to share in the net income of the issuing companies.

Each row lists a type of financial asset (column 1) in ascending order of risk (column 2). Investment objectives (column 3) include capital preservation, current income, and capital appreciation (i.e., future income), either singly or in some combination. Stability of principal, stability of current income, and potential capital appreciation, which help describe specific investment characteristics of these securities, are listed in columns 4–5. In the text, we also discuss the degree of inflation protection provided by each type of financial asset.

Money Market Securities

Money market securities are very short-term debt obligations issued mostly by the federal government and large, very secure banks and nonfinancial corporations. Because they have very low default risk and very short maturities, they also offer the lowest returns of any security listed in Table 5.3. Money market securities, which are normally issued in denominations of $100,000 or more, include U.S. Treasury and federal government agency securities, large certificates of deposit, commercial paper, repurchase agreements, and bankers' acceptances. Due to the large minimum denominations, most individuals find it is more convenient to invest in shares of portfolios of money market securities offered by banks, savings and loans, and credit unions, or money market mutual funds offered by insurance companies, brokerage firms, and mutual fund companies. For money you don't need for day-to-day expenses, money market funds represent a convenient alternative to holding currency or checking account balances. And unlike currency and checking deposits, money market securities provide full inflation protection.

The risk of capital loss with money market securities is very low, but it's not zero. Investing in individual money market securities or money market funds involves two types of risk: Default risk and portfolio mismanagement risk. There are occasional instances where an issuer of these securities has defaulted. Franklin National Bank and Penn Central are prominent examples. Default risk is minimized by holding shares in a diversified portfolio, rather than owning individual securities.

Capital losses due to portfolio mismanagement risk occur when money market securities must be sold before maturity. As with all debt securities, the market value of money market instruments will fall if interest rates rise after the securities are issued. Because these securities have very short terms to maturity (when they will be paid in full), their market values will not fall very much, even if interest rates rise a great deal. In any case, even small capital losses due to fluctuations in market value can be eliminated easily by holding the securities to maturity.

But if interest rates rise and holders must sell these securities before maturity, there is some risk of capital loss. Because the purpose of holding money market securities is capital preservation, any circumstance where such a capital loss occurs represents portfolio mismanagement—that is, incorrect anticipation of the need for liquidity. A money market security owner who is forced to sell before maturity has underestimated his or her need for liquidity and should have acquired a security with a shorter term to maturity to protect against the risk of loss.

The possibility of such mismanagement is not limited to individual holders. In 1979, the investors in a small money market mutual fund,

TABLE 5.3 The Financial Investment Menu for Marketable Securities

	(1) Type of Security	(2) Risk Level	(3) Investment Objective	(4) Stability of Principal	(5) Stability of Current Income: Dividends and Interest	(6) Potential Capital Appreciation
			Debt Securities			
(1)	Money market securities (very short-term maturity)	Lowest	Capital preservation	Highest	Low	Not an appropriate investment objective
(2)	Short-term bonds (1–5 year maturity)	Low	Primary: Capital preservation Secondary: current income	High	Low to moderate	Not an appropriate investment objective
(3)	Long-term bonds (5–30 year maturity)	Low to moderate	Primary: current income Secondary: capital preservation	Moderate	High	Not an appropriate investment objective

Common Stock

(4)	Blue chip stock	Moderate	Primary: current income Secondary: capital appreciation	Moderate	Moderate to high (plus some growth of income)	Moderate
(5)	Growth stock	High	Primary: capital appreciation Secondary: current income	Low	Moderate (plus growth of income)	High
(6)	Maximum-growth stock	Highest	Capital appreciation	Lowest	Low (plus high growth of income)	Highest

99

First Multifund, experienced a loss of about 15 percent when fund managers guessed wrong about interest rates. First Multifund's portfolio managers tried to lock in what they believed were unusually high interest rates by investing in longer-term money market securities. They were wrong. Interest rates subsequently went much higher, and redemption requests rose sharply as shareholders began shifting their money to higher-yielding securities. Because the mutual fund had insufficient liquid assets to meet these redemptions, the managers were forced to sell some securities at a loss, and this loss was borne by the shareholders. More recently, the managers of the Institutional Liquid Assets fund guessed wrong on the direction of interest rates and got into a liquidity bind. In this case, however, well-heeled institutional sponsors covered the losses, so investors didn't suffer capital losses. This risk can be minimized by investing in money market funds that have a short average term to maturity—40 days or less.

As column 3 indicates, money market securities should be purchased with the sole investment objective of capital preservation. The principal (dollar amount) invested is very stable (column 4) and immediately convertible into cash. In the money market fund form, stability of principal is virtually complete because fund managers can usually offer continuous redemption in constant dollar unit values. Fund managers are able to offer continuous redemption by staggering the maturities of the securities they buy for the portfolio. In so doing, they have enough securities maturing on any given day to meet the normal requests for redemptions without selling any securities before maturity.

The interest return on money market securities has averaged $2\frac{1}{2}$ percent over the past 50 years, which matches the $2\frac{1}{2}$ percent average annual rate of inflation over the same period. The level of interest rates on money market securities reflects the market's estimation of future inflation rates and, *on average*, the interest income on money market securities is just high enough to keep pace with inflation. The inflation premium in interest rates is *not* interest income, but rather a repayment of principal that was eroded by inflation. Thus money market securities provide capital preservation (stability of principal) and preservation of the purchasing power of money capital—but nothing more.

If one of your financial objectives is to earn current income to meet regular current expenses, you may want an investment with stability of *current income* payments. Column 5 indicates that the stability of interest income from money market securities is low. A particular market rate of interest cannot be "locked in" for very long because of the short-term nature of these securities. Money market interest rates fluctuate constantly and often by large amounts, which mainly reflects changes in the market's estimation of future inflation rates.

How about capital appreciation with money market securities? Column 6 states that capital appreciation is *not* an appropriate investment objective for any type of debt security. Unlike common stock, debt securities earn only a fixed rate of interest to their maturity dates. That's all the borrower is obligated to pay, regardless of changes in economic or financial conditions. With common stock, on the other hand, an improved earnings and dividend paying capacity of the corporation will lead to a higher stock price and hence capital gains to the holder.

In order to earn capital gains with debt securities, you must be able to accurately forecast interest rates. If you expect interest rates to fall and you guess correctly, you could buy debt securities and earn capital gains. Conversely, if you expect interest rates to rise, you could sell short and also earn capital gains—again, if you're correct. But forecasting interest rates is considerably less reliable than forecasting the weather. (With the weather, at least, you'd know if it was going to be summer, fall, winter, or spring. With interest rates, you wouldn't know that much.) Regardless of what anyone might tell you, there is no known way to accurately forecast interest rates. Trying to do so is closely akin to trying to beat the market with common stocks. You'll end up earning below-average returns, while taking above-average risk. Thus capital appreciation should not be an investment objective for *any* debt security.

Short-Term Bonds

If you can commit your investment funds for a longer period of time and are willing and able to bear a little more risk in exchange for a higher-interest income, you could buy short-term bonds. There are a few mutual funds that specialize in bonds with one to five year maturities. These mutual funds provide convenient and low-cost portfolio and time diversification services.

With short-term bonds, the primary investment objective is still capital preservation (column 3), but there is now a secondary objective of earning some current income over and above the amount needed to compensate for inflation. Because the period for which the loan will be committed is longer than with money market securities, there is somewhat less stability of principal (column 4), but there is a little more stability of income over the holding period (column 5).

Long-Term Bonds

If your primary objective is current (and stable) income, but capital preservation is somewhat important, long-term bonds provide a way to gain that additional current income by assuming additional risk. For individuals with this combination of investment objectives, there are a large number of diversified bond mutual funds available.

Historically, long-term bonds have yielded, on average, about 2 percent more than money market securities. (Short-term bond yields fall between money market securities and long-term bonds.) Given the long-term maturities of these securities, interest income is stable (column 5), but there is less stability of principal (column 4) than with money market securities. Small changes in market interest rates cause relatively large changes in the current market prices of long-term bonds. If an emergency arises and these securities must be sold, it might be at a time when bond prices are temporarily depressed, which would cause a significant loss of invested capital. But if your holding period is long term and the likelihood of selling on short notice is small, this instability of principal may be a worthwhile tradeoff for higher and more stable income.

Long-term bonds, however, create considerable risk of inflation loss. If after you buy long-term bonds (or bond mutual funds), inflation unexpectedly increases, the purchasing power of both current interest income and the original investment capital will decline. (*Expected* inflation is already reflected in current bond prices and interest rates and does not have this effect.) So, while you lock in stable current interest income with long-term bonds, the tradeoff is greater exposure to inflation risk. Money market securities do not have this inflation risk because they mature quickly, allowing the investor to continually reinvest at the market rate of interest, which will adjust to changes in the rate of inflation. Because you are not locked into a long-term contract with money market securities, unexpected changes in inflation do not lock you into long-term losses.

In summary, all debt securities offer a contractual rate of interest and provide tradeoffs between stable principal and stable current income. As the length of time to maturity increases, however, you must assume more inflation risk as the tradeoff for obtaining higher and more stable income. Tax-exempt state and local government bonds (not specifically mentioned) have the same investment characteristics and tradeoffs for comparable maturities as those listed in Table 5.3, and they are exempt from federal and sometimes state and local income taxes. This special feature will be discussed in Chapter 8.

Common Stock

Based on variability of investment returns, the risk level is higher for common stock than for debt securities. Unlike interest income from bonds, dividend income from stock is not a contractual obligation of the corporation and tends to be less stable. (Remember that this is a generalization. There are some very risky bonds that have high risk of default of principal and interest and some very safe stocks whose dividend payments have been stable over long periods of time.) The reward for accepting the generally higher risk involved with variable dividend income and lower stability of principal is that dividends can grow over time, whereas interest is contractually fixed. The potential for dividend growth allows for the *possibility* of some protection against unexpected inflation.

Do common stocks, therefore, provide protection against inflation? Well, yes—and no! Viewed over longer time spans, corporate profits have more than kept pace with inflation, so stockholders, who own the rights to those profits, have had inflation protection. But there have been periods of time when investment returns on stocks (dividends plus capital appreciation) have lagged behind the growth in corporate profits. The 1970s were one of those times when the holding period yield on stocks did not provide effective protection against inflation. Why? Slow economic growth, back-to-back recessions, erratic and debilitating government intervention, and sharply rising energy prices combined to make the *entire economy more risky*. Investors therefore demanded a higher rate of return as compensation for the greater overall risk of owning stocks. That in turn meant that stock prices had to be lower per dollar of corporate profits. As stock prices fell (or failed to rise as fast as inflation), investment returns did not keep up with the rate of inflation.

As discussed in Chapter 2, once the economy gets back on a stable, high-growth track, this "entire economy" risk effect and the risk premium it necessitated will decrease. At that point, stock returns will once again provide general protection against inflation. Thus the yes-and-no answer: In the short run, common stock investments may not provide inflation protection. In the long run, however, stocks provide both inflation protection *and* a way to share in the growing productivity of the U.S. economy. And it's in the long run that common stocks are the "investment for all seasons."

Table 5.3 divides common stocks into three classes: blue chip, growth, and maximum growth. These classes correspond to low, medium, and high risk levels. The table does not include such stock–bond hybrids as convertible bonds and preferred stock, which are not widely held and are only of interest to investors in special circumstances. In terms of investment characteristics, however, they would fall into the strip between the top and bottom halves of the table.

Blue Chip Stocks

Stocks, taken as a whole, are more risky than bonds. This does not mean that *any* stock is more risky than *any* bond, but it does mean that a stock issued by a particular company is more risky than a bond issued by that company. For bearing this additional risk, the investor has a chance to earn a higher holding period return, composed of some combination of dividend payments and capital appreciation. How much higher this investment return is depends on the degree of riskiness of the stocks involved. Stocks in general (representing average risk) have yielded about 5 percentage points more than long-term bonds and 7 percentage points more than money market securities over the past 50 years. Because the risk is generally lower than average for blue chips, however, the average yield for these securities falls somewhere between the long-term bond rate and the average rate for all common stocks.

The dividend rate on blue chip stocks is somewhat lower than the interest rate on comparable long-term bonds, but the rate of dividend growth and capital appreciation on blue chip stocks more than makes up for the difference. From an investor's perspective, therefore, *current* income should be a somewhat less important objective, and dividend growth, capital appreciation, or both should be somewhat more important. This is often an attractive choice for someone at or near retirement. Stability of principal for blue chip stocks (column 4) is about the same as for long-term bonds. The stability of current dividend income (column 5) is also comparable to long-term bonds because the net earnings (and hence dividend-paying ability) of most blue chip corporations are relatively stable. Because most blue chip companies reinvest some net earnings to expand productive capacity, dividend growth and capital appreciation (column 6) will tend to exceed the rate of inflation.

Growth Stocks

Growth stock corporations are generally involved in more risky fields and pay out a smaller portion of their earnings in dividends than do blue chip companies. The primary investment objective for owning these stocks should be capital appreciation, but in a context where some current dividend income is still considered important. The stability of principal (column 4) is lower, but current dividend income is still fairly stable (column 5) because most companies in this category cut dividends only as a last resort. Although dividend payments will be lower, by retaining a larger share of net earnings and reinvesting them into the corporation, these companies tend to produce higher dividend growth rates and capital appreciation (column 6) than do blue chip companies.

Growth stocks correspond to the average-risk category for common stocks. They are more risky than blue chip and less risky than maximum growth stocks. Their overall holding period return correspondingly falls in the middle also, being close to the 5 percentage point historic differential between stocks in general and long-term bonds.

Maximum Growth Stocks

The most risky securities are maximum growth common stocks. Here, current dividend income is not an objective. The investment objective is almost exclusively capital appreciation, and the investor is willing to take fairly large risks in return for the possibility of earning a large dividend income in the future. With these stocks, dividend payments are zero or low and very uncertain. Needless to say, these stocks put you on the *big* rollercoaster! On the other hand, the historic record suggests that you will *probably* earn a higher return over the long haul with a diversified portfolio of such stocks than with any other financial asset—something on the order of 11 percent.

6

PUTTING IT ALL TOGETHER: TIPP IN ACTION

The first half of this book explained what is fact and what is fiction (or folklore) about available investment opportunities. The second half, which begins with this chapter, explains how to translate the known facts into an effective investment program. This chapter presents a practical guide for establishing and maintaining an efficient portfolio, based on the TIPP principles of financial investing. The chapter is organized around a Portfolio Worksheet, which is designed to accomplish two basic objectives:

1. Develop a portfolio with the degree of systematic risk that meets your financial goals.
2. Minimize the amount of unsystematic risk in the portfolio.

MANAGING SYSTEMATIC RISK

First, let's take a quick review of financial risk, which was discussed in Chapter 5. The total risk of a stock can be divided into two components, systematic and unsystematic risk. Systematic risk, which is the risk in the return–risk tradeoff of the first principle of TIPP, depends on the extent to which the investment return of a stock is sensitive to average stock market returns. It is called systematic risk because all stock returns are affected systematically by changes in overall economic conditions. Beta is the widely used measure of this component of risk. If the returns on a stock fluctuate more than average, it has high systematic risk, indicated by a beta larger than 1.00. Stocks with returns that fluctuate less than average have low systematic risk—that is, they have a beta of less than 1.00. Systematic risk, measured by the beta method, explains about 30 percent of the total risk of an average stock.

The unsystematic risk component, which accounts for the other 70 percent of risk, is caused by a wide array of factors that affect the investment returns of a specific company or industry. Because these events *do not* affect all companies systematically, when stocks of companies that are not closely related are combined in a portfolio, unsystematic risk is reduced by the balancing-out effect of diversification. In a fully or efficiently diversified portfolio, all unsystematic risk is eliminated; what remains is only systematic risk. Thus the risk of a diversified portfolio can be measured by the average beta of the stocks in the portfolio.

Portfolio Beta

The focus of financial investment management centers on achieving and maintaining the appropriate level of systematic risk to meet personal objectives and circumstances.[1] Table 6.1 provides an example of calculating the systematic risk of a portfolio (which is obviously not fully efficient or TIPP efficient, given the small number of stocks in the ex-

---

[1] We are concentrating on financial investment choices. These decisions, of course, are affected by broader personal finance issues not covered in this book, such as your age, income, present wealth, family characteristics, spending behavior, employer and individual pension funds, and prospects for inheritance. Your choices are also affected by your investment goals, such as education expenses, starting a business, down payment on a house, or funds for a secure and rewarding retirement. Personal finance also includes decisions on savings accounts, insurance, housing, and monthly budgeting.

TABLE 6.1 Calculating Portfolio Risk

Name of Stock	(1) Current Price per Share	×	(2) Number of Shares	=	(3) Current Market Value	(4) Fraction of Portfolio	×	(5) Beta	=	(6) Weighted Beta
Jungle Jim's Cookies	$20		600		$12,000	.194		.80		.155
General Sand and Gravel	40		350		14,000	.226		.85		.192
Space Cadets	100		200		20,000	.322		1.35		.435
Amalgamated Fashions	10		1600		16,000	.258		1.20		.310
			Totals		$62,000	1.000				
							Averages	1.05		1.09

ample). The entries in column 3 are calculated by multiplying the current price per share (column 1) by the number of shares held of each stock (column 2). The total value of the portfolio is $62,000, which is simply the sum of the market values of each of the four stocks in the portfolio. Column 4, which lists the fractional values of each stock in the portfolio, is calculated by dividing the total value of the portfolio into the current market value of each stock (i.e., dividing $62,000 into the values of each stock in column 3).

The beta values provided in column 5 can be obtained from Appendix A or from other sources (see the section on "Searching for Beta" later in this chapter). Although the simple average portfolio beta of the four stocks in Table 6.1 is 1.05, this will not be an accurate measure of portfolio beta except in the unlikely case where the current market value of each stock is the same. What is required is a *weighted* average. This is calculated by using the fractional values in column 4 as weights. Each beta value in column 5 is multiplied by its fractional share of the entire portfolio (column 4), creating the weighted betas in column 6. The sum of the weighted betas is 1.09, which is called the *weighted portfolio beta*. This portfolio has above-average risk because its investment returns will fluctuate by 9 percent more than the average of the overall stock market.

Is beta the best way to measure portfolio risk? There is a lively debate about this question, and a good deal of research is being conducted to refine risk measurement. The use of beta assumes that the future risk of a stock can be estimated on the basis of its past risk. Typically, high betas are associated with companies that have high growth rates, cyclical revenues, high fixed costs, and large amounts of debt. Low beta companies are usually larger, more mature, or in regulated industries. As long as the company does not drastically change its business practices or line of products, its past beta is likely to be a good estimate of its future beta. But *do* betas persist? Will a stock's past variability of investment return be a good guide to the future? After all, it's the future you're interested in, not the past.

The evidence is that betas of individual companies do tend to persist over time, but they are not constant. Just as an individual's personality may change over time, the "risk personality" of a company (and its stock) can also change. Management personnel come and go. New managers may have different preferences for taking business and financial risk. They may borrow a lot of money and guide the company into new product lines and expand into promising but risky ventures, or they may move in the opposite direction, becoming much more cautious than earlier management teams.

Studies have shown that the betas of diversified portfolios, such as a TIPP portfolio of 12–15 stocks, remain relatively constant because of the "law of large numbers." While the betas of some stocks in a diversified portfolio may decline, others will probably rise. Because of this offsetting effect, the average portfolio beta tends to be much more stable than the betas of the individual stocks in the portfolio. And because it's the portfolio beta that is important for managing systematic risk, beta is considered to be a good approximation of risk. Although it's not perfect, it provides an operational measure of the systematic risk of a portfolio that is sufficiently accurate for most investors.

How often should you adjust a portfolio that has strayed from your target beta level? Remember that you must weigh the benefits of achieving your target level of risk against the transaction costs of buying and selling stocks to rebalance a portfolio. Studies on this subject report that rebalancing about every 6 or 7 years is about optimal under ordinary circumstances, which illustrates the fact that diversified portfolio betas are relatively stable. As a safeguard against extraordinary circumstances, portfolios should be reviewed every five years.

Fine-Tuning Portfolio Risk

Building a portfolio to achieve a target return–risk level is just a matter of selecting a diversified list of stocks with the appropriate betas. Fine-tuning portfolio risk is equally straightforward. You would increase your portfolio's risk composition by adding stocks with betas higher than the existing weighted portfolio average, and you would reduce it by adding stocks with lower betas.

There is a second way to fine-tune portfolio risk, using a combination of money market securities and common stocks. Let's say your target level of portfolio risk is a weighted beta of 0.5. With half of your funds, you buy a well-diversified portfolio of stocks with average market risk (i.e., beta = 1.00). This is called a *market portfolio* because it resembles average market risk. An index mutual fund (discussed in Chapter 7) approximates the characteristics of a market portfolio. With the other half of your funds, you buy risk-free money market debt securities, which have beta values of 0.0. If half of the portfolio has a beta of 1.00 and the other half is 0.0, the weighted average is the target level of 0.5. This procedure is called *leveraging down*. By purchasing money market securities, you are loaning (leveraging down) at the risk-free rate of interest.

It can be shown that the investment return on a leveraged-down portfolio will be somewhat higher than on a nonleveraged portfolio of common stocks with the same beta value.[2] The nonleveraged portfolio is not as efficiently diversified, so its risk-adjusted return is lower. In addition to the benefit of a somewhat higher return, the technique of leveraging down is especially attractive if you want a low portfolio beta. As shown in Figure 6.1, only 6 percent of the nearly 1700 stocks covered by Value Line have betas of 0.60 or lower, and nearly two-thirds of these low beta stocks are gold mining companies or public utilities. Because you can't get sufficient diversification by investing only in stocks from these two groups, leveraging down is usually the best way to go if you want a very low risk portfolio.

If your objective is a portfolio beta between 0.80 and 1.00, you could still follow the procedure of leveraging down as an alternative to the all-stock portfolio with the same weighted beta. In this range, however, the gains (measured as the additional risk-adjusted investment return) would be quite small for the average investor, meaning that it does not matter which way you go.

The leveraging principle can also be used to increase portfolio risk above average. The procedure would be to borrow (leverage up) at the risk-free rate of interest and buy more of the market portfolio of stocks. Investors can usually borrow from a brokerage firm, using the market value of their stock as collateral for the loan. This is called a *margin loan*. The interest rate on a margin loan is generally the call rate (a risk-free money market rate), plus some small premium that varies from broker to broker. Currently, you can borrow up to 50 percent of the market value of your stock holdings, which means that you could buy $30,000 of a market portfolio of stocks with a cash payment of $15,000 and a margin loan of $15,000. This would increase your weighted portfolio beta from 1.00 to 2.00, and your expected investment return would be somewhat higher than with an all-stock portfolio that has a beta of 2.00.

---

[2]Most advanced finance textbooks provide a proof of this statement.

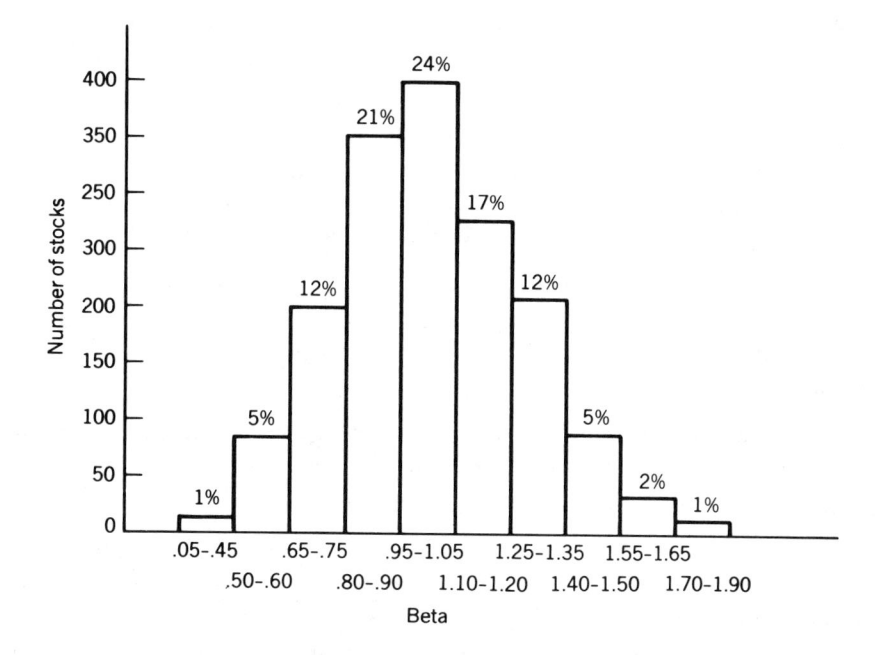

FIGURE 6.1 Number of stocks, classified by beta

There is a serious objection to leveraging up, however, that doesn't exist for leveraging down: *It increases the investor's vulnerability to the greed–fear cycle.* Suppose you have a margin account at a time when stock prices are rising rapidly. As the market value of your portfolio increases, you can buy more stock simply by borrowing against the rising value of your present stock. In the euphoria of a raging bull market, this can turn a mild condition of greed into an ugly case of avarice. If you are susceptible to this emotional trap, the availability of borrowing on margin just adds fuel to the fire. You'll be apt to plunge at just the wrong time.

In an all-out bear market, the opposite effect occurs. Stock bought with borrowed money is often in shaky hands. As your paper wealth melts away, fear can turn into full-blown panic. That's bad enough. But if you bought a stock on margin, you may have to put up more cash as collateral for the margin loan. This is the dreaded margin call. If you are unwilling or unable to meet a margin call, your stocks will be sold to satisfy the margin requirement. Thus you could be selling at just the wrong time. Getting whip sawed by the greed–fear cycle, which is further accentuated by the pitfalls of margin borrowing, can tip the odds in favor of buying high and selling low.

Is this realistic? Can leveraging up really create serious problems? You bet it can. The Great Stock Market Crash in 1929 is the most prominent example of the complications caused by financial leveraging. Margin calls accentuated the steep decline in stock prices just as margin buying helped fuel the earlier spectacular rise in prices. As prices plummeted, panicky investors dumped their stocks or were sold out to meet margin calls. Many were completely wiped out because their margin loans were greater than the market value of their tumbling stocks. In these cases, they also lost their homes, savings accounts, and other assets in bankruptcy proceedings. Even more tragically, in some cases they lost their marriages, self-esteem, and even their lives.

The Great Crash may never be repeated. Today, legal limits on margin loans prevent leverage pyramiding from reaching the extremes it achieved in the late 1920s. But the same psychological leverage trap lurks in every stock market swing. Although the scale of price fluctuations has been smaller in recent decades, the losses are nonetheless real, and the imprudent can still be deeply, even fatally, hurt. The basic problem is that financial leverage magnifies stock price fluctuations, which sorely tests one's nerves. Moreover, in a declining market, you may lose the option of riding out the storm if you can't meet the margin calls.

Does this mean you should never buy stocks on margin. In a word, yes.[3] There is a better way. Again, let's use the worst-case scenario, the Great Crash of 1929, as an illustration. If you had bought and fully paid for a diversified portfolio of stocks just before the October 1929 stock market crash, you would have paid close to top dollar for many of those stocks, and you would have suffered a serious loss of wealth in the ensuing months. But you would *not* have been wiped out. In the stock market "battle," it is vital that you survive today's setback so you can return to "fight another day." By surviving 1929 and holding the stocks you bought at the peak of the 1920s bull market, you would have

---

[3]Note, however, that ruling out the use of leveraging up means that it will be very difficult to develop a diversified portfolio of stocks with a weighted beta much above 1.35 (see Figure 6.1). We think that the problems associated with buying stock on margin far outweigh the benefits. But if you really want a very high beta portfolio and you recognize the risks that are involved, financial leveraging is your best way to achieve the objective.

begun to show a profit on your original investment by about 1950. Not too hot, you say? We agree. But it's still a lot better than having been wiped out in 1929 and not even being in the game in 1950.

This example grossly overstates the potential losses that a judicious investor would have incurred during those turbulent times. Most people did not buy all of their stocks at peak prices just before the Crash. Typically, investors were accumulating stock throughout the 1920s. Consequently, the *average* prices they paid were far less than the peak prices in 1929. Where many investors went awry was to buy on margin, and therefore, they were unable to withstand the steep price decline. Those who followed the TIPP principle of time diversification and avoided margin buying throughout the entire decade of 1920–1929 would have fared much better. Even if they had stopped investing after October 1929, stocks accumulated through a TIPP program would have regained their original value by about 1936.[4] And this is in addition to the dividends many companies continued to pay right through the depths of the Depression.

Thus if you used TIPP and did *not* use financial leverage in the 1920s and 1930s, tragic times would have been converted into merely trying times for your financial investment program. (Of course, you still had to contend with high unemployment during the Depression.) *The point is this*: If your investment practices would have enabled you to survive such a chaotic event as the Great Crash, you can confidently expect to survive and prosper in any financial situation you are likely to face. Common stocks *are* the investment for all seasons.

MANAGING UNSYSTEMATIC RISK

"Don't put all your eggs in one basket" is an adage people generally follow when making decisions that affect their financial, economic, and social lives. They believe it. Yet when they buy stocks, they use far too

---

[4]The decline in stock prices, which began in October 1929, continued throughout most of 1930, 1931, and 1932, but then stocks rose sharply during 1933–1936. If you continued buying stocks in those years, your investment returns would have been much higher by 1936 because of the stocks you would have bought at bargain prices in the depths of the Crash. In our example, we made the conservative assumption that during the Depression, you would not have had sufficient funds for additional saving and investment. But remember, *someone* was buying those stocks that were being sold at fire-sale prices in 1931 and 1932.

few "baskets." Marshall Blume and Irwin Friend[5] have shown that most individuals who buy common stocks end up with very poorly diversified portfolios. Seventy percent of the investors in the Blume and Friend study owned only one or two stocks; this included many investors who had portfolios valued at more than $100,000 and even some with market values exceeding $1 million. *This type of mistake is totally unnecessary.* Even if you begin investing with a small amount of money, you can get adequate diversification without paying large commissions.

In a fully or efficiently diversified portfolio, all unsystematic risk is eliminated, leaving beta as a reasonably accurate measure of the remaining (systematic) risk. In a TIPP-diversified portfolio, which is designed for the needs of an individual investor, however, the risk-reducing advantages of *full* diversification are not deemed to be worth the transaction costs involved. About 90 percent of all unsystematic risk can be eliminated with a TIPP-diversified portfolio of 12–15 individual stocks. As explained in Chapter 5, diversification to eliminate *all* unsystematic risk would require 500 or more different stocks. That's a lot of paper to shuffle and a lot of files to keep.

A basic principle of economics states: "A job worth doing is *not* necessarily worth doing well." This means you must pay attention to both benefits and costs. If the size of a diversified portfolio was more than tripled—from 15 stocks to 50 stocks—unsystematic risk would be reduced by an additional one-half of one percent, compared to the 90 percent of unsystematic risk that is eliminated with the first 15 stocks. That's not much gain for a lot of work! A TIPP-diversified portfolio of 12–15 stocks is a manageable list that provides a good balance between too few stocks (too much unsystematic risk) and too many stocks, where bookkeeping and transaction costs become onerous. In this section, we provide the practical steps involved in developing a TIPP-diversified portfolio.

Diversification by Industry

A portfolio will not provide adequate diversification if the investment returns on its stocks are closely related to each other in terms of eco-

---

[5]Marshall Blume and Irwin Friend, *The Changing Role of the Individual Investor* (New York: John Wiley, 1978).

nomic, financial, and political events. Sincere and informed professionals in the field of finance disagree on exactly the best way to select an efficiently diversified portfolio. There are complex statistical procedures available, but these techniques are only economical when one is managing very large amounts of money.

One easy way to achieve a diversified portfolio is to choose stocks from a number of different industries that are relatively unrelated. Very often, economic or financial events affect the investment returns of stocks in one industry but have little or no impact on those in other industries. The intense foreign competition facing the U.S. automobile industry, for example, has little effect on our soft drink industry. Likewise, a technological breakthrough in computer design, leading to sharply higher profits for computer and electronics companies, would not appreciably affect the investment returns in the insurance industry. Rising or falling interest rates affect electric utilities much more than toy manufacturers.

Figure 6.2 contains an industry classification system that provides a useful guide for selecting a diversified portfolio. All stocks are divided into six basic sectors:

I. Financial, Insurance, Real Estate
II. Consumer
III. Services
IV. Capital Goods and Technology
V. Materials
VI. Public Utilities

Within each basic sector, there are a number of industries or groups of industries, broadly classified by type of product or service. For example, under the basic Consumer sector, there are four industry groups:

II. Consumer
    A. Consumer goods—food
    B. Consumer goods—nonfood
    C. Drug, health care, and supplies
    D. Wholesale and retail trade

I. Financial, Insurance, Real Estate
   A. Bank, savings and loan (East, Midwest, South, West)
   B. Insurance, financial services
   C. Real estate
II. Consumer
   A. Consumer goods—food
   B. Consumer goods—nonfood
   C. Drug, health care, and supplies
   D. Wholesale and retail trade
III. Services
   A. Advertising and publishing
   B. Business equipment and services
   C. Recreation, hotel
   D. Transportation
IV. Capital Goods and Technology
   A. Aerospace
   B. Automotive and transportation equipment
   C. Building materials and construction
   D. Computer, electronics, and precision instruments
   E. Machinery, equipment, and supplies
V. Materials
   A. Chemical
   B. Mining, refining
   C. Iron and steel mills, metal fabricating
   D. Paper, forest products, packaging
   E. Petroleum, oilfield services
VI. Public Utilities
   A. Electric (East, Midwest, South, West)
   B. Gas
   C. Water
   D. Telecommunications

FIGURE 6.2 Industry Classification for portfolio diversification

Each industry group contains a wide variety of companies that are somewhat related with respect to economic and financial factors. For example, consumer goods—food includes, among others, companies involved in brewing, food processing, and soft drinks. Within the category consumer goods—nonfood, there are companies producing such products as home appliances, clothing, and cosmetics. Although both of these industry groups would be affected by overall economic conditions that influence consumer spending (i.e., systematic risk), sales of companies in the nonfood sector would be more sensitive to economic fluctuations than those in the food group. Thus investment returns for companies in these two industry groups would be somewhat unrelated, providing the balancing-out effect necessary for efficient diversification.

There are three rules to follow for using the industry classification provided in Figure 6.2:

1. Select at least 12–15 stocks that meet your investment objectives.
2. Each of the six basic sectors should be represented in the portfolio.
3. Stocks should be drawn from at least 12 different industry groups.

Furthermore, because no industry classification system can take into account every conceivable possibility, you should use reasonable judgment when making selections. Clearly, you shouldn't buy two soap manufacturers or two oil companies. Most of the time, the investment returns of two stocks this similar will fluctuate together as if they were one stock, giving you little or no effective diversification.

If possible, try to avoid selecting companies in different industries that are connected by a common element. Don't choose a company that manufactures only snowmobiles (consumer goods—nonfood), along with a second that specializes in selling ski equipment (wholesale and retail trade), and a third that operates winter resorts (recreation, hotel). Obviously, investment returns of all three companies depend on a common element—the amount of snow each winter. Usually, you won't have this problem because most companies are themselves somewhat diversified and often their products and services overlap two or more of the industry groups listed in Figure 6.2. Although there can be hidden common elements connecting the investment returns of two or more companies, if you are careful to spread your stock investments throughout the list in Figure 6.2, the mistakes you may make will be minor. The worksheets discussed in the next section will assist in the selection process.

IMPLEMENTING THE INVESTMENT PLAN

We stated at the beginning of this chapter that investment planning requires both knowledge about investment opportunities *and* the ability to translate that knowledge into an effective investment program that is

120 PUTTING IT ALL TOGETHER: TIPP IN ACTION

tailored to your personal objectives. In the translation or implementation phase, you need very specific information about the risk and industry characteristics for individual stocks. This section provides an introduction to the resource materials provided in Appendix A on the investment characteristics of about 800 individual stocks. This information will help you accomplish the implementation phase of portfolio management.

Portfolio Worksheet

Figure 6.3 is a Portfolio Worksheet that will be the primary organizational tool used in the implementation phase. The objective is to fill in the worksheet by selecting 12–15 (or more) individual stocks from at

Basic Sector	Industry Group	Market value	Portfolio Share	Beta	Weighted Beta
I. Financial, insurance, real estate					
II. Consumer					
III. Services					
IV. Capital goods/ technology					
V. Materials					
VI. Public utilities					

FIGURE 6.3 Portfolio Worksheet

IMPLEMENTING THE INVESTMENT PLAN   121

Basic Sector	Industry Group	Market value	Portfolio Share	Beta	Weighted Beta
I. Financial, insurance, real estate					
Bank America	A. Banks, Savings and Loan			0.95	
II. Consumer					
Holly Sugar	A. Consumer Goods—Food			0.60	
Champion Products	B. Consumer Goods—Nonfood			1.15	
III. Services					
Brunswick	C. Recreation, Hotel			1.15	
Ryder System	D. Transportation			1.10	
IV. Capital goods/ technology					
Rockwell International	A. Aerospace			1.20	
General Motors	B. Automotive and Transport Equip.			1.00	
V. Materials					
Dupont	A. Chemical			1.15	
Union Camp	D. Paper, Forest Products, Packaging			1.05	
Exxon	E. Petroleum, Oilfield Services			0.85	
VI. Public utilities					
Middle South Utilities	A. Electric (South)			0.80	
Western Union	C. Telecommunications			1.15	
	Totals $				
			Averages	1.01	

FIGURE 6.4   Portfolio Worksheet

least 12 different industry groups, distributed among the six basic sectors. In addition, the overall portfolio risk of the stocks selected must meet your risk objective. With the procedure outlined in Table 6.1, the portfolio beta is calculated from information entered on the worksheet.

For purposes of illustration, let's assume you are just beginning to invest and wish to achieve an average level of risk—that is, a beta of approximately 1.00. Turn to Appendix A, which provides industry and beta information for about 800 stocks. Although you are not limited to stocks in Appendix A, this list is sufficiently comprehensive to meet the objectives of most investors. If you already own some stocks, but have not yet achieved efficient diversification, Appendix A will be a useful tool for balancing your portfolio. Selection techniques are described in the section "Shopping for Stocks," later in this chapter.

Let us say that after considering your overall investment objectives, you decide to purchase equal amounts of the 12 stocks listed on the worksheet in Figure 6.4. (The information listed on this worksheet was obtained from Appendix A.) In this example, the stocks are distributed among all six basic sectors and in 12 different industry groups. This satisfies the TIPP principle of portfolio diversification. Because you initially invested equal amounts of money in each stock, the unweighted portfolio beta shown in Figure 6.4 would be the same as the weighted beta. The portfolio beta is 1.01, which is close enough to the objective beta of 1.00.

At this point, you have established your investment objective and designed a diversification strategy. What remains is to purchase initial amounts of the stocks selected using time diversification and cost minimizing techniques. Time diversification was discussed in Chapter 5 and cost efficient investing will be covered in Chapter 7.

Five-Year Review

It is important to conduct a thorough review of the portfolio about every five years. This will be done by repeating the portfolio management steps outlined earlier.

Let's assume that after five years your Portfolio Worksheet looks like the one in Figure 6.5. The total market value of the portfolio is $38,700, and as expected, the market values of the individual stocks are not equal. Using the procedure developed in Table 6.1, you recalculate the weighted beta of the portfolio. In this example, it turns out to be 1.02, which is still very close to the original risk objective of 1.00.[6] Hence, as long as your investment objectives haven't changed during this five-year period, no adjustments are necessary.

A portfolio can lose its diversification efficiency if there is an exceptionally large change in the prices of several of its stocks. Likewise, a number of individual beta values of the portfolio stocks may change in the same direction, rather than in an offsetting manner. In either case,

---

[6]For this example, we assumed that the betas of the individual stocks were unchanged over the five-year period. As discussed earlier, individual betas may change over time, so revised beta values would be used in the portfolio review phase.

Basic Sector	Industry Group	Market value	Portfolio Share	Beta	Weighted Beta
I. Financial, insurance, real estate					
Bank America	A. Banks, Savings and Loan	3000	.078	0.95	.074
II. Consumer					
Holly Sugar	A. Consumer Goods—Food	3500	.090	0.60	.054
Champion Products	B. Consumer Goods—Nonfood	4200	.109	1.15	.125
III. Services					
Brunswick	C. Recreation, Hotel	3100	.080	1.15	.092
Ryder System	D. Transportation	3900	.101	1.10	.111
IV. Capital goods/ technology					
Rockwell International	A. Aerospace	4100	.106	1.20	.127
General Motors	B. Automotive and Transport. Equip.	2500	.065	1.00	.065
V. Materials					
Dupont	A. Chemical	3000	.078	1.15	.090
Union Camp	D. Paper, Forest Products, Packaging	2700	.070	1.05	.074
Exxon	E. Petroleum, Oilfield Services	2800	.072	0.85	.061
VI. Public utilities					
Middle South Utilities	A. Electric (South)	2800	.072	0.80	.058
Western Union	C. Telecommunications	3100	.080	1.15	.092
	Totals $	38,700	1.00		
			Averages	1.01	1.02

FIGURE 6.5 Portfolio Worksheet

the weighted portfolio beta may diverge significantly from the original target level. Finally, your long-term financial objectives may change. Rebalancing the portfolio, which may entail changing the proportions of existing stocks or adding new ones, should be based on the TIPP principles of time diversification and minimizing transaction costs.

FINISHING TOUCHES

This completes the presentation of the basic information you'll need to establish and manage a profitable financial investment program. In conclusion, we'll address three questions that investors frequently ask as they begin to apply the principles of TIPP.

Shopping for Stocks

"How do I get the names of *specific* companies? There are thousands of corporations with publicly traded stock. If Whizbang Whistles, Ltd. and Dandy Diapers, Inc. both have the same industry and risk characteristics, and these are the qualities that are suitable for my investment objectives, how do I choose between them? Someone told me I should pin a list of names to the wall and throw a dart at it!"

As discussed in Chapters 3 and 4, with the conventional beat-the-market approach to financial investing, stocks are selected on the basis of a story:

> "Whizbang Whistles has just completed a capital modernization program. This will sharply increase their earnings, so their stock price is going to take off."
>
> "Dandy Diapers will benefit from the trend of young mothers going back to work. This stock is underpriced."
>
> "The economy will improve next year, and automobile stocks will be big gainers."
>
> "Interest rates will rise, which will hurt electric utilities and bank stocks. It's time to switch to food processing and tobacco companies."

The story approach tries to establish comparative values (discussed in Chapter 4), which provides a reason for choosing one stock over another. But there is one unusual feature about modern portfolio management presented in this book. There aren't any hard-and-fast rules for stock selection beyond the broad guidelines of risk and diversification (and tax considerations, which are discussed in Chapter 8). Because there are usually hundreds of stocks that are equally suited to every type of investment objective, you can make up your own selection rules based on the "personality" of a company. If you like Big Macs, buy some McDonalds stock. If you feel that the airline industry is too risky, just avoid airline stocks. If you think railroads are dull, don't buy railroad stocks. If you need a substantial amount of current income, select companies that pay high dividends. One place to begin learning about the personality of a company is to read its annual report, which you can obtain on request. (Addresses are provided for the companies listed in Appendix A.) There are a number of investment advisory services that provide statistical and product information on corporations (see Figure 6.6).

Searching for Betas

"Where do I get information on betas for individual stocks?" We provide betas for over 800 stocks listed in Appendix A. There are several other readily available sources of data on betas for individual stocks.

Security Owner's Stock Guide (monthly, Standard and Poor's, 25 Broadway, New York, NY 10004).

The *Stock Guide* provides basic information on over 5000 stocks, including the corporation's principal business, dividend and earnings data, and the S&P quality ranking for over 3000 issues. It also includes summary data on nearly 400 mutual funds. Small, medium, and large libraries usually subscribe to this service.

Stock Reports (quarterly, Standard and Poor's, 25 Broadway, New York, NY 10004).

These are two-page reports on about 4000 stocks that are traded on the principal exchanges and over the counter. Each report provides a detailed summary of the corporation's principal lines of business and major products, a 10-year summary of pertinent income and balance sheet data, and the S&P quality ranking. Charts record price and trading volume information on the corporation's common stock. Many medium-to-large libraries subscribe to this service.

The Value Line Investment Survey (weekly, Value Line, Inc., 711 Third Avenue, New York, NY 10017).

Value Line provides detailed information on about 1700 stocks, including historical financial data, price and trading volume charts, beta estimates, and a description of the principal lines of business and major products. The data on each stock and industry is updated every 13 weeks and is supplemented, when necessary, on a weekly basis. Large libraries often subscribe to this service.

The Media General Financial Weekly (weekly, Media General Financial Services, P.O. Box C-32333, Richmond, VA 23291).

This weekly newspaper provides a wide range of statistical data on most publicly traded stocks, including an industry classification for each stock and betas for most stocks.

FIGURE 6.6 Selected sources of investment information

Value Line publishes betas for the 1700 or so stocks it covers. The *Media General Financial Weekly* provides betas on over 3000 stocks. Some of the large full service brokerage firms regularly compute betas on a wide list of stocks. Standard and Poor's assigns "quality rankings" to a list of over 3000 stocks. These rankings, which are estimates of risk, are available in the S&P *Stock Reports* and *Security Owners Stock Guide*. The S&P quality rankings can be used as a rough proxy for a numerical measure of beta. Robert Haugen[7] found that portfolios composed of stocks with identical S&P quality rankings had the following betas:

S&P Ranking	Beta	Risk Level
A+	0.77	
A	0.78	Below average
A−	0.80	
B+	0.93	Average
B	1.13	
B−	1.21	Above average
C	1.38	

Thus a diversified portfolio made up of stocks with S&P quality rankings of B would be equivalent to a portfolio beta of about 1.13.

Be aware that financial services use a variety of methods to compute beta, so that actual estimates will differ somewhat from source to source. Some services use total investment returns (dividends plus stock price changes), whereas others use only price changes. Because betas are estimated by measuring the past variability of investment returns, the length of time covered in the measurement is important. Betas estimated from very recent data may reflect a temporary condition that is not representative of the true risk level of the stock. But if the historical time period covered is too long, there is a greater chance that the beta values are out of date. Opinions of analysts vary as to the optimum length of time to use when measuring beta.

[7]Robert Haugen, "Do Common Stock Quality Ratings Predict Risk?" *Financial Analysts Journal*, March–April, 1979.

Foreign Connection

"Should I also invest in foreign stocks to increase the diversification of my portfolio?" Changes in economic conditions and stock markets around the world are not closely related. Because stock markets in different countries are not synchronized, you can get additional risk-reducing or balancing-out effects by adding foreign stocks to your portfolio. Canadian stocks are an exception. Because the U.S. and Canadian economies are closely tied together, the U.S. and Canadian stock markets are also highly correlated, so that Canadian stocks provide little additional diversification.

Foreign stocks can significantly improve the diversification of the portfolio. Bruno Solnick[8] found that unsystematic risk was reduced by about one-third when sample portfolios were diversified evenly across eight countries rather than containing stocks solely from the United States. But he found that international diversification couldn't be achieved by investing in U.S.-based multinational corporations. Although these companies may derive 25 percent or more of their earnings from sales in foreign countries, their investment returns still march to the tune of the United States stock market. So to acquire the benefits of international diversification, you must buy companies based in foreign countries.

Achieving international diversification, however, creates new complications and causes some additional costs. The following should be considered:

1. When you invest in foreign stocks, you may become liable for additional taxes, which will reduce your investment return and complicate your income taxes.

2. Holding foreign stocks may subject you to currency controls, possibly tying up dividend payments or delaying the retrieval of your financial capital if you need to sell the stocks.

3. Because international investments are denominated in foreign currencies, foreign ownership subjects you to the additional financial risk of exchange rate fluctuations.

---

[8]Bruno Solnick, "Why Not Diversify Internationally Rather Than Domestically?" *Financial Analysts Journal*, July–August, 1974.

4. If your stock transactions are small, commission costs will be significantly higher because you will not be able to use dividend reinvestment plans discussed in Chapter 7, which are largely a U.S. institution.

Also, with the exception of the Canadian stock exchanges, it is more difficult to buy foreign stocks that aren't traded in the United States. This highly specialized financial service is only provided by a limited number of retail brokerage firms. There are over 300 foreign stocks traded in U.S. securities markets, but approximately 70 percent of them come from just three countries—Japan (30 percent), Canada (25 percent), and South Africa (13 percent).[9] Because the Canadian and U.S. stock markets are closely related, the Canadian stocks will not significantly improve the diversification of your portfolio. And the South African stocks are primarily gold mining companies. This narrows your choice of foreign stocks traded in the United States to about 100 Japanese companies, 20 or so companies each for Australia, the United Kingdom, and Israel, and a smaller number of companies from 15-20 other countries.

For an average-size portfolio, the additional costs and complications of owning *individual* foreign stocks exceeds the benefits of improved diversification. If you want to add international diversification to your portfolio, the best way is to invest in one or more foreign stock mutual funds. A mutual fund provides dividend reinvestment services and the ability to make small periodic purchases, and the fund management has the special knowledge required for transacting on foreign stock exchanges. This is one case where the added management and transaction expenses of mutual funds are well worth the cost. A list of some foreign stock mutual funds is provided in Appendix C.

---

[9]The majority of foreign stocks traded in the United States are American Depository Receipts (ADRs). An ADR is a certificate representing ownership in shares of a foreign stock. The actual shares are held in a trust account by a bank in the foreign country. Thus when ADRs are bought or sold, ownership changes hands, but the actual certificates remain in the trust account.

7

A PENNY SAVED IS A PENNY EARNING

We have now covered the three risk management principles of TIPP:

1. Selecting an appropriate return–risk objective;
2. Achieving adequate diversification of the assets in your portfolio;
3. Diversifying through time by making periodic purchases.

Our final task is to accomplish these risk management objectives in a cost effective way. This is the fourth principle of TIPP:

4. Minimizing transaction costs.

The first rule for minimizing transaction costs is to avoid paying for things the investor doesn't need. The principal–agent contract (see Chapter 2) and the efficient markets hypothesis (see Chapter 3) clearly demonstrate that paying for beat-the-market advice is counterproductive. The unnecessary advisory fees and taxes incurred because of in-and-out trading in an effort to beat the market will lower investment returns. A buy-and-hold strategy, with the principles of financial risk management, will yield the best investment return.

The second rule for minimizing transaction costs is to avoid overpaying for what the investor does need. Even a buy-and-hold investment program requires financial services. A diversified portfolio of stocks must be purchased. Dividends must be reinvested if your investment objective is long-term capital growth. Transactions may be required to rebalance your portfolio if the return–risk characteristics of your portfolio diverge from your target level or if your investment objectives change. And stocks must be sold when the objectives for which you initially invested are reached. At each stage, every penny saved by careful selection and use of transaction services increases investment returns.

Until recently, mutual funds provided the only feasible way an average investor could buy a diversified portfolio of stocks and obtain both dividend reinvestment services and the ability to periodically invest small sums of money. As discussed later in this chapter, mutual funds make sense in some cases. But now there is an alternative. Dividend reinvestment plans (DRPs) offered by many corporations provide the average investor with an economical way to acquire and manage a portfolio of individual stocks. The majority of DRPs charge no commissions or service fees for reinvesting dividends and purchasing additional stock. In some cases, you can even buy stock directly from the company at a 5 percent discount from the current market price. Moreover, with DRPs you avoid the unnecessary advisory and management fees and tax costs associated with most mutual funds.

First offered by a few corporations in the late 1960s, DRPs quickly became a popular stockholder service. About 800 companies, representing over 50 percent of the market value of all publicly traded stock in the United States, now have DRPs, and the list continues to grow. Appendix A provides the names and addresses of most of the corporations who have DRPs and the specific provisions and services offered by the various plans.

Generally, stock purchases can be handled most easily and economically through DRPs or no-load mutual funds (also discussed later in this chapter). Any large one-time purchase or sale of stock, however, should be made through a discount broker. When you buy or sell stock through a full service broker like Merrill Lynch or Dean Witter, a large part of the commission rate is a fee for investment service. Full service doesn't mean *better* service, but rather a bundling of brokerage services (buying, selling, and transferring titles) with investment advisory services, which are then sold together for one commission price. (This practice also creates the serious conflict of interest discussed in Chapter 4.) Discount brokers have unbundled these two separate functions and provide investors with the option of buying and paying for the brokerage or title transfer service alone. Thus by using discount brokers, you will be able to avoid paying for advisory services you don't need.

This chapter contains a description of the discount brokerage industry and provides a shoppers' guide for the commission rates of about 100 discount brokers. With this information, you'll be able to shop nationwide for the best title transfer services at the least cost. If you prefer to transact with a local discount broker, you'll be able to find one that charges the best price in your area. This information is important because, although they all call themselves *discount* brokers, their commission rates vary widely. So shopping around can result in considerable cost savings.

With the information on individual DRPs in Appendix A, the commission cost information for individual discount brokers in Appendix B, and a no-load mutual fund directory, you will be able to fully satisfy the fourth principle of TIPP—minimizing transaction costs.

DIVIDEND REINVESTMENT PLANS

There are two major features of most DRPs, automatic dividend reinvestment and the option to purchase additional shares of the stock. With the dividend reinvestment option, common stock dividends (and, in some DRPs, preferred stock dividends and bond interest) are automatically reinvested.

In order to qualify for a DRP, one must normally own at least one share of stock in the company.[1] It is often more economical to purchase the initial shares through a full service broker rather than a discount broker, who will charge a minimum commission of $25–$35 per transaction. Once you qualify, you can invest any dollar amount within the

---

[1]W. R. Grace and Control Data have no restrictions. Anyone can establish a DRP account by submitting an application form and a check for the initial voluntary cash investment. A few public utility companies allow their customers to make an initial voluntary cash investment without first becoming a stockholder. These include Central Maine Power, Cleveland Electric, Philadelphia Electric, Portland General Electric, San Diego G&E, and Union Electric.

minimums and maximums specified by the DRPs without going through a broker. If the dollar amount of your dividend or additional investment is not equal to full shares of stock, fractional shares will be credited to your account. The price you pay for this additional stock will be the average market price for all shares of the company traded that day. Your participation is voluntary and may be terminated at any time.

Voluntary cash payments are invested on the quarterly dividend payment dates, along with dividends that are being reinvested. In addition, most DRPs establish one or two voluntary cash investment dates between quarterly dividend payment dates. (Sometimes this feature is contingent on the administrator receiving enough money from all participants to buy at least 100 shares of stock.) A DRP with frequent investment dates helps investors achieve the TIPP principle of time diversification. Voluntary cash investments are usually limited to minimum and maximum amounts for each quarter, with a $10 minimum and $5000 maximum being typical. You can send a check or money order to the administrator for any amount within the minimum and maximum limits.

Advantages of DRPs

A DRP is particularly advantageous for investors who want to buy individual stocks or reinvest dividends, save and invest on a regular basis, or receive quarterly dividend checks but still have the option to buy additional stock from time to time. These services are very inexpensive. Eighty percent of the companies listed in Appendix A offer cost-free DRPs. In these plans, the company pays the service fees and commissions incurred to maintain the program. In the remaining DRPs, investors pay the transaction costs incurred by the administrator, which typically involves a service fee of 4–5 percent of the amount invested, up to a maximum of $2.50 per transaction, plus a proportionate share of brokerage costs. Because the DRP administrator consolidates all funds to be invested and buys large blocks of stock at volume-discount commission rates, brokerage costs are normally 1 percent or less of the new money invested. This is substantially lower than if each investor separately purchased small amounts of stock through a broker.

Another advantage of DRPs (and mutual funds, which we'll get to soon) is that dividends are automatically reinvested and monthly savings and other small checks can be invested without delay. This provides an important element of self-discipline to your savings program. Even with the best of intentions on your part, it is easy for money that you plan to save to slip into your checking account and mysteriously disappear. Alternatively, if you buy stock directly through a broker, you must diligently make deposits in a savings or money market account until you have accumulated enough to buy additional stock at a reasonable commission rate. While it is being accumulated, your money will earn a lower rate of return (see Appendix to Chapter 5), and by investing large sums at one time, you will not be fully achieving the TIPP principle of time diversification.

A DRP also provides a convenient record-keeping service. After each purchase, you receive a statement listing the full and fractional shares credited to your account. It shows the amount of the last dividend and any voluntary cash payment invested since the last statement, the number of shares purchased in the last transaction, the price paid for those shares, and the total number of shares you own. There is no need to record these amounts each time because the statement is cumulative. You will also receive a statement at the end of each year showing the total amount of taxable dividend income earned during the year.

The custodial service of a DRP provides protection against stock certificates being lost, misplaced, or stolen. As an added custodial service, many administrators will accept a deposit of stock certificates not presently held in the DRP at no cost or for a very low one-time fee. Stockholders retain all voting rights for stock accumulated in DRPs and may request delivery of their stock certificates at any time. At your request, most administrators will arrange to sell the shares and send you a check for the proceeds, less any service fee and commission. If the amount involved is substantially more than $800, however, you will be better off having the stock certificates delivered and then selling them through a discount broker.

Specific Provisions of DRPs

Although most DRPs have both dividend reinvestment and voluntary cash options, the individual plans have a number of variations in the specific provisions and services offered to stockholders. Table 7.1 provides a sample of companies, drawn from Appendix A, that illustrates

TABLE 7.1 Sample of Dividend Reinvestment Plan Provisions (selected from Appendix A)

	Cost		Dividend Reinvestment Plans Voluntary Cash		
	Service Fee	Commission	$ Minimum/ $ Maximum	Frequency (per year)	Special Features
IBM	0	0	$10/5000q	12	OI
CBS	5-2.50	Y	25/1000m	12	
Emerson Electric	0	Y	25/2500q	4	
FMC	0	0	10/1000m	8	PRF
Caterpillar Tractor	4-2.00	Y	10/unlim	12	
Atlantic City Electric	0	Y-VC	0/20,000y	12	
Sperry	0	0	25/3000q	12	5-D SSO BOND OI
Hospital Corp. of America	0	0	25/12,500q	12	5-D+VC OI
Humana	0	0	none		

Note: See text or Appendix A for key to table abbreviations.

DIVIDEND REINVESTMENT PLANS 135

these differences. The table is divided into three parts: Cost, Voluntary Cash, and Special Features. The first line contains the major features of the DRP offered by IBM. The Cost column shows that there are no service fees or commissions. The Voluntary Cash column lists the minimum and maximum payments allowed per time period and the number of times voluntary cash payments are invested. The minimum payment is $10, and the maximum is $5000 per quarter (q). Voluntary cash payments are invested 12 times a year. Under the Special Features column, OI means this is an original-issue DRP. Your reinvested dividends and voluntary cash payments are used to buy new stock issued by the company.

The DRP for CBS has both a service fee and commission costs. The numbers 5-2.50 under the service fee column mean that the fee is 5 percent of the amount being invested up to a maximum of $2.50 per transaction. The letter Y under the commission column means that the investor pays his or her proportionate share of commissions. The minimum voluntary cash payment is $25, and the maximum is $1000 per month (m). Voluntary cash payments are invested 12 times per year.

Emerson Electric pays the service fees, but the stockholder pays the commission charges. Voluntary cash payments are invested four times per year, with minimums and maximums of $25 and $2500.

The FMC Corporation invests voluntary cash payments eight times per year, once on each quarterly dividend payment date and again halfway between each quarterly dividend payment. Under the Special Features column, PRF means that owners of preferred stock are eligible to participate in the DRP. Preferred stock dividends can be reinvested in common stock, and preferred stockholders can also participate in the voluntary cash option for purchasing common stock.

The Caterpillar Tractor DRP has a 4 percent service charge, with a maximum of $2.00 per transaction. Voluntary cash investments are unlimited (unlim).

Atlantic City Electric has no minimum payment for voluntary cash investments. The maximum is $20,000 per year (y). Although there are no commissions on reinvested dividends, Y-VC under the Commission Cost column means that commissions are charged on voluntary cash payments.

Under the Special Features column for Sperry Corporation, the term 5-D means that dividends will be reinvested at a 5 percent discount from the current market value. In addition, Sperry offers a split share option (SSO), meaning the investor can reinvest part of the dividends and receive the rest as income. BOND means that investors who own Sperry Corporation bonds are eligible to join the DRP. Bond interest is reinvested in additional shares of common stock, and bondholders can purchase common stock through the DRP. This is an original issue (OI) DRP.

Hospital Corporation of America has an original-issue DRP that offers a 5 percent discount on both reinvested dividends and voluntary cash payments (5-D+VC).

The Humana Corporation offers a cost-free DRP for reinvesting dividends, but does not have a voluntary cash payment option (none).

Some of these special features have tax implications. The IRS has ruled that certain benefits received by stockholders from DRPs must be counted as taxable dividend income. If you purchase the stock through a DRP in the open market, you must include as taxable income your share of any commissions and expenses paid by the company on your behalf. However, the service fee may be taken as an itemized deduction when computing your tax liability, and commissions may be included in the cost basis of the stock you purchase. The cost basis will be important in computing capital gains tax liability when you subsequently sell the shares (see Chapter 8).

In an original-issue (OI) DRP, now offered by about one third of the companies listed in Appendix A, new stock is purchased by investors directly from the company, so there are no commission costs, and thus no tax liability is incurred because of the cost-free nature of the DRP. If the company sells the shares at a discount, however, the difference between the fair market value and the discounted price is considered taxable dividend income to the investor. Because taxes are paid on the differential at the time of the transaction, the cost basis for calculating capital gains when the stock is eventually sold is the fair market value, not the discounted price actually paid.

NO-LOAD MUTUAL FUNDS

A mutual fund is a financial service that pools the resources of a number of investors and develops a portfolio of securities that meets one or a combination of the basic investment goals discussed in the Appendix to Chapter 5: capital preservation, current income, or capital appreciation. An investor selects mutual funds that meet his or her return–risk objectives and shares proportionately in dividend and interest income, capital gains or losses, and expenses of the fund, based on the number of shares held in the fund. Here, we are interested in common stock mutual funds as an alternative to maintaining a TIPP diversified portfolio.

As explained in Chapter 3, mutual fund managers cannot outperform an efficient financial market. Before transaction costs are accounted for, professionally managed portfolios have investment returns that are no better than buy-and-hold investment strategies that use diversified portfolios of equally risky stocks. Consequently, after transaction costs are subtracted, mutual funds yield lower investment returns than buy-and-hold portfolios of equal risk. Thus the true *cost* of buying mutual fund financial services is a lower investment return. How much lower for any specific mutual fund depends on how much money the fund wastes on unnecessary management fees, commissions, and other operating expenses incurred in attempting to beat the market.

In exchange for this cost, the *benefits* of mutual funds are ready-made portfolio diversification, access to a number of useful ancillary financial services (discussed later in this chapter), and convenience. Whether you should manage your own portfolio of stocks, buy shares in one or more mutual funds, or choose some combination of individual stocks and mutual funds depends on the benefit–cost calculation as it affects you. Because objectives and preferences vary between individuals, this is a choice only you can make. The remainder of this chapter discusses the benefits and costs of alternative ways to achieve particular investment objectives. The first choice is between load and no-load mutual funds.

Load or No-Load Mutual Funds?

There are two kinds of mutual funds, load funds and no-load funds. The term *load* refers to the commission paid to a salesperson when an investor buys shares in a mutual fund. In a no-load fund, investors deal directly with the management rather than through a separate sales organization, so there is no need to pay a sales commission. Instead of being contacted by a salesperson who provides information about a mutual fund, you must take the initiative. This means writing for the prospectus and latest financial report, evaluating the material, and mailing a check to the fund or funds of your choice. The selection of an appropriate mutual fund should be made using the TIPP principles of financial investing. The No-Load Mutual Fund Association has a directory entitled *Your Guide to Mutual Funds*, which provides the names, addresses, telephone numbers, investment objectives, and other pertinent information for about 200 no-load mutual funds. (To order, write No-Load Mutual Fund Association, 11 Penn Plaza, New York, NY 10001. Include $2.00 for postage and handling.)

With load funds, the typical nominal commission rate is 8.5 percent of the amount invested. Because the load, or commission, is paid to a sales organization for selling stock in the mutual fund, it is subtracted from the amount you invest. This means that the actual commission rate is 9.3 percent of the funds invested. For a purchase of $1000, for example, a commission of 8.5 percent is $85, leaving $915 to be invested in mutual fund shares; $85 is 9.3 percent of $915, which is the actual commission rate. In most load funds, the commission rate gradually declines as the size of the investment increases. Except for a visit from a friendly sales representative, there aren't any good reasons for investing in a load fund. The commission, which is taken out when you invest, permanently reduces your investment return because managers of load mutual funds have no special secrets for outsmarting an efficient market. Assuming a holding period return of 9 percent, a $10,000 investment in a no-load mutual fund would outperform a similar load mutual fund by nearly $9000 in 25 years. The $9000 difference is the amount of earnings lost on the $915 initially paid to a sales representative rather than invested.

Benefits of Mutual Funds

Mutual funds provide several important financial services:

1. Each mutual fund furnishes a formal statement of its investment objective, which roughly corresponds to its portfolio risk. Examples of average betas for mutual funds, classified according to their investment objectives, are as follows:[2]

[2]John G. McDonald, "Objectives and Performance of Mutual Funds, 1960–1969," *Journal of Financial and Quantitative Analysis*, June 1974, pp. 331–333.

Mutual Fund Objective	Average Beta
Income	0.55
Balanced	0.68
Income–growth	0.86
Growth–income	0.90
Growth	1.01
Maximum capital gains	1.22

Thus by using the stated investment objectives, an investor can select a mutual fund that meets his or her return–risk goal, satisfying the first principle of TIPP. Although the relationship is not perfect, a mutual fund's stated objective is a good approximation of its portfolio risk. Most funds maintain the same level of risk from year to year.

2. Most mutual funds have well-diversified portfolios, which substantially reduces unsystematic risk while providing the convenience of owning a single security instead of many. This achieves the portfolio diversification principle of TIPP.

3. You can spread out purchases and sales of mutual fund shares in amounts that fit your budget and financial objectives. Mutual funds also provide low-cost record keeping and custodial services and offer a variety of convenience services. Dividends can be automatically reinvested, if you wish, and many funds allow additional money to be invested, shares redeemed by telephone, and automatic investing by periodic bank drafts on your checking account or through payroll deduction plans. Also available are systematic withdrawal plans, whereby you can receive a monthly or quarterly check. Most funds may also be used for IRAs, Keogh Plans, and other tax-sheltered retirement accounts (see Chapter 8). All of these services help achieve the time diversification and minimum transaction cost principles of TIPP.

Mutual Fund Costs

There are three major types of costs involved in mutual fund investments: operating expenses, commissions, and taxes. Operating expenses can be measured by the expense ratio, which is the ratio of operating costs to average net assets in the fund during the year. The expense ratio is calculated and published in the prospectus and annual report of each mutual fund. Operating expenses include the salaries of directors, executives, portfolio managers, and clerical personnel, the rent and maintenance expenses for office facilities, and fees for custodial, accounting, and legal services. These expenses are not affected very much by the amount of money being managed—$10 million or $100 million can be managed with about the same staff and facilities. Expenses that vary according to the size of the portfolio and number of investors, such as correspondence with stockholders, printing, and mailing, are a relatively small part of the total. Consequently, operating expenses per dollar of funds managed are smaller for large portfolios. Average expense ratios of common stock mutual funds, ranked by size of fund, are as follows:

Size of Mutual Fund (millions of dollars)	Average Expense Ratio
Below 20	1.5%
20–50	1.2
50–200	1.0
200–500	0.8
Over 500	0.6

The average expense ratio for all common stock mutual funds is about 1.0 percent. Thus if you own shares valued at $10,000 in a typical mutual fund, your share of the annual operating costs will be about $100, while in a very small mutual fund operating costs would average $150, and in very large funds it would be about $60 per year. On a size-adjusted basis, operating expenses are the same in load and no-load funds.

Commissions on portfolio transactions are the second cost of a mutual fund investment. The typical common stock fund replaces about 75 percent of its portfolio each year. This is known as its portfolio turnover rate. Your proportionate share of commission costs is related to portfolio turnover. A mutual fund manager who tries to beat the market with a lot of in-and-out trading will incur, to your detriment, a lot of commissions. It is difficult to generalize, however, about which types of mutual funds have high or low portfolio turnover commissions costs.

Although the average portfolio turnover rate for most mutual funds is about 75 percent, funds range from zero to over 200 percent in individual cases. There is some tendency for smaller mutual funds to have somewhat higher portfolio turnover rates, but you will find both small and large funds with low or high turnover rates. Specific funds, however, tend to have consistent turnover rates from year to year.

There are other things besides turnover rates that affect the commission costs a mutual fund incurs on your behalf. Commission costs in funds with large investments in foreign stocks will be higher than those in funds that invest in stocks that are traded in U.S. securities markets. This is because commission costs in many foreign stockmarkets are not determined competitively and are higher than those in the United States. Another reason for higher-than-expected commission costs is that mutual fund managers do not always transact with brokers offering the lowest commission rates. They sometimes give preference to full service brokers, who provide the fund's managers with investment advice. Because the cost of this advice is included in the full service broker's commission rate, which is ultimately paid by mutual fund stockholders, the higher commission cost is actually an additional (hidden) investment advisory fee. Portfolio managers often prefer this arrangement because they would otherwise have to pay for this information out of their own pockets.

A typical mutual fund with a $100 million portfolio will have about $300,000 in commission costs per year. In this case, the commission cost ratio, which is equal to commission costs divided by average net assets, would be 0.3 percent.[3] When the commission cost ratio is added to the typical operating expense ratio of 1.0 percent, the total transaction expense ratio for a typical mutual fund would be about 1.3 percent. Because professional managers cannot outperform an efficient market, it follows that the average rates of return on mutual funds would be below the average for comparable portfolios without these expenses. And that is exactly what the studies discussed in Chapter 3 demonstrate. Total expenses vary widely between mutual funds, but the expected return on a risk-adjusted basis will always be lower than for an equivalent portfolio not subject to these transaction costs.

The payment of unnecessary taxes is the third type of cost associated

---

[3]Commission cost ratios are not published, but they can be calculated from data provided in the fund's prospectus.

with mutual funds. If capital gains are realized when fund managers use a buy-and-sell strategy in an attempt to beat the market, they become the tax liability of the mutual fund shareholders in the year in which they occur. Alternatively, with a buy-and-hold investment strategy, capital gains taxes are deferred until you reach your investment goal. As explained in Chapter 8, any time you defer paying taxes, that's equivalent to receiving an interest-free loan from the government. This "loan" earns the market rate of return until you finally pay the tax. Moreover, you may also obtain a lower overall tax rate if the capital gains are postponed until you are in a lower tax bracket. Except in the case of index funds (discussed in the next subsection), all mutual funds incur some unnecessary capital gains tax liability on behalf of their shareholders. This cost varies in proportion to both the turnover rate of the mutual fund and your tax bracket.

An Index Mutual Fund

There is an alternative to either maintaining your own portfolio of individual stocks or paying the high costs of a conventional managed mutual fund. This alternative is an index fund. The objective of an index fund is to match—rather than beat—the investment performance of the overall stock market. This is accomplished by designing a portfolio that duplicates the stocks in a broadly based stockmarket index—hence the term *index fund*. It is an approach used by many institutional investors, including banks, insurance companies, and pension funds. In an index fund portfolios are designed to match the performance of, say, the S&P 500 (which includes over 70 percent of the market value of all publicly traded stocks). The portfolio risk, or beta, of an index fund is 1.00. The Vanguard Index Trust, which uses the S&P 500 as its model, is a no-load index mutual fund that is available to individual investors. (For further information on the Vanguard Index Trust, write to Vanguard Financial Center, Valley Forge, PA 19482 or call their investor information center: 1-800-523-7025; in Pennsylvania, 1-800-362-0530.)

An index mutual fund avoids several of the major objections to conventional managed mutual funds. With conventional beat-the-market investing, mutual fund managers unbalance their portfolios by "betting" on some stocks more heavily than others. These bets increase the unsystematic (uncompensated) risk of the portfolio and also reduce investment returns because of high transaction costs for advisory fees and commissions. In contrast, an index fund provides efficient diversification because the portfolio is balanced, which minimizes unsystematic risk. And because it's unmanaged in the traditional sense, its investment return will be higher than those on a managed fund because there are no investment advisory fees or commissions for in-and-out trading. The rate of return is lower than that of the index of stocks it seeks to duplicate because there are some management fees, but the differential is much smaller than with conventional mutual funds.

MUTUAL FUNDS OR DO-IT-YOURSELF?

Mutual funds were designed to provide financial services for investors who do not have the time, inclination, technical knowledge, or sufficient capital to effectively manage their own financial investments. Before the development of DRPs, mutual funds provided the only economical way for average investors to obtain adequate portfolio and time diversification. In that era, transaction costs associated with investing small amounts of money in individual stocks were too high. But with the advent of DRPs, investors now have a choice between managing their own portfolio, paying for the financial services of a mutual fund, or selecting a combination of individual stocks and mutual fund shares. The choice you make depends, of course, on your financial circumstances and personal preferences.

Weighing the Benefits and Costs

If you choose to build your own portfolio, you must select stocks in such a way that the combination substantially reduces unsystematic risk. As explained in Chapter 6, it is relatively easy to build a TIPP-diversified portfolio of 12–15 stocks, but this does take some time and effort on your part. A mutual fund provides ready-made diversification. With the exception of an index fund, however, mutual funds are not fully diversified because they unbalance the fund's portfolio in an attempt to beat the market. But the typical mutual fund will still have somewhat less unsystematic risk than a TIPP diversified portfolio because it is usually impractical for an individual investor to obtain and manage a very large number of stocks. So you will give up some diversification efficiency if you choose a TIPP portfolio over a mutual fund.

Mutual funds also provide several services that are not generally available to investors who buy stock through DRPs. These include:

Bank drafts and payroll deduction authorizations that make systematic investing easier

Systematic withdrawal plans for retirees

Custodial services for IRA, Keogh, and other tax-sheltered retirement plans

Thus the benefits of a mutual fund are ready-made diversification, slightly better diversification efficiency, and several convenience options not available with a TIPP-diversified portfolio. The cost of a mutual fund is the lower investment return that results from higher transaction costs. A $5000 TIPP portfolio of average risk stocks with a 9 percent annual holding period return will grow to approximately $11,500 in 10 years. In contrast, a no-load index mutual fund with a total transaction expense ratio of 0.5 percent will grow to approximately $11,200 over the same period. In this instance, then, the cost of obtaining the portfolio diversification services and convenience options of the index mutual fund is $300 for the 10-year period, or an average cost of $30 per year.

This modest cost difference, however, becomes much greater if the holding period increases, the amount invested increases, or a conventional mutual fund is used instead of an index mutual fund. Table 7.2 provides a rough estimate of the net cost involved in using a mutual fund rather than a TIPP-diversified portfolio; the table uses the transaction cost ratios discussed earlier. For a $5000, 10-year investment (column 1), the financial services provided by a no-load index mutual fund (row 1) will result in a net cost of $30 per year, compared to a do-it-yourself TIPP portfolio. The same investment in a conventional no-load mutual fund with a 1.0 percent total transaction expense ratio (row 2) will lower investment returns by about $70 a year. With a 1.3 percent total transaction expense ratio (row 3), the net cost is about $100. The costs here are modest. But if the holding period is increased to 25 years, the average annual cost of a $5000 investment in an index no-load mutual fund rises from $30 to $150, reflecting the impact of compound-

TABLE 7.2 Average Annual Net Cost Using Mutual Fund Financial Services Instead of a TIPP-Diversified Portfolio

	(1) $5000 Investment for 10 years	(2) $5000 Investment for 25 years	(3) $50,000 Investment for 10 years	(4) $50,000 Investment for 25 years
1. No-load index mutual fund with 0.5% total transaction expense ratio[a]	30	150	250	1100
2. No-load mutual fund with 1.0% total transaction expense ratio[b]	70	300	900	3100
3. No-load mutual fund with 1.3% total transaction expense ratio[b]	100	400	1200	4100

Note: Assumptions used in computing the data are as follows: (1) Holding period return before costs is 9 percent. Dividend rate is 4 percent of the initial investment. (2) The TIPP portfolio used for comparative purposes consists of 75 percent cost-free DRPs and 25 percent DRPs with 5 percent service fee, maximum of $2.50 per transaction, and 1 percent commission cost. The example reflects the initial commission cost to establish DRPs and the tax cost of commissions paid by the company at 40 percent marginal tax bracket. The $50,000 portfolio was established with initial purchases through a discount broker.

[a]Reflects estimated total transaction expense ratio of 0.5 percent for a $5000 portfolio and 0.39 percent for a $50,000 portfolio.

[b]Does not reflect the possibility of capital gains tax liability due to in-and-out trading, which would increase the cost (decrease the return) of a mutual fund investment, compared to a buy-and-hold TIPP portfolio or an index mutual fund.

ing on the loss of investment dollars to transaction expenses. Likewise, if the amount invested is increased from $5000 to $50,000, the cost is increased from $30 per year to $250 per year, even though the actual cost of managing a portfolio (yours or the mutual fund's) doesn't increase in proportion to the amount of money invested. When the effects of a larger investment and a longer holding period are combined, a $50,000 investment in a no-load index mutual fund for 25 years results in an average annual cost of $1100 per year.

The other entries in Table 7.2 show what happens if a conventional no-load mutual fund is used instead of an index mutual fund. Lines 2 and 3 assume transaction expense ratios of 1.0 and 1.3. Here, the average annual cost for a $50,000 investment for 25 years rises to $3100 and $4100, respectively.

Thus if you are investing $5000 or less on a one-time basis, for an expected holding period of 10 years or less, a no-load mutual fund may be the most desirable option. Under these circumstances, the additional financial services of a mutual fund, especially an index fund, can be purchased at a modest price. Moreover, an index fund avoids the additional capital gains tax liability incurred when conventional mutual funds use a buy-and-sell investment strategy, a cost not reflected in Table 7.2. But if you plan to save and invest over a long period of time, or if your investment fund is expected to grow much beyond $5000, it may be well worth the minimal time and effort required to maintain a TIPP portfolio of stocks yourself rather than using the mutual fund option.

Customizing Your Portfolio

Because investors often have multiple financial goals, a combination of a TIPP-diversified portfolio of individual stocks and one or more mutual funds may be an appropriate investment strategy. At the present time, mutual funds—but not DRPs—offer custodial services for IRAs, Keoghs, and other tax-sheltered retirement plans. Because it is usually advantageous for investors to take full advantage of the benefits provided by tax sheltering, mutual funds will be an important component of many investment portfolios (see Chapter 8).

Further, as discussed in Chapter 5, international stocks can contribute important diversification to your portfolio. Because a DRP is a financial service offered primarily by U.S. corporations and commission costs for individual stock transactions in foreign countries may be relatively high, an international mutual fund is often the best way to obtain international diversification.

If some of your portfolio stocks do not have DRPs, but you still want to reinvest small dividend checks received from these stocks, they can be reinvested in other portfolio stocks with DRPs or in a mutual fund. If you want to invest small amounts of money on a periodic basis in a stock that doesn't have a DRP, Merrill Lynch offers a dividend reinvestment and voluntary cash payment service called the Sharebuilder Plan, which covers most publicly traded stocks. The initial minimum purchase is $100, and additional purchases can be made in amounts ranging from $25 to $5000. The number of additional investments is unlimited. Commission rates, which depend on the dollar amount invested, are 6.5 percent on purchases up to $300, and decline to 1.6 percent on a $5000 investment. Single transactions over $5000 are charged regular Merrill Lynch commission rates. Dividends are reinvested at a lower commission rate. The cost of purchasing stock and reinvesting dividends through the Sharebuilder Plan is substantially higher than with corporate DRPs, so it should be used only for investing in stocks that do not have DRPs. (For further information, write to: Sharebuilder, P.O. Box 520, Church Street Station, New York, NY 10008, or call 1-800-221-2856.)

If you reinvest all dividends, you must use income from other sources to pay the taxes due on the dividend income. Some people prefer this arrangement because it helps force them to save. But for others, this may present problems. If so, the split share option offered by some DRPs or the systematic withdrawal option available with mutual funds may be useful. You can have enough dividend income passed through to cover the tax liability on your investment income.

If your sole investment objective is current income, you can either select a TIPP-diversified portfolio of high yield stocks or buy one or more mutual funds that specialize in high yield securities—or you could use some combination of the two. The monthly withdrawal option offered by most mutual funds is an attractive financial service for investors whose only investment objective is to receive regular income payments.

Finally, if you select an index mutual fund as your principal investment, but you want below-average risk, you can add a money market mutual fund or money market account to your portfolio so that the overall portfolio risk (beta) is lowered to the level of risk you want to take.

This technique, which was discussed in Chapter 6, is called *leveraging down*. You can also leverage down with a TIPP-diversified portfolio of individual stocks. If you want above-average risk, you can develop a TIPP-diversified portfolio of stocks with a portfolio beta above 1.00, leverage up a TIPP-diversified portfolio or an index mutual fund by borrowing money and buying additional shares, or select one or more conventional mutual funds that provide above-average risk.

As you customize your portfolio, adding mutual funds and other financial assets, such as money market funds, pension funds, and tax-sheltered limited partnerships (see Chapter 8), you are effectively adding two basic sectors to the classification list for portfolio diversification provided in Chapter 6 (see Figure 6.2):

VII. Mutual Funds
 A. Common stock
 B. International common stock
 C. Corporate/government bonds
 D. Tax-free bonds
 E. Money market
VIII. Other Financial Investments
 A. Cash management accounts
 B. Pension funds
 C. Other

DISCOUNT BROKERS

From its beginning in 1792 and until 1975, the New York Stock Exchange (NYSE) established minimum commission rates that brokerage firms were required to charge for transactions on the NYSE. A brokerage firm that dared to engage in commission price cutting would have been denied use of the NYSE to execute buy-and-sell orders for its customers. Because a majority of the dollar value of transactions involve stocks listed on the NYSE, this would have put the brokerage firm out of business. (It would be the same thing as not allowing a heart surgeon to use hospital facilities.) Because of the dominant position of the NYSE, its commission schedule was used throughout the brokerage industry, whether or not transactions involved a stock listed on the NYSE. This eliminated direct commission price competition between brokers.

The NYSE commission rate structure bundled title transfer (brokerage) and investment advisory services together, so investors didn't have the option of buying title transfer services alone. In the early 1970s, a few small firms began offering a separate title transfer service to individual investors at a discount from NYSE commission rates. (Thus a firm that specialized in title transfer services became known as a "discount broker.") They traded exchange-listed stocks in the over-the-counter (OTC) market, so the NYSE couldn't enforce its rules on them. The discount brokerage industry remained small, however, because the OTC market couldn't handle the order flow as efficiently as the traditional stock exchanges. But in 1975 the SEC adopted a rule that abolished the fixed commission rate system, so discount brokers could use the NYSE and other stock exchanges to execute trades for their customers. By the early 1980s, there were about 150 discount brokerage firms, and beginning in 1982 many commercial banks and thrift institutions began offering discount brokerage services. Discount brokers now handle about 20 percent of retail securities transactions, and with the recent entry of banks and thrifts into the industry, this percentage share of the market is expected to continue to rise.

What Is Title Transfer?

A title transfer service involves two relatively simple tasks. First, when a broker receives an order to buy or sell a stock, the broker relays it to a dealer, who specializes in executing transactions for this particular security. A dealer provides a liquidity service, standing ready to buy stock from people who want to sell and sell stock to people who want to buy. (Some brokers also provide dealer services for some stocks.) The difference between the prices at which the broker offers to buy and sell is called the bid-ask spread. This is the fee paid by investors for the dealer's service. After the order is executed, the broker sends a confirmation of the trade to the investor and handles the routine paperwork to obtain transfer of ownership of the security from the seller to the buyer and the payment of money from the buyer to the seller. By maintaining low overhead, eliminating the investment research department, and replacing the traditional commission salespeople with salaried order specialists, discount brokers are able to offer substantially lower commission rates for title transfer services. Depending on the size and type of order, discount brokers' commission rates are 50 to 80 percent lower than full service brokers' rates.

Most discount brokers offer the same array of title transfer services as full service brokers. They accept all types of orders—market, limit, margin, stop, day, week, month, and good-until-cancelled—on all types of securities. They provide custodial services, and most of them pay interest on idle cash balances. Discount brokers operate under the same SEC regulations as full service brokers, and all firms are members of the Securities Investors Protection Corporation (SIPC), which provides up to $500,000 insurance coverage per account ($100,000 on cash balances) in the event the brokerage firm is forced into liquidation. Some firms supplement this insurance with private policies that provide as much as $2.5 million additional coverage for each account.

What about quality of execution? Can you expect to get as good a price from a dealer with an order placed through a discount broker as one placed through a full service broker? Yes. All brokerage firms use approximately the same type of facilities and techniques for sending orders to the dealers who perform the liquidity service. In fact, trades of less than 1100 shares of stocks listed on the NYSE receive exactly the same execution service because they are all entered into a computerized order routing system called DOT (Designated Order Turnaround). The other stock exchanges and the OTC market also have automated systems for routing orders to dealers. All trades are executed in an open, competitive market. There is no evidence that a particular brokerage firm, whether it is large or small, full service or discount, member of the NYSE or not, can get better bid-ask prices from dealers than any other brokerage firm. Most orders submitted through DOT are executed in about 2 minutes, regardless of which broker places the order. Some brokers claim they can get orders reported back faster than their competitors—perhaps while you are still on the telephone. For an investor using the TIPP principles of financial management, however, it doesn't make any difference if the order is reported back a couple of minutes faster.

Will confirmations, monthly statements, and stock certificate delivery be as accurate and prompt with a discount broker? Yes. After a trade is completed, the title transfer process involves a lot of routine paperwork, much of which is handled by computers. Because all brokerage firms either own or have access to computers, the quality of this aspect of title transfer is quite similar between firms. Many discount brokers and small full service brokers use a specialized clearinghouse firm to handle the paperwork. In fact, some discount brokers use the wholesale division of large full service brokers like Merrill Lynch to execute trades and handle the paperwork for them. But not all firms are exactly alike. Some brokers (both full service and discount) have more efficient back office record keeping facilities than others. Because the paperwork involved in title transfer is a highly standardized, routine operation, most firms do a good job, so you shouldn't tolerate a broker who provides sloppy service or makes a lot of paperwork errors.

Selecting a Discount Broker

Although discount brokers offer approximately the same quality of title transfer service, commission costs for identical trades often vary widely between firms because they use different rates and methods to compute commission charges. Some discount brokers charge over twice as much as others for exactly the same transaction. Commission rates generally increase as the number of shares in the transaction increases, and many firms also charge higher rates for higher-priced stocks. Moreover, brokerage firms use a variety of minimum and maximum charges, sliding rate scales (such as the price per share or the increase in number of shares), and special fees and volume discounts in arriving at the final commission cost for a transaction.

The most price competitive discount brokers charge a flat commission rate per share, regardless of the price per share, and use a sliding rate scale that declines sharply as the number of shares for a single order increases. Because there is very little difference in the cost of handling a single order for, say, 100 shares or 1000 shares of stock or 300 shares of a $20 stock compared to 300 shares of an $80 stock, this type of commission schedule more accurately reflects the broker's cost of providing a title transfer service.

Table 7.3 compares the commissions charged by the most price competitive discount brokers to those charged by average discount brokers, bank discount brokers, and full service brokers. Column 1 lists the average commissions for 11 "typical transactions"—that is, trades ranging from 100 to 500 shares of stocks selling between $20 and $50 per

TABLE 7.3 Brokerage Commissions by Transaction Size for Selected Groups of Firms

	(1) Typical Transaction[a]	(2) Large Transaction[b]	(3) Low-Priced Stock Transaction[c]
1. 20 price competitive discount brokers			
a. Average Cost Per Transaction	$48	$153	$53
b. Percentage of Dollar Value of Transaction	0.5%	0.2%	1.3%
2. Average of all discount brokers			
a. Average Cost Per Transaction	$73	$232	$69
b. Percentage of Dollar Value of Transaction	0.8%	0.3%	1.7%
3. Average bank discount broker			
a. Average Cost Per Transaction	$80	$238	$70
b. Percentage of Dollar Value of Transaction	0.9%	0.3%	1.8%
4. Average full service broker			
a. Average Cost Per Transaction	$181	$746	$166
b. Percentage of Dollar Value of Transaction	2.0%	1.0%	4.2%

[a]Includes trades of 100, 200, 300, and 500 shares of a $20 stock; 200, 300, and 400 shares of a $30 stock; 200 and 300 shares of a $40 stock; and 200 and 500 shares of a $50 stock. The average transaction size is $9500.
[b]Includes trades of 1000 and 1500 shares of a $50 stock; 2000 shares of a $40 stock; and 2000 shares of a $50 stock. The average transaction size is $76,000.
[c]Includes 2000 shares of a $2 stock; 1000 shares of a $4 stock; 500 shares of an $8 stock; and 400 shares of a $10 stock. The average transaction size is $4000.

share. The 20 most price competitive brokers (row 1) charge, on average, $48 for a typical transaction, which represents a commission rate of one-half of one percent (0.5 percent) of the dollar value of the transaction. The average discount broker (row 2) charges $73 for a typical transaction, which is about 50 percent higher than what the most competitive firms charge. Commercial banks that offer discount brokerage services (row 3) generally have commission rates that are close to the average rates charged by independent discount brokers. Full service brokers (row 4) charge commissions that are over $3\frac{1}{2}$ times higher than those of the most price competitive discount brokers for typical transactions.

Column 2 lists the average commission cost for a sample of large transactions ranging from $50,000 to $100,000. The 20 most price competitive discount brokers for typical transactions are also the most competitive for large transactions. Note that commission costs as a percentage of the dollar value of the transaction decline sharply for large transactions. Commissions charged by full service brokers for large transactions, however, are nearly five times higher than those of the most competitive discount brokers.

Column 3 lists the average commission cost for a sample of trades involving low-priced stocks. About one half of the 20 most price competitive firms for typical and large transactions are also in the most competitive group for low-priced stocks. But some brokers, who are otherwise competitive, are expensive for low-priced stock transactions because they charge a minimum rate per share regardless of the share price. There are other brokers, however, who are relatively expensive for typical and large transactions, but have very competitive rates for transactions involving low-priced stocks.

Although it would be possible to find the one brokerage firm that would have the lowest commission cost on each trade, it's usually not worth the time and effort. Generally, if a broker is competitive for a representative sample of trades, his commission cost on any particular trade in that group will be within $10 or so of the firm charging the lowest rate for that trade.

Table 7.4 provides examples from Appendix B of commission cost data for individual discount brokers for the three types of trades we have discussed. You can use these data to locate price competitive brokers or to see how your broker measures up to price competitive firms. The first column lists the minimum commission charge per order,

TABLE 7.4 Sample of Commission Cost Data for Individual Brokerage Firms (selected from Appendix B)

Name, Address, Telephone	(1) Minimum Commission	(2) Typical Trade	(3) Large Trade	(4) Low-Priced Stock Trade	(5) States with Offices
1. First Heritage Co., 5 Hanover Square, New York, NY 10004 NATL 800-621-7011 LOCAL (212)668-1776	$35	64%	63%	85%	CA IL NY
2. LaSalle Street, 175 W. Jackson, Chicago, IL 60604 NATL 800-621-5393 LOCAL (312)427-4242 STATE 800-572-5568	$25	78	80	107	IL OH WI
3. Schwab (Charles), One Second St., San Francisco, CA 94105 NATL 800-648-5300 LOCAL (415)546-1000 STATE 800-792-0988	$30	113	97	84	Nationwide

Note: See text and notes to Appendix B for full description of table entries.

which is $35 for First Heritage. The average commission charged by First Heritage for a typical transaction (column 2) is listed as 64 percent, which means you can expect to pay about 36 percent below the commission charged by the average discount broker on typical trades at this brokerage firm. For example, on a trade where the average discount broker charges a commission of $60, you would pay about $38 (i.e., $60 x 0.64) at First Heritage. Moreover, a full service broker would charge about $150 on a trade that costs $60 at an average discount broker. First Heritage also charges competitive rates for large transactions (37 percent below average—column 3) and for low-priced stocks (15 percent below average—column 4). Column 5 indicates that First Heritage has offices in California, Illinois, and New York, so if you're out of state but wish to trade with this firm, you'll have to call or write to find out if they are registered in your state. Many brokers are registered in all or nearly all states even if they don't maintain an office in that state. You'll also want to get their latest commission schedule because brokers occasionally change their rates.

LaSalle Street (row 2) offers below-average commission rates for typical and large transactions, but is relatively expensive for transactions involving low-priced stocks. LaSalle Street has offices in Illinois, Ohio, and Wisconsin. Schwab (row 3) has above-average rates for typical transactions, about average rates for large transactions, and below-average rates for low-priced stocks. Schwab has an extensive branch office system and is registered in every state.

When selecting a discount brokerage firm, many investors are willing to pay somewhat higher commission rates for special service characteristics offered by some firms. Many people feel that reputation is an important attribute for a brokerage firm, so they prefer to trade with large, prominent companies who have a "brand name," such as Fidelity, Quick and Reilly, Rose, or Schwab. Some people prefer to do business with local companies even though brokerage services are conducted predominately over the telephone (with toll-free service) and through the mails, so it is just as easy to trade with a company located 2000 miles away as it is with a local firm. (Sometimes it's faster to mail a letter cross country than cross town.) In addition to the intangible quality of dealing with a local firm, investors may feel it's important to have the option of direct contact with people to resolve problems such as transaction or paperwork errors. With a local office, you can go pound on someone's desk. Some firms advertise that they provide check clearance with local banks and next-day receipt of transaction confirmations. Some people prefer to trade with the brokerage division of their bank because they can do business with a company they know and trust. In addition, banks may offer the convenience of crediting dividends, interest, and the proceeds of stock sales, and debiting stock purchases to your checking or savings account at the bank.

Let's say you live in Chicago and have the choice of placing an order with any of the three firms listed in Table 7.4 or with your local bank. A typical transaction that would cost $100 at an average discount broker would cost, on average, $64 at First Heritage, $78 at LaSalle, $110 at your bank, and $113 at Schwab. Is it worth $14 per transaction to you to do business with a local firm (LaSalle) rather than First Heritage, which is located in New York? For this transaction, your bank will charge about $32 more than LaSalle and $46 more than First Heritage. Does this cost justify the benefits of trading with your bank? Schwab can be considered a local firm because it has a branch office in Chicago. Is it worth an additional $35 to deal with Schwab, which is one of the largest and most prominent (i.e., heavily advertised) discount brokerage firms, rather than LaSalle? Obviously, for large or frequent transactions, the benefit–cost calculation may change. If a discount broker has the type of service characteristics that appeal to you, the information in Appendix B provides a rough estimate of how much more, if any, you'll pay to obtain them.

8
PUTTING TAXES IN PERSPECTIVE

The U.S. tax system has evolved into an unbelievably complex jumble of exemptions, exceptions, credits, and penalties, reflecting conflicting social policy goals and the political influence of myriad special interest groups. People are taxed at widely differing rates because some qualify for tax breaks and others don't. Homeowners receive tax breaks that aren't available to renters. Capital intensive industries have lower tax rates than high technology and service industries. Employees who receive insurance or pension benefits as part of their compensation packages pay less taxes than employees who receive the same total compensation, but without the tax-free or tax-deferred benefits.

Tax preferences are meant to encourage certain desirable activities, but regardless of the intended objectives and however worthwhile, there have been serious unintended results. First, because the tax system is not economically neutral, billions of dollars of valuable resources are diverted *from* profitable and efficient investments *into* expenditures made primarily because they receive tax preferences. The glut of office buildings and condominiums in the 1980s was caused by the lure of real estate tax shelters, which parlay accelerated depreciation and high leverage into large paper losses that reduce taxes on other income. Overinvestment in oil and gas projects, citrus groves, and race horse breeding are other prominent examples. Tax shelter investments in Bible deals, bait worm farms, and bull semen are among the more bizarre byproducts of tax gimmicks gone wild.

A large number of investment advisors, accountants, and tax lawyers earn their living by interpreting the tax complexities that lead to these inefficient but tax-sheltered investments. All the time and resources they and their clients expend on tax avoidance schemes, however, don't produce a dime's worth of goods and services that contribute to our economic well-being as a nation. They just temporarily relieve the pain of the self-inflicted wound—the tax complexity we created in the first place. The resulting misallocation and wasteful use of resources reduces overall productivity, weakens our ability to compete with other countries, and lowers our standard of living.

A second consequence of the growing complexity and uneven treatment of the tax system has been an erosion of voluntary compliance. People will not obey laws they don't understand or believe to be unfair. This attitude of tax defiance has been exacerbated by inflation, which pushes people into higher and higher tax brackets and reduces their after-tax incomes. Because they didn't vote for this inflation-based tax increase, many of them feel justified in "repealing" it by reducing their tax burdens by whatever means available. Rising social security taxes also provoke people to protect their steadily eroding after-tax income. In the process, there has been a blurring of the difference between tax evasion, which is a crime, and tax avoidance, which is simply taking full advantage of the tax code.

Tax avoidance is not only legal, it is encouraged—indeed, it is required if you are to avoid paying more than your legal and fair share of taxes. But taxpayers have begun to bend the rules to make the system "fair" in their own eyes. Barter and cash transactions are used to reduce reportable income. Expenditures for personal use are arranged so they appear to be deductible business expenses. Items donated to charity are appraised at artificially inflated values. Tax shelters are concocted that use incorrect or extreme interpretations of the tax code or the facts of the activity to obtain tax savings that are disproportionate to the economic reality of the investment.

Taxpayers are assisted by the tax experts—those investment advisors, accountants, and lawyers who earn hefty fees and commissions by supplying the means to beat the tax system. They are further encouraged by widely publicized stories about profitable tax dodges and the declining odds of an audit. The odds of an audit have declined because creative interpretations of the tax code and outright tax evasion have grown much faster than the IRS's ability to monitor the system. Tax defiance is also encouraged by the congested tax courts, which postpones the day of reckoning for questionable or fraudulent tax practices.

TAX PLANNING UNDER UNCERTAINTY

There has been a slow but spreading recognition that the tax system is too complex and that the erosion of voluntary compliance and the tax shelter boom are getting out of control. As this book is going to press, Congress is wrestling with several sweeping tax simplification plans. Although the outcome is uncertain, it is likely that the tax reform that emerges will be a product of political tradeoffs that will leave at least some tax preferences intact. The mortgage interest deduction on your principal residence, for example, is not likely to be eliminated. Tax deductions for charitable contributions will remain in some form. Tax preferences for certain types of investments will probably always be part of our tax code. Thus investors will still have to take taxes into consideration when making investment plans. Moreover, revising the tax code appears to be a favorite pastime of Congress. So investors who don't have the time, expertise, or inclination to evaluate whether the continual flow of new tax rulings or tax preference schemes are profitable must either pay for tax advice, which is often very expensive, or select "safe" tax preferences that have been thoroughly tested by time and experience, such as capital gains on stocks, IRAs, and municipal bonds.

Although taxes are an important consideration in any financial plan, personal preferences for return and risk vary widely; the impact of tax preferences depends on an individual's marginal tax bracket; and the future make-up of the tax code is always uncertain. Thus it is impossible to cover all of the ins and outs of tax management as it relates to investment decisions. But the TIPP principles of financial management provide the general rules for evaluating the advisability of a given tax shelter investment. The goal of effective tax planning is not simply to pay zero taxes, but to obtain the best after-tax *net* return for the amount of risk taken. (The net return for a tax shelter is the sum of tax savings plus cash return—current income plus capital appreciation—on the investment, less expenses associated with the project.)

Tax shelters must be scrutinized very carefully because many of them have very high transaction costs and risk or invite trouble from the IRS. As a result, tax-sheltered investments often offer no yield advantages over comparable taxable investments. And for the incautious, a tax shelter that concentrates primarily or solely on reducing taxes without considering the economic merits and financial risk of the investment may ultimately earn lower after-tax returns than comparable traditional investments.

GENERAL FRAMEWORK OF TAX SHELTERS

A tax shelter must either defer taxes or reduce taxes. Some tax shelters do both. The objective is a total return, combining tax benefits with the economic profit on the investment, that exceeds the return on a comparable investment that is fully taxed.

Tax Deferral

Deferred taxes are equivalent to interest-free loans from the government. The benefits of tax deferral are the returns earned on the loan until the taxes are finally paid. Tax deferral is a major feature of the popular limited partnership tax shelters in real estate, energy, equipment leasing, and farm and livestock operations. Tax deferral is achieved in these investments by creating an imbalance of costs over revenue in the early years of the project involved. If the majority of the accounting costs for depreciation and depletion and, where possible, other expenses, can be shifted into the present, costs can be made to exceed current income. These paper losses are then used by the investor to reduce tax liability on other income. The investor's tax liability is only deferred, however, because in the latter phase of the project's life, there will be an imbalance of revenue over cost, producing taxable income. Tax-sheltered retirement programs, such as IRAs and Keoghs, are also based on the tax deferral principle. Income invested in a qualified retirement program is fully tax deferred, as are the earnings from the investment. Taxes are paid as the money is withdrawn during retirement years. (Most common stock investments involve some degree of tax deferral.)

The earnings on deferred taxes can significantly increase returns. Assume you have $10,000 of income that is subject to a marginal tax rate of 40 percent. Your options are to put that $10,000 into a tax-deferred investment or into an investment that confers no deferral advantages. With the nondeferred investment, you must pay taxes of $4000 on the $10,000 of income, leaving $6000 to invest. Assume further that the rate of return will be 10 percent regardless of whether the investment is tax deferred or fully taxable. But on the fully taxed investment, the actual after-tax return is 6 percent because 4 percent will be paid in taxes at the 40 percent marginal tax rate. At 6 percent, compounded annually, an initial investment of $6000 will grow to about $10,700 in 10 years.

If, on the other hand, you put the $10,000 into a tax-deferred investment, you can invest the full $10,000 (which includes the government loan of $4000 in deferred taxes). This $10,000 will earn the full 10 percent of its return each year, growing to about $25,900 by the end of the 10-year period. At that point, we assume you are liable to 40 percent taxes on the full amount of $25,900, leaving you with about $15,500 after taxes. This illustrates the power of tax deferral. In this example, even without a reduction in tax rates, tax deferral increases the after-tax value of your investment funds by $4800 ($15,500 versus $10,700) in just 10 years! The additional $4800 represents earnings on the initial interest-free government loan of $4000 and the anuual interest-free loans represented by the tax deferral of earnings in each year.

Tax Reduction

Tax shelters can reduce or eliminate taxes in several ways. They can take advantage of the special tax treatment of certain types of investments, or they can reduce tax rates, either by converting tax payments to a time period when the taxpayer is in a lower marginal tax bracket or by converting higher-taxed ordinary income to lower-taxed capital gains income. Income from municipal bonds, for example, receives special tax treatment. By law, interest income on bonds issued by state and local governments, called *municipal bonds*, is not taxed by the federal government (unless it is taxed indirectly through the alternative minimum income tax) and is generally free from state and local income taxes in the state where the bonds are issued. (Municipal bond investments are discussed in more detail later in this chapter.) Similarly, sometimes Congress confers special tax preferences on certain types of investments. Investment tax credits for historic structure rehabilitation and the purchase of energy conservation equipment are examples of specially favored investments.

A second way taxes can be reduced is by converting tax liability from a high to a low marginal tax bracket. Tax-sheltered retirement accounts offer this type of tax reduction, in addition to the tax deferral advantages discussed earlier. If individuals are in lower tax brackets after they retire, income withdrawn from tax-sheltered retirement accounts will be taxed at lower rates than would have applied when the income was earned. The reverse might be true, however, if your savings became large enough so you were in a higher tax bracket than before. Because capital gains income can be realized at the discretion of the investor, converting tax liability from a high to a low marginal tax bracket also can be used to reduce taxes with limited partnership and common stock investments.

A third way to reduce taxes is by converting ordinary income to lower-taxed capital gains income. Under current tax law, only 40 percent of capital gains are treated as income for tax purposes. Thus converting a dollar of ordinary income into a dollar of capital gains income will eliminate tax liability on 60 cents of the dollar. Note that, in some cases, it is possible to simultaneously convert tax liability to a lower marginal tax bracket *and* convert income to capital gains income, thus obtaining a double tax shelter effect. The capital gains conversion tax shelter, however, depends on preferential tax rates for capital gains income, which is always subject to change by Congress.

There are two primary ways ordinary income can be converted to lower-taxed capital gains income. The first way to obtain a capital gains conversion tax shelter is to have deductions that reduce the cost basis of the investment for tax purposes. In limited partnership real estate investments, for example, depreciation expenses, which are written off against other sources of income, also reduce the cost basis of the investment for tax purposes. When the property is sold, depreciation expenses are subtracted from the original purchase price to determine the cost basis from which the capital gain is determined. In effect, the owner has written these deductions off against current income in the early years of the investment and then pays taxes on this income in later years at capital gain rates. Investments in mineral property and timber are some other ways to obtain a capital gains conversion tax shelter. Tax-sheltered retirement accounts, however, *do not* have a capital gains conversion feature. Money withdrawn is taxed at ordinary income tax rates.

The second type of capital gains conversion tax shelter is with common stock. Corporate earnings that are retained and reinvested in the company, rather than being paid as fully taxed dividends, increase the earnings capacity and the stock price of the corporation (see Chapter 5). The stock price appreciation allows the stockholder to realize the investment return on the stock in the form of more lightly taxed capital gains rather than as dividend income.

CHOOSING TAX SHELTERS THAT DON'T LEAK

In this section, we examine the general economic and financial characteristics of so-called tax-advantaged investments. These tax shelters, usually offered as limited partnership shares, provide tax deferral and tax conversion benefits, and limited liability for investments in such things as real estate, oil and gas, agriculture and livestock, equipment leasing, and research and development. The partnership form of business allows accelerated depreciation, depletion, deductible expenses, and investment tax credits to be passed through the partnership as tax benefits to the individual partners. Leverage is commonly used to increase the tax benefits of the investment. In subsequent sections, we will cover the more traditional—and generally lower-risk—tax shelter features of common stocks, individual retirement programs, and municipal bonds.

Tax shelters promising extraordinary returns are generally exploiting a loophole in the tax code. If Congress or the IRS don't plug the loophole (which they eventually do in many cases), market forces will reduce the opportunity to earn above-average returns compared to other investments of similar risk. Why? Because the market pricing process always moves to eliminate situations where investment returns are not proportional to risk. This was the basic message of the TIPP principle of return–risk tradeoffs discussed earlier.

There are several ways the market adjusts to circumstances where tax-sheltered investments initially earn a higher after-tax return than comparable taxable investments. First, if higher returns are available on tax-sheltered investments, promoters can charge investors high fees and commissions for the privilege of buying into the deal. This reduces the cash return component of a tax shelter. Second, as promoters scramble to invest the money that pours into these tax shelters, they bid up the market price for the investment goods involved—such as real estate or oil and gas properties. As the cost of acquiring investment goods rises, this also reduces the cash return of the tax shelter. Thus the tax benefits of a shelter are reduced by high transaction costs and lower returns on the investments themselves. Only the initial investors who take advantage of a newly discovered scheme to beat the tax system will earn above-average after-tax investment returns.

There is evidence that the market pricing process tends to equalize after-tax returns on tax-sheltered and comparable fully taxed investments. Sales commissions, consultants' fees, legal and accounting expenses, and management costs often total 30 percent or more of a tax shelter deal. These transaction costs are far greater than those on conventional investments. The soaring popularity of real estate investment trusts (REITs) in the early 1970s led to overbuilding of offices, shopping centers, and industrial buildings. Real estate prices for many of these properties rose sharply and then later fell as vacancies accumulated. Then again in the early 1980s, bidding wars developed for the available real estate properties as promoters of limited partnership tax shelters were faced with investing billions of dollars annually that were flowing into these tax shelters. Price inflation under similar circumstances has been noted for oil and gas acreage, drilling rights, and drilling equipment.

The IRS Cometh

The prospect of lucrative fees will attract more promoters into the tax shelter business. But as the competition for investors' funds heats up and cash returns decline on the latest generation of tax shelters, inevitably some promoters will begin to hatch new tax shelter schemes (promising higher yields) that may cross that vague line between tax avoidance and tax evasion. (The investors are fellow travelers because they think they'll get something for nothing.) Then if the IRS determines that the tax write-offs are not valid, investors must pay back taxes *and* penalties. This special tax risk, which is unique to tax shelter investments, can lower yields below conventional taxable investments of similar risk.

In recent years, the IRS has focused much of its energy on auditing tax shelters and has become quite adept at striking down what it terms "abusive" tax shelters. If the IRS determines that a tax deficiency exists, the taxpayer must pay the taxes due, plus an interest penalty on all taxes ruled to be improperly deferred or reduced. The interest rate is based on the prime rate in the preceding quarter when the penalty is assessed. As a small consolation, the interest penalty is tax deductible. In some cases, additional penalties for "valuation overstatements" and negligence are assessed; these are not tax deductible, resulting in a serious loss of wealth for the investor. To this must be added the loss of income that could have been earned on a comparable taxable investment, as well as the aggravation, stress, and cost of an IRS audit.

Risk

Tax-oriented investment programs are often financed with large amounts of debt relative to the money people have invested in the project. This is done to magnify the tax preference benefits of accelerated depreciation, investment tax credits, and large start-up costs. Leverage financing, which is equivalent to buying stocks on margin, increases potential returns, but also increases financial risk (see Chapter 6). In addition, there is usually more business risk with the typical tax-sheltered investment in something like a shopping center or oil exploration project than with conventional investments like stocks and mutual funds. The typical limited partnership tax shelter also carries much more liquidity risk than traditional financial investments. An investor in a limited partnership deal, for example, may face heavy tax liabilities for premature withdrawal, incur discounts of 25 to 30 percent when selling partnership shares in the thin secondary markets for these investments, or find that the shares are impossible to transfer even if a willing buyer is found. There is also the danger of overloading your portfolio with tax shelters in real estate or oil drilling investments, which increases unsystematic—that is, uncompensated—financial risk.

There are other pitfalls for the unwary tax shelter investor. A limited partnership tax shelter, for example, may not be as limited as advertised. In the small print of some tax shelter contracts, there are clauses holding the limited partners liable for more than their initial investments, which may force them to subsequently put up more money to cover investment losses. At the very least, a prudent investor should pay for independent legal advice before investing. The worst place to learn about a tax shelter is from some guy trying to sell you one. And, as usual, crooks abound wherever there's a lot of money floating around. Some unsuspecting investors have suffered sizable losses in tax shelter deals because crooks don't play by the same rules as the rest of us. Such niceties as legally binding contracts and promises to perform certain duties mean nothing to them. Here, a healthy dose of suspicion is often a better defense than legal advice.

In summary, the seemingly higher yields promised by tax shelters are due, in large part, to higher business and financial risk, not superior investment return. Tax risk, legal risk, and fraud are additional occupational hazards for investors in tax-oriented programs. Finally, there is no assurance that a tax shelter will be able to deliver the total yield promised by the promoter because the market pricing process tends to compete away above-average returns.

TAX SHELTERS IN COMMON STOCKS

Common stocks can use both tax deferral and tax reduction techniques to reduce tax liability on investment income.[1] This is also a "safe" tax shelter because there are no gray areas of law to worry about. The deferral aspect arises from the fact that the capital gain from a stock investment is not taxed until the stock is sold. With a TIPP buy-and-hold strategy, capital gains are deferred until you have reached your financial goal. Alternatively, with a beat the market strategy, you must pay taxes on all transactions that result in capital gains. You lose the investment returns that could have been earned on those tax dollars if you had deferred paying them with a buy-and-hold investment strategy. With TIPP, taxes can also be reduced if the investor is in a lower marginal tax bracket when the stocks are sold.

Common stocks can also reduce taxes by converting higher-taxed dividend to lower-taxed capital gains income. If corporate income is

---

[1]Parents can also shelter dividend income by shifting tax liability to their children through a trust account. The Uniform Gift to Minors Act makes it very easy to establish a trust account with DRPs and mutual funds.

retained and reinvested rather than paid out as dividends, this increases the corporation's earning power and its stock price. When investors subsequently sell the stock at the higher price, they are essentially taking delayed dividend payments in the form of more lightly taxed capital gains income. This process is not automatic, however. Corporate income that is reinvested rather than paid to stockholders is at risk, so the investor is only successful in converting dividend income to capital gains income if the corporate investments are successful.

Deferral and reduction tax shelters with common stocks depend on the proportion of corporate income paid out as dividends, which is called the *payout ratio*. The lower the payout ratio, the greater the tax shelter effect. Thus investors who want a substantial amount of tax sheltering with common stocks should buy low-payout stocks. However, low-payout stocks are generally more risky than high-payout stocks. So investors who want high tax sheltering but also want low-risk portfolios should buy a portfolio of high-risk, low-payout stocks, but leverage it down by adding municipal bonds, which are low risk and tax free, to obtain the desired level of portfolio risk. (See the discussion of leveraging in Chapter 6.)

The tax code usually contains other tax preferences for common stocks. For example, the first $100 of dividend income ($200 on joint returns) is tax free. From 1981 to 1985, investors could defer taxes on dividends of qualified public utilities up to $750 on single returns and $1500 on joint returns by reinvesting them through DRPs. These provisions have value on a year-to-year basis, but they are always subject to change by Congress.

TAX-SHELTERED RETIREMENT PROGRAMS

For money you plan to invest for retirement income, some of the best tax shelters available are the tax-sheltered retirement programs, such as IRAs and Keoghs. These programs are particularly attractive for people who are unwilling to assume the substantial risks involved in limited partnership tax shelters. In all of these programs, the principle is the same: Tax liability is deferred on the qualifying part of income invested, as are earnings from the investment. As explained above, this type of tax deferral is equivalent to the government granting you an interest-free loan and then increasing the compound return on the investment by deferring taxes on the earnings. Withdrawals are taxed at the ordinary tax rate, but because the money will normally be withdrawn after retirement or in some other low-income period, you may be able to reduce taxes by converting income to lower marginal tax brackets. Because the money can be withdrawn at your discretion anytime after age $59\frac{1}{2}$, you have control over when the money will be eligible for taxation. Withdrawal must begin, however, by age $70\frac{1}{2}$.

There are several reasons why these are "safe" tax shelters. First, there is no need to use—and perhaps misuse—the artificial device of creating an imbalance of costs over revenue in the early years of an investment project to shelter other income from tax liability, thereby deferring taxes. With tax-sheltered retirement progams, tax deferral is automatically granted for the qualifying part of income invested. Second, there is little or no tax or legal risk. Third, it isn't likely that these programs will be abolished or amended in a way that reduces their tax benefits. Rather, based on recent developments, the prospect is that they will be further liberalized in future years. Legislation that provides tax subsidies for these private retirement programs is intended to encourage individuals to take more responsibility in planning for retirement. Investing today for a satisfactory retirement standard of living is very important, especially since social security is designed to replace only about 40 percent of an average person's preretirement income.

Individual Retirement Accounts

Any wage earner can invest up to $2000 per year in an IRA or the full amount of his income if it is less than $2000. If a spouse does not have wage income, a wage earner can contribute an additional $250 to a "spousal IRA" if the marital couple files a joint tax return. Contributions to an IRA are not affected by participation in any other pension plan. IRAs may be set up through commercial banks, thrift institutions, brokerage firms, insurance companies, mutual funds, or anyone else who meets the IRS qualifications for custodianship. At the present time, however, corporate DRPs do not provide the type of custodial service required for tax-sheltered retirement accounts.[2] The investment itself may be in a wide variety of assets, such as stocks, bonds, mutual funds,

---

[2]There is at least one exception. An IRA is available to stockholders of Cleveland Electric as part of its DRP.

savings accounts, certificates of deposit, financial futures contracts, limited partnerships, and real estate. Investments in tangible or collectible assets, such as art, coins, stamps, antiques, rugs, and metals, are not eligible.

Investing through tax-sheltered retirement programs should be based on the same TIPP principles as any other type of investment. The selection should meet your return–risk objectives, contribute to overall portfolio diversification, and be based on the rules for time diversification and minimizing transaction costs. The TIPP principle of time diversification is quite often violated by investors who frantically scrape together $2000 in early April to invest in an IRA by the April 15th tax return deadline. Ideally, money should be put into an IRA in equal payments spread over the entire year. You should also be very careful about transaction costs. Stay away from investments that have large sales commissions, withdrawal penalties, back end loads, and management fees that can substantially reduce your overall rate of return.

Tax-sheltered retirement programs have liquidity risk. Because these programs are designed to encourage people to plan and provide for a substantial part of their own retirements, Congress included a penalty for early withdrawal. If you must withdraw funds from an IRA before age $59\frac{1}{2}$, the special nondeductible penalty is 10 percent of the amount withdrawn. This penalty is waived if you become totally disabled or die. In addition, you must pay taxes at the ordinary income tax rate on the amount withdrawn. This isn't actually a penalty because these taxes would have been due earlier if they hadn't been deferred. It could be a penalty, however, if the withdrawal pushes you into a higher marginal tax bracket than the one you were in when the taxes were originally deferred.

Although the basic objective of an IRA is for retirement income, the money is not permanently locked away, and the 10 percent penalty is not an insurmountable obstacle if you have a compelling reason to withdraw the funds early. The cost of the penalty must be compared to a similar investment that is not tax sheltered that could be sold without penalty. At some point, the penalty is more than offset by the additional savings that have accumulated tax free in the IRA from the date of investment. Generally, the savings from tax deferral will completely offset the penalty within 6–10 years. The exact breakeven point depends on your marginal tax bracket, the rate of return on the IRA investment, and the amount of income from the non-IRA investment alternative that is eligible for lower capital gains taxes.

Some people view an IRA as both a tax-sheltered retirement program and a contingency private unemployment insurance fund. Assume you contributed $6000 to an IRA over a 3-year period when you were in a 40 percent tax bracket and withdrew $6000 during a time period of unemployment when your marginal tax rate after withdrawal was 30 percent. Your effective tax rate on the $6000 is 10 percentage points lower, which exactly offsets the 10 percent penalty. As a bonus, you keep the additional earnings that accumulated tax free over the investment period.

Keogh and Other Plans

Keogh plans are for self-employed people and their employees in single proprietorships and partnerships, but not corporations. Income from part-time self-employment that is in addition to your regular job is also eligible for a Keogh plan. People who qualify for a Keogh plan can also contribute to an IRA. Your employees must be included in the plan, and all partners in a partnership must be treated equally. The basic principle underlying a Keogh plan is the same as for an IRA. A tax subsidy is given to encourage people to provide for their own retirements. Income contributions and earnings on those contributions are tax deferred. The penalty conditions are similar. Otherwise, Keogh plans are quite different from IRAs. They apply to far fewer people, and the maximum annual contribution to a "defined contribution" Keogh plan is $30,000 or 25 percent of eligible earnings, whichever is smaller. This is much larger than the $2000 allowed for IRAs.

Even larger deductions are possible with "defined benefit" Keogh plans, where the amount to be paid out after retirement is defined in the plan, rather than the amount to be paid in, as under a defined contribution plan. With a defined benefit plan, contributions may be as large as necessary to finance the annual defined benefit payments; these can be as large as $200,000 per year. The maximum payment is adjusted annually for cost-of-living increases. In general, the provisions for qualification, tax treatment, contributions, payment of benefits, and filing are more complicated for Keoghs than for IRAs. Anyone interested in setting up a Keogh plan must read the rules carefully or have the plan administered by an experienced trustee.

There are several other tax-sheltered retirement plans that are based on the same principles as IRAs and Keoghs. For example, a Simplified Employee Pension (SEP) IRA is a special type of IRA created by Congress to simplify employer pension plans. With this program, an employer makes contributions directly to the IRA accounts of employees. A SEP-IRA allows contributions up to 25 percent of earnings, with an annual maximum of $30,000. This parallels the provisions in a Keogh plan, but an employer cannot set up both. There are also several types of "salary reduction" tax-sheltered retirement programs, which also accomplish the same objectives.

MUNICIPAL BONDS

Is a municipal bond a tax-sheltered investment? Maybe! Interest income on municipal bonds is not subject to federal income tax, and it is generally free from state and local taxes in the state of issue. In that sense, a municipal bond *is* a tax-sheltered investment. The market yield on a municipal bond, however, is lower than on a similar taxable bond because the market pricing process works to equalize after-tax yields on comparable securities. If the after-tax yield on municipal bonds was higher than after-tax yields on comparable corporate bonds, bond investors could increase their after-tax interest income by selling corporate bonds and buying municipal bonds. But this change in the demand-supply balance would cause corporate bond prices to fall and municipal bond prices to rise, which increases yields on the corporate bonds and decreases yields on municipals. This process of adjustment would continue until after-tax yields were equal.

This is exactly what we see in the market. In recent years municipal yields have varied between 25–35 percent below comparable corporate bonds, which reflects the average tax advantage differential. Thus, in effect, you pay a "tax" on municipal bond interest income by accepting a lower market interest rate. Or in other words, you pay your taxes ahead of time. In that sense, a municipal bond *may not* be a tax-sheltered investment.

But the tax or lower yield on municipal bonds is not the same for everyone because people are in different marginal tax brack market pricing process can capture only the average tax municipals, not the marginal advantage for persons in high If the market yield on municipals is 30 percent below corpo son in the 40 percent bracket would pay a 30 percent tax (lower yield) by investing in municipal bonds but would save 40 percent in taxes because the interest income is tax free. Thus a municipal bond *is* a tax-sheltered investment, but only for people in high marginal tax brackets.

When to Buy Municipals

There are two steps in deciding whether a municipal bond is a good investment for you. First, you must decide if a bond investment provides the return–risk characteristics that meet your preferences. On an after-tax basis, the average yield on municipals is always lower than the yield on average common stocks because bonds in general and municipal bonds in particular have lower risk. Thus bonds are an appropriate investment only if you wish to obtain a risk level or degree of income stability that you can't obtain from a diversified portfolio of stocks (see Appendix to Chapter 5). Bonds are also useful for leveraging down a portfolio of stocks.

Second, if you decide to invest in bonds, then you must calculate whether a tax-exempt or a taxable bond will yield a higher after-tax return. The following formula provides the way to compare tax-exempt and taxable investment yields:

$$\frac{\text{Tax-free investment yield}}{1 - \text{your top tax bracket}} = \frac{\text{Taxable investment yield needed}}{\text{to exceed a tax-free yield}}$$

The right side of the formula shows what the yield on the tax-free investment would have been if it was taxable. (If the investment is also exempt from state and local taxes, the taxable equivalent of the tax-free yield is increased.)

Let's say the current yield on a municipal bond is 9 percent and you are in the 40 percent marginal tax bracket (stated as a decimal, which is .40). Insert these numbers in the formula:

$$\frac{9\%}{1 - .40} = \frac{9\%}{.60} = 15\%$$

You will need an investment return of more than 15 percent from a taxable bond to get a better return than a 9 percent yield from a municipal bond. If taxable bonds of comparable risk were currently yielding 13 percent, you would choose the municipal bond. If you are in the 20 percent marginal tax bracket, however, then

$$\frac{9\%}{1-.20} = \frac{9\%}{.80} = 11.25\%$$

In this case, you would be better off to invest in the taxable bond and pay taxes on the interest income rather than pay "taxes" in the form of a lower yield on the municipal bond. Over time, the relationship between tax-exempt and taxable yields can change, and so can your marginal tax rate. So you should make this calculation each time you buy additional bonds.

How to Buy Municipals

Because municipal bonds have default risk and their yields can fluctuate, diversification is just as important with these securities as with stocks. If a tax-exempt bond investment meets your return–risk preferences, a municipal bond no-load mutual fund is usually the best way to satisfy the TIPP rules regarding portfolio and time diversification and minimizing transaction costs. Mutual funds offer a choice of regular interest income payments or automatic interest reinvestment. Some funds offer a checkwriting option and telephone or bank wire transfers. So you get a number of convenience options in addition to portfolio diversification.

You pay for these benefits by earning a lower return than would be possible with an individually held portfolio of comparable securities. The lower yield results from three factors. First, you pay an annual management fee. Second, mutual funds continually receive new money and requests for redemptions, which requires maintaining a low yield liquidity reserve and incurring additional commission costs. Third, fund managers may buy and sell securities when they believe interest rates and credit conditions are going to change. But because the efficient markets hypothesis holds true for bond markets as well as st~ ' kets, this activity simply reduces the investment return be necessary commission costs. These cost factors are partia. savings from the quantity discounts on commissions paid for necessary transactions to maintain a well-diversified portfolio of securities.

An alternative to a mutual fund is a unit investment trust for municipal bonds. A unit trust buys a portfolio of securities with the proceeds of a single subscription and then holds the securities until they reach maturity, when proceeds are paid to shareholders. There is a very small annual trustee fee, but no management fee because there is no professional management in the traditional sense. With a unit trust, you pay a one-time sales commission that ranges between 2–5 percent. Normally, however, the sales commission and trustee fee for a unit trust are lower than the annual management fee and additional commission costs associated with a no-load municipal bond mutual fund. As a result, you will earn a somewhat higher yield with a unit trust than with a comparable mutual fund. Except for the sales commission, a unit trust is similar to a no-load index mutual fund. But it is more difficult to achieve time diversification with a unit trust. The minimum purchase is usually $1000 or more, they are not offered on a continuous basis, and some of them do not have an interest reinvestment option.

9

SUCCESS!

All get-rich-quick schemes involve committing a large share of your life's assets to a single figurative spin of the roulette wheel. The odds on losing are great, but if the right number comes up, you *are* instantly rich. By the law of averages, it happens for a few people. Betting on long odds is one way to obtain wealth, and there are many people ready to sell you "secrets" to beat the odds and become wealthy—quick and easy. As we have discussed at length, however, these "secret" methods don't work. It all comes back to luck. And for the vast majority of us, Lady Luck is no lady! She teases. But inevitably, she delivers the losses that the law of averages predicts we should expect.

If you are truly poor—that is, you have little or no prospect of ever getting ahead through hard work or inheritance—then your only chance of financial success is to take enormous risks by betting a couple of dollars on a long shot. This fact, by the way, helps explain the widespread and enduring success of the illegal numbers game, the Irish Sweepstakes, and the Trifecta at your local racetrack. If you are at least a moderately productive person, however, you don't have to accept the lousy odds and bleak chances of success offered by such lotteries. You *can* control the outcome of your financial plans.

Besides the obvious attraction of financial independence, get-rich-quick schemes are enticing *because* they are exciting, while prudent investment programs that will inevitably work are dull. Some investors object to a buy-and-hold investment strategy because it's dull. They want excitement and the chance to make a million dollars. Let's face it. If it wasn't fun to gamble, Las Vegas would be a dusty spot in the desert and state lotteries would be a big yawn. If you've got a speculative temperament, financial markets can provide all the action you want—and often more! You can set up your own little home casino and trade in stock options, penny stocks, and stock index and financial futures contracts. The odds, after all, aren't any worse than those offered by Las Vegas, state lotteries, or horse races. If you enjoy gambling, and the stock market is your game, just make sure to separate your gambling funds from your investment funds. Gambling is consumption. It's an enjoyable pastime. But remember, when you gamble you are spending money to obtain enjoyment now, not to receive a return in the future.

FORMULA FOR FINANCIAL SUCCESS

There are three steps to financial success, and prudent investing is only the third. In order to gain financial wealth, you must first earn a large enough income, then save enough of it and, finally, carefully invest what you save. (If you inherit wealth, of course, you can skip the first two steps. But regardless, step three is equally important for everyone.) Our focus in this book has been on the TIPP investment strategy. TIPP uses the tried-and-true principles of effective financial investing and will "tip" the scales of financial success in your favor. We have also described how to use dividend reinvestment plans, mutual funds, and discount brokers as inexpensive but highly effective ways to implement and maintain your investment program; and we have explained how to handle tax matters. But TIPP can only work with the funds you earn and save. In the remainder of this chapter, we will discuss how TIPP can help you achieve the "adequate income" and "sufficient savings" steps to financial success.

ADEQUATE INCOME

Playing stock market games—where you are actively engaged in buying, selling, chasing rainbows, scheming, *and* worrying—is not a good use of your time and other resources. With beat-the-market games, you can lose in two important ways. First, the evidence is overwhelming that the chances of winning the game by earning above-average investment returns are remote. And it's possible to get caught up in the greed-fear cycle and inadvertently begin to take unnecessary risk. All the while, you continually pay the high price of admission to the stock market game—advisory fees, commissions, and unnecessary taxes—that will result in below-average investment returns. All of these things can lead to a serious loss of wealth, as well as being emotionally draining. So why play the stock market game when it offers little or no chance to win, but lots of ways to lose?

Second, playing stock market games diverts time and energy from other, more important pursuits. Throughout this book, there has been an emphasis—often overlooked in financial planning—on properly valuing your own time and energy. Playing stock market games limits the amount of time and energy available for the development of your most important income-earning asset—you. Underinvesting in human capital decreases the ability to achieve the first and all-important "adequate income" step to financial success.

As discussed in Chapter 2, the U.S. economy is in the midst of a revitalization and a technological revolution that is expected to produce very rapid economic growth in the latter 1980s and into the 1990s. As the economy moves into this postindustrial state, the potential exists for your human capital to earn higher rates of return than in the slow-growth 1970s and early 1980s. So forget the stock market games and prepare for the future. The chances for a very good income are certainly within your grasp!

SUFFICIENT SAVINGS

A higher income increases the ability to save. In addition, the expected high-growth economy will increase the profitability of the corporate sector, providing higher rates of return on common stocks. The compound effect of higher rates of saving and higher rates of return for each dollar saved and invested will enable you to set and reach higher financial goals. This doesn't change the basic fact, however, that saving requires self-discipline. Regardless of the size of your income, wants in the present are always more immediate than wants in the future. When the money is there, it is difficult to deny yourself things you want now.

For this reason, personal finance advisors suggest treating your saving and investment program as a set of bills that must be paid on a regular basis. If these "bills" are paid first rather than from whatever income is left at the end of the month, the temptation to overspend is considerably reduced. The TIPP investment program is especially suited to this type of personal budget planning. By emphasizing periodic investing and automatically reinvesting dividends, TIPP provides an easy, economical, and effective way to build a sound, profitable, financial investment portfolio.

When making a financial plan, keep in mind the difference between attempting to do something and success in accomplishing what you attempt. The plan must recognize the real limits of life. Many people have a grossly exaggerated notion of the rate of return on invested capital. Opinion polls suggest that the public believes corporations earn profits in the range of 30–40 percent! The Wall Street crowd helps perpetuate this myth by promising extraordinary rates of return if you buy *their* investment advice. But the facts are different. The average rate of return on common stocks during the last 50 years has been about 9 percent. This financial investment return directly reflects the average earnings power of corporations. Because inflation averaged about 2 percent during this time period, *real* returns (i.e., adjusted for inflation) have been on the order of 7 percent per year.

Knowing the investment return you can expect is very useful for financial planning. But how much saving is enough? It depends, of course, on your goals. In turn, whether your goals are reasonable depends on the size of your current income, health, number of dependents, and other factors. These are topics typically discussed in books on personal budgeting. In establishing your goals, however, there are three useful rules to follow:

1. Think in *real* terms, rather than just in terms of dollars. Then you don't have to make complicated and perhaps faulty inflation forecasts. Remember that in the long run the *real* return on stocks has averaged 7 percent. That's just an average. There are going to be time periods when rates are far below and far above that average, but it's the best planning guide available.

2. Use simple multiples. Given a 7 percent average real rate of return in the long run, a dollar invested today will double in 10 years, quadruple in 20 years, and increase 8 times in 30 years. Without trying to guess the rate of inflation, you can project the amount of money you will need in the future, based on what money will buy today, and then save accordingly, using these 7 percent multiples. (Recall from Chapter 5 that these multiples only apply if you are investing in common stocks that have average risk. With low-risk stocks, bonds, or money market funds, the multiples are smaller; with high-risk stocks, they are larger.)

3. Remember that financial goals may change. Make sure to take time out each year to reconsider whether your current rate of saving will enable you to meet your current long-run goals.

POSTSCRIPT

Although there is a great deal of agreement about the basic principles of financial investing, we do not want to imply that all financial economists would agree with everything in this book. In any field of study, there are always areas of controversy that remain to be resolved through theoretical advancement, improving analytical tools, and collecting and refining data bases. For those who want to read further in the exciting field of financial investing, a good place to begin is with R. J. Towles and E. S. Bradley, *The Stock Market*, 4th ed. (New York: John Wiley, 1982). This book provides a practical guide to the terminology, structure, and operations of the stock market.

A very readable summary of what we know—and don't know—about how securities markets price common stocks is provided in R. A. Brealey, *An Introduction to Risk and Return from Common Stocks*, 2nd ed. (Cambridge, Mass: MIT Press, 1983). This book and the following sample of more comprehensive works contain extensive bibliographies of the technical literature for the field of financial investing: K. D. Garbade, *Securities Markets* (New York: McGraw-Hill, 1982); J. H. Lorie, P. Dodd, and M. H. Kimpton, *The Stock Market: Theories and Evidence*, 2nd ed. (Homewood, Ill.: Dow Jones-Irwin, 1985); W. F. Sharpe, *Investments*, 2nd ed. (Englewood Cliffs, N.J.: Prentice-Hall,

1981); and S. M. Tinic and R. R. West, *Investing in Securities: An Efficient Markets Approach* (Boston: Addison-Wesley, 1979). The classic article on portfolio selection of financial assets is H. M. Markowitz, "Portfolio Selection," *Journal of Finance*, 7, 77–91 (1952). Basic data for the investment returns of securities in the United States is provided in R. G. Ibbotson and R. A. Sinquefield, *Stocks, Bonds, Bills and Inflation: The Past and the Future* (Charlottesville, Va.: Financial Analysts Research Foundation, 1982). The reader who wants to study how portfolio theory, the capital asset pricing model, and efficient markets theory fit into the wider field of corporate finance should begin with R. Brealey and S. Myers, *Principles of Corporate Finance*, 2nd ed. (New York: McGraw-Hill, 1984).

APPENDIXES

appendix A

COMPANIES WITH DIVIDEND REINVESTMENT PLANS, CLASSIFIED BY INDUSTRY

Dividend Reinvestment Plans

I. Financial, Insurance, Real Estate

A. Bank, savings and loan (East)

	Ticker Symbol	Beta	Service Fee	Commission	$Minimum/ $Maximum	Frequency (per year)	Special Features
American Security, 730 15th St., N.W., Washington, D.C. 20013	ASEC	0.85	0	0	25/5000q	4	5-D+VC OI
Bank New England, 28 State St., Boston, MA 02109	BKNE	0.70	0	0	50/5000m	12	5-D+VC SSO OI
Bank New York, 48 Wall St., New York, NY 10015	BK	0.80	0	0	25/1000q	12	5-D+VC SSO BOND OI
Bankers Trust New York, Box 9007, New York, NY 10249	BT	0.70	0	0	25/5000q	12	5-D+VC PRF OI
Bay Banks, 175 Federal St., Boston, MA 02110	BBNK	0.70	0	Y	10/1000m	12	
CBT, One Constitution Plaza, Hartford, CN 06115	CBCT	0.85	0	0	10/1000m	12	
Chase Manhattan, Chase Manhattan Plaza, New York, NY 10081	CMB	0.95	0	0	100/3000q	12	5-D SSO OI
Chemical New York, 277 Park Ave., New York, NY 10172	CHL	0.90	0	0	25/5000q	12	5-D PRF BOND OI
Chittenden, 2 Burlington Square, Burlington, VT 05402	CNDN	0.95	0	Y	10/2000q	8	
Citicorp, 399 Park Avenue, New York, NY 10043	FNC	1.10	5-2.50	Y	10/1000m	8	
Citizens First, 208 Harristown, Glen Rock, NJ 07452	CFB	0.75	Y	Y	10/unlim	12	
Citytrust, 945 Main St., Bridgeport, CT 06602	CITR	0.60	0	0	10/1000m	12	SSO OI
Colonial, 81 W. Main St., Waterbury, CT 06726	CBCN	0.90	0	0	25/3000q	4	
Commercial, 15 Exchange Pl., Jersey City, NJ 07302	CBSH	0.70	0	0	10/2000m	12	
Conifer/Essex, 370 Main St., Worcester, MA 01608	CNFG	0.70	0	0	25/1000q	8	
Continental, 1500 Market St., Philadelphia, PA 19102	CBRP	0.65	0	0	25/1000m	12	
First Empire State, 1 M&T Plaza, Buffalo, NY 14240	FEMP	0.70	5-2.50	Y	10/1000q	4	
First Maryland, Box 1596, Baltimore, MD 21201	FMDB	0.80	0	0	25/5000q	12	5-D OI
Fleet Financial, Box 368, Providence, RI 02901	FLT	0.75	0	0	10/1000q	4	OI
Hartford National, 777 Main St., Hartford, CT 06115	HNAT	1.05	0	0	25/5000q	12	5-D+VC OI
Horizon, 334 Madison Ave., Morristown, NJ 07960	HZB	0.75	0	0	10/2500q	12	5-D+VC PRF OI

Irving Bank, One Wall St., New York, NY 10015	V	0.70	0	25/5000q	8	5-D SSO OI
Key Banks, 60 State St., Albany, NY 12207	KEY	0.75	0	10/1000m	12	
Marine Midland, 140 Broadway, New York, NY 10015	MM	0.95	0	Y	25/1000m	12	
Maryland National, Box 987, Baltimore, MD 21203	MDNT	0.75	0	50/5000q	12	5-D SSO OI
Mellon National, Box 15629, Pittsburgh, PA 15244	MEL	0.90	0	50/5000q	4	5-D OI
Merrill Bancshares, Exchange St., Bangor, ME 04401	MERB	0.75	0	Y	10/1000m	8	
Midlantic, Box 600, Edison, NJ 08818	MIDL	0.75	0	10/3000q	4	PRF
Morgan (J P), 23 Wall St., New York, NY 10015	JPM	0.85	5-2.50	Y	10/3000q	4	
Multibank Financial, 1400 Hancock, Quincy, MA 02169	MLTF	0.75	0	.25/5000q	12	5-D+3-DVC SSO OI
New Jersey National, 1 West State, Trenton, NJ 08603	NJNB	0.95	0	25/5000q	4	5-D+VC OI
Norstar, 1450 Western Ave., Albany, NY 12203	NOR	0.60	0	10/10000q	4	OI
Old Stone, Box 1536, Providence, RI 02901	OSTN	1.10	4-2.50	Y	25/1000m	8	
PNC Financial, Foster Plaza, Pittsburgh, PA 15220	PNCF	0.75	0	50/1000m	12	5-D OI
State Street Boston, 225 Franklin, Boston, MA 02110	STBK	0.70	5-2.50	Y	10/1000m	8	
Summit, 367 Springfield Ave., Summit, NJ 07901	SUBN	0.65	0	10/3000q	8	PRF
United Jersey, Box 2066, Princeton, NJ 08540	UJB	0.75	0	10/6000q	12	BOND OI

A. *Bank, savings and loan (Midwest)*

American Fletcher, 111 Monument, Indianapolis, IN 46277	AFLT	0.85	0	25/5000m	12	SSO
Ameritrust, 900 Euclid, Cleveland, OH 44101	AMTR	0.80	0	10/5000q	12	
Banc One, 100 E. Broad St., Columbus, OH 43271	ONE	0.55	0	10/5000q	4	PRF
Boatmen's, Box 236, St. Louis, MO 63166	BOAT	0.65	0	100/5000q	4	OI
Centerre, One Centerre Plaza, St. Louis, MO 63101	CTBC	0.75	0	10/1000m	8	
Central Banc, Central Trust Ctr., Cincinnati, OH 45202	CBAN	0.80	0	10/1000m	12	
Comerica, 211 W. Ford, Detroit, MI 48226	CMCA	0.75	0	10/3000q	4	
Fifth Third Bancorp, Box 478, Cincinnati, OH 45201	FITB	0.55	5-3.00	Y	25/1000m	12	
First of America, 108 E. Michigan, Kalamazoo, MI 49007	FABK	0.75	0	25/5000q	12	5-D+VC PRF OI

Note: Examples from this appendix are discussed in Chapter 7.

Abbreviations: m = per month; q = per quarter; y = per year; unlim = unlimited; PRF = owners of preferred stock eligible to participate; BOND = owners of bonds eligible to participate; SSO = split share option whereby less than 100 percent of dividends can be invested; 5-D = 5 percent discount on reinvested dividends; 5-D+VC = 5 percent discount on reinvested dividends and voluntary cash contributions; OI = original issue; Y-VC = commission charged only on voluntary cash contributions; 3 EA VC = $3 service fee for each voluntary cash contribution.

Dividend Reinvestment Plans

	Ticker Symbol	Beta	Cost Service Fee	Commission	Voluntary Cash $Minimum/ $Maximum	Frequency (per year)	Special Features
First Bancorp of Ohio, 106 S. Main, Akron, OH 44308	FBOH	0.70	0	0	none		
First Chicago, One First National Plaza, Chicago, IL 60670	FNB	1.05	0	0	25/5000q	4	5-D+VC OI
First National Cincinnati, Box 2058, Cincinnati, OH 45201	FNAC	0.75	0	0	50/5000q	4	
First Wisconsin, 777 E. Wisconsin, Milwaukee, WI 53202	FWB	0.65	4-2.50	Y	25/1000m	12	
Hawkeye Bancorp, 7th & Locust, Des Moines, IA 50307	HWKB	0.85	0	Y-VC	unlim	unlim	5-D OI
Huntington Bancshares, Box 5065, Cleveland, OH 44101	HBAN	0.60	0	0	50/5000q	12	5-D PRF SSO OI
Marine Corp., Box 481, Milwaukee, WI 53201	MCRP	0.85	0	0	25/3000q	4	
Mark Twain, 8820 Ladue, St. Louis, MO 63124	MTWN	0.60	0	0	10/2000m	4	BOND
Marshall & Isley, 777 N. Water, Milwaukee, WI 53202	MRIS	0.80	0	0	10/1000m	12	
Mercantile, Box 321, St. Louis, MO 63166	MTRC	0.75	2.00	Y	25/1000m	12	3 EA VC
Money Management, 1000 E. 80th, Merrillville, IN 46410	MGT	1.10	5-2.00	Y	25/unlim	12	
National City Corp., Box 5756, Cleveland, OH 44101	NCTY	0.75	0	0	20/2500m	12	
NBD Bancorp, 611 Woodward, Detroit, MI 48226	NBD	0.90	0	0	10/10000q	8	
Norwest Corp., 1200 Peavey Bldg., Minneapolis, MN 55479	NOB	0.80	0	0	25/3000q	12	5-D SSO OI
Security Bancorp, 16333 Trenton, Southgate, MI 48195	SECB	0.75	0	0	10/1000m	12	SSO
Valley Bancorp, Box 1061, Appleton, WI 54912	VYBN	0.80	0	0	10/1000m	4	

A. Bank, savings and loan (South)

	Ticker Symbol	Beta	Service Fee	Commission	$Minimum/ $Maximum	Frequency (per year)	Special Features
AmSouth Bancorp, 1400 First National, Birmingham, AL 35203	ASO	0.80	0	0	10/5000q	4	5-D OI
Bank of Virginia, 7 N. 8th St., Richmond, VA 23260	BKV	0.75	0	0	10/1000m	12	5-D PRF OI
Bankers Trust, Box 2307, Columbia, SC 29202	BTSC	0.65	0	Y	25/1000m	12	
Barnett Banks of Florida, 100 Laura, Jacksonville, FL 32202	BBF	0.90	0	0	25/10000m	12	OI
Branch Corp., 223 W. Nash, Wilson, NC 27893	BNCH	0.80	0	0	25/1000m	12	
Central Fidelity, Box 27602, Richmond, VA 23261	CFBS	0.70	0	0	25/1000m	12	5-D PRF OI

188

Citizens Fidelity, Citizens Plaza, Louisville, KY 40202	CFDY	0.80	5-2.50	Y	10/3000q	8	
Citizens & Southern, 1801 Main, Columbia, SC 29222	CITS	1.05	0	0	20/2000m	12	5-D BOND OI
Dominion Bankshares, Box 13327, Roanoke, VA 24040	DMBK	0.80	0	0	10/5000q	12	
First Alabama, Box 1448, Montgomery, AL 36102	FABC	0.70	0	0	20/3000m	12	
First American, First American Center, Nashville, TN 37237	FATN	0.50	0	0	25/2000q	12	5-D+VC PRF OI
First Kentucky, Box 36000, Louisville, KY 40232	FKYN	0.85	0	0	10/1000m	4	
First Security, 1 First Security Plaza, Lexington, KY 40507	FSCK	0.65	0	0	none		OI
First Tennessee, 165 Madison, Memphis, TN 38103	FTEN	0.60	0	Y	25/5000q	12	SSO
First Union, First Union Plaza, Charlotte, NC 28288	FUNC	0.80	0	0	25/10000q	12	5-D+VC OI
First Virginia, 6400 Arlington Falls, Church, VA 22042	FVB	0.80	0	0	25/5000q	12	5-D
Great American, 1 American Plaza, Baton Rouge, LA 70825	GTAM	0.60	2.00	Y	25/1000m	12	3 EA VC
Landmark Bank, Box 5367, Fort Lauderdale, FL 33310	LBKF	0.85	0	Y	10/1000m	12	
NCNB Corp., One NCNB, Charlotte, NC 28255	NCB	0.85	0	0	20/3000q	8	5-D OI
Northwestern, Box 21527, Greensboro, NC 27420	NWFN	0.85	0	0	10/5000q	12	
Planters, Box 1220, Rocky Mount, NC 27801	PNBT	0.60	0	Y	10/1000m	12	
Southeast, Box 012500, Miami, FL 33101	STB	0.70	0	0	25/5000q	4	5-D SSO OI
Southern, Box 1329, Greenville, SC 29602	STBN	0.70	0	0	20/3000q	12	PRF OI
Sovran Financial, Box 600, Norfolk, VA 23501	SOVN	0.75	0	0	25/5000q	12	5-D+VC SSO OI
Sun Banks, Box 3631, Orlando, FL 32802	SU	0.90	0	0	10/1000m	12	
Trust Co. of Georgia, Box 4625, Atlanta, GA 30302	TRGA	0.80	0	Y	10/1000q	12	5-D OI
United Virginia, Box 26665, Richmond, VA 23261	UVBK	0.60	0	0	10/5000q	4	PRF
Wachovia, Box 3001, Winston-Salem, NC 27150	WB	0.75	0	Y	10/5000m	12	

A. *Bank, savings and loan (West)*

Affiliated Banc., 1101 Arapahoe, Boulder, CO 80302	AFBK	0.70	0	Y	25/1000q	4	
Allied, 808 Travis, Houston, TX 77002	ALBN	0.85	5-3.00	Y	25/1000m	12	
Arizona Bancwest, 101 N. First, Phoenix, AZ 85003	AZBW	0.80	0	0	25/5000q	12	5-D+VC OI
BancOklahoma, Oklahoma Tower, Tulsa, OK 74192	BOKC	0.80	0	0	25/2500q	4	
Bancorp Hawaii, 111 S. King, Honolulu, HI 96813	BNHI	0.80	0	0	25/5000q	12	5-D SSO OI
BankAmerica, BankAmerica Ctr., San Francisco, CA 94104	BAC	0.95	5-2.50	Y	25/1000m	12	SSO BOND

			Cost		Dividend Reinvestment Plans Voluntary Cash		
	Ticker Symbol	Beta	Service Fee	Commission	$Minimum/ $Maximum	Frequency (per year)	Special Features
Banks of MidAmerica, Box 25848, Oklahoma City, OK 73125	BOMA	1.05	0	0	20/20000q	12	5-D+VC PRF BOND
Colorado National, 950 Seventeenth, Denver, CO 80202	COLC	0.80	0	0	50/1000m	12	5-D SSO OI
First City Texas, 1001 Bannin, Houston, TX 77002	FBT	1.00	5-2.50	Y	25/1000m	12	
First Interstate, Box 54068, Los Angeles, CA 90054	I	1.05	0	0	10/5000q	4	5-D SSO OI
First Security, 79 S. Main, Salt Lake City, UT 84130	FSCO	0.90	0	0	10/5000m	12	5-D OI
First Wyoming, 18th & Carey, Cheyenne, WY 82001	FWO	0.70	0	0	100/5000q	12	5-D+VC BOND OI
Interfirst Corp., 1201 Elm, Dallas, TX 75270	IFC	0.85	0	0	25/5000q	4	OI
MCORP, Box 225415, Dallas, TX 75265	MBK	0.85	0	0	10/5000q	12	5-D OI
Rainier Bancorp, Box 3966, Seattle, WA 98124	RBAN	0.80	0	0	25/5000q	12	5-D OI
RepublicBank, Box 225961, Dallas, TX 75265	RPT	0.80	0	0	25/3000q	24	PRF
Security Pacific, Box 3546, Los Angeles, CA 90051	SPC	0.95	5-2.00	Y	25/1000m	24	
Texas American, Box 2050, Fort Worth, TX 76113	TXA	0.85	0	0	100/2000q	12	5-D SSO OI
Texas Commerce, Box 2558, Houston, TX 77252	TCB	0.70	0	0	25/2000q	12	5-D+VC OI
US Bancorp, 309 S.W. 6th, Portland, OR 97204	USBC	0.85	5-2.50	Y	50/1000q	4	
Valley National, Box 71, Phoenix, AZ 85001	VNCP	0.85	0	0	10/1000m	8	
Victoria, 120 Main Pl., Victoria, TX 77902	VICT	0.80	0	0	0/3000q	4	SSO OI
Wells Fargo, 420 Montgomery, San Francisco, CA 94104	WFC	0.90	0	0	25/5000q	12	SSO OI

B. *Insurance, financial services*

Advest Group, 6 Central Row, Hartford, CT 06103	ADV	1.50	0	0	20/2500q	4	
Aetna Life, 151 Farmington, Hartford, CT 06156	AET	0.95	0	0	10/3000q	4	
American Express, American Express Plaza, New York, NY 10004	AXP	1.35	0	0	0/3000m	12	5-D SSO OI
American Family, American Family Center, Columbus, GA 31999	AFL	0.85	0	0	25/3000q	4	

Company	Ticker						
American General, Box 3247, Houston, TX 77253	AGC	0.90	0	0	10/3000q	4	
American Heritage, 11 E. Forsyth, Jacksonville, FL 32202	AHL	0.55	0	0	none		
Beneficial Corp., Box 911, Wilmington, DE 19899	BNL	0.90	0	0	10/1000m	12	PRF
H&R Block, 4410 Main, Kansas City, MO 64111	HRB	0.95	0	Y	25/2500q	4	
Business Men's Assurance, BMA Tower, Kansas City, MO 64141	BMAC	1.05	0	0	25/5000q	4	
Capital Holding, Commonwealth Bldg., Louisville, KY 40202	CPH	0.85	0	0	10/3000q	12	
Chubb Corp., 15 Mountain View Rd., Warren, NJ 07061	CB	0.85	5-2.50	Y	10/3000q	8	
CIGNA, 1185 Avenue of the Americas, New York, NY 10036	CI	1.00	0	0	10/1000m	12	PRF SSO
Cincinnati Financial, Box 145496, Cincinnati, OH 45214	CINF	0.85	5-3.00	Y	25/1000m	12	
Combined International, 707 Combined Ctr., Northbrook, IL 60062	PMA	1.00	0	0	20/1000m	12	PRF
Hartford Steam Boiler, 1 State St., Hartford, CT 06102	HBOL	0.80	0	Y	10/3000q	8	
Household International, 2700 Sanders, Prospect Heights, IL 60070	HI	0.90	5-2.50	Y	10/5000q	8	PRF
Jefferson-Pilot, Box 21008, Greensboro, NC 27420	JP	0.90	4-2.50	Y	20/1000m	12	5-D OI
Kemper Corp., Long Grove, IL 60049	KEML	0.95	0	0	25/5000q	12	5-D OI
Monumental Corp., 1111 N. Charles, Baltimore, MD 21201	MONU	0.85	0	0	20/5000q	12	
Ohio Casualty, 136 N. 3rd, Hamilton, OH 45025	OCAS	0.80	5-2.50	Y	10/5000m	12	
St. Paul Co., 385 Washington, St. Paul, MN 55102	STPL	0.95	0	0	10/60000y	12	5-D OI
Seibels Bruce Group, Box 1, Columbia, SC 29202	SBIG	1.00	0	0	20/3000q	4	5-D SSO OI
SRI Co., Box Q. Branchville, NJ 07826	SRIC	1.15	0	0	100/1000q	4	
Stewart Info., 2200 W. Loop South, Houston, TX 77027	SISC	1.40	5-3.00	Y	25/1000m	12	
Transamerica Co., Box 2118, San Francisco, CA 94126	TA	1.05	0	0	10/5000m	12	SSO
Travelers Corp., 1 Tower Sq., Hartford, CT 06115	TIC	1.10	0	0	5/5000m	12	5-D SSO OI
USLICO, 1701 Penn N.W., Washington, D.C. 20006	USVC	1.15	0	0	25/1000m	12	
USF&G Co., Box 1138, Baltimore, MD 21203	FG	0.90	0	0	50/5000q	12	
USLIFE Co., 125 Maiden Lane, New York, NY 10038	USH	0.95	0	0	10/4000q	12	
Washington National, 1630 Chicago, Evanston, IL 60201	WNT	0.85	0	0	25/5000q	4	5-D PRF SSO OI

Dividend Reinvestment Plans

	Ticker Symbol	Beta	Cost Service Fee	Commission	Voluntary Cash $Minimum/$Maximum	Frequency (per year)	Special Features
C. Real estate							
California REIT, 601 Montgomery, San Francisco, CA 94111	CT	0.65	0	0	25/10000q	4	5-D+VC OI
Commonwealth Financial, Box 1529, Houston, TX 77001	CFGRS	0.65	2.00	Y	25/1000m	12	
Federal National Mort., 3900 Wisconsin N.W., Washington, D.C. 20016	FNM	1.50	5-2.50	Y	10/1000m	12	5-D OI
Federal Realty, 5454 Wisconsin, Chevy Chase, MD 20815	FRT	0.50	0	0	50/15000q	12	
First Union, 55 Public Sq., Cleveland, OH 44113	FUR	0.65	5-3.00	Y	20/5000m	12	
Hotel Investors, 5530 Wisconsin, Chevy Chase, MD 20815	HOT	0.35	0	0	25/3000q	4	
Hubbard Real Estate, 125 High, Boston, MA 02110	HRE	0.60	0	0	50/3000q	12	
IRT Property, 6540 Powers Fury, Atlanta, GA 30339	IRT	0.60	0	0	none		5-D SSO OI
Koger Co., Box 4520, Jacksonville, FL 32201	KGR	0.75	0	0	100/5000m	12	5-D SSO OI
Koger Properties, Box 4520, Jacksonville, FL 32201	KOG	0.95	0	0	100/5000m	12	5-D+VC OI
Lincoln National, 1300 S. Clinton, Fort Wayne, IN 46801	LNC	0.85	0	0	25/5000q	12	5-D+VC OI
Mass Mutual, 1295 State, Springfield, MA 01111	MML	0.75	5-2.50	Y	10/1000m	8	
MONY Mortgage, 1740 Broadway, New York, NY 10019	MYM	0.80	0	0	50/1500q	12	5-D SSO OI
New Plan Realty Trust, 469 5th Ave., New York, NY 10017	NPR	0.40	0	0	100/5000q	4	5-D SSO OI
Property Trust of America, Box 1372, El Paso, TX 79948	PTRAS	0.80	0	0	25/2000q	12	5-D+VC OI
R.E.I.T. of America, 615 Battery, San Francisco, CA 94111	REI	0.70	0	0	10/1000q	4	
Washington REIT, 4963 Fairmont, Bethesda, MD 20814	WRE	0.55	0	0	100/3000q	4	
Wells Fargo, Box 44031, San Francisco, CA 94144	WFM	0.80	0	0	25/5000m	12	SSO

II. Consumer

A. *Consumer goods—food*

Company	Ticker						
American Brands, 245 Park Ave., New York, NY 10167	AMB	0.70	0	O	10/10000q	8	5-D+VC SSO BOND OI
American Filtrona, Box 34668, Richmond, VA 23234	AFIL	0.95	0	O	25/1000m	12	5-D+VC SSO OI
AMFAC Inc., 700 Bishop, Honolulu, HI 96801	AMA	0.95	0	O	25/1000m	12	5-D+VC PRF OI
Beatrice Co., 2 N. LaSalle, Chicago, IL 60602	BRY	0.80	0	O	1/1000m	8	
Bob Evans Farms, 3776 S. High, Columbus, OH 43207	BOBE	0.80	0	O	10/unlim	8	
Borden, 277 Park Ave., New York, NY 10172	BN	0.70	0	O	10/10000q	12	5-D SSO OI
Castle & Cook, 130 Merchant, Honolulu, HI 96802	CKE	0.80	0	O	10/1000m	12	SSO OI
Clorox, 1221 Broadway, Oakland, CA 94612	CLX	0.95	0	O	10/3000q	4	
Coca-Cola, Box 1734, Atlanta, GA 30301	KO	0.75	0	O	10/3000q	12	
Coca-Cola Consolidated, Box 31487, Charlotte, NC 28281	COKE	0.80	4	Y	10/1000m	12	SSO OI
Colgate-Palmolive, 300 Park Ave., New York, NY 10022	CL	0.75	0	O	10/1000q	4	
ConAgra, 1 Central Park Plaza, Omaha, NE 68102	CAG	0.70	0	O	10/1000m	8	
Consolidated Foods, 3 First National Bldg., Chicago, IL 60602	CFD	0.60	5-3.00	Y	10/1500q	8	
Conwood Corp., Box 217, Memphis, TN 38101	CWD	0.80	5-2.50	Y	10/3000q	4	
CPC International, International Plaza, Englewood Cliffs, NJ 07632	CPC	0.80	4-2.00	Y	25/3000q	4	
Curtice-Burns, Box 681, Rochester, NY 14603	CBI	0.65	0	O	10/1000m	12	
Dart & Kraft, 2211 Sanders, Northbrook, IL 60062	DKI	0.75	0	O	10/5000q	4	5-D+VC PRF OI
Dean Foods, 3600 River, Franklin Park, IL 60131	DF	0.75	0	O	25/3000q	4	
DiGiorgio, 1 Maritime Plaza, San Francisco, CA 94111	DIG	0.95	0	O	5/2500m	12	PRF BOND OI
Economics Lab, Osborn Bldg., St. Paul, MN 55102	ECON	0.85	5-3.00	Y	10/3000q	12	
Federal, Box 17236, Memphis, TN 38187	FFF	0.55	0	O	10/5000m	12	5-D+VC OI
General Foods, 250 North St., White Plains, NY 10625	GF	0.80	0	O	10/1000m	8	5-D+VC PRF OI
General Mills, Box 1113, Minneapolis, MN 55440	GIS	0.85	0	O	10/1000q	12	5-D SSO OI
Gerber, 445 State, Fremont, MI 49412	GEB	0.65	0	O	25/3000q	4	
Heinz (HJ), Box 57, Pittsburgh, PA 15230	HNZ	0.75	0	O	25/1000m	12	
Hershey, Box 814, Hershey, PA 17033	HSY	0.60	0	O	0/2000y	12	
Holly Sugar, Holly Sugar Bldg., Colorado Springs, CO 80903	HLY	0.60	4-3.00	Y	10/3000q	12	

	Ticker Symbol	Beta	Cost Service Fee	Cost Commission	Voluntary Cash $Minimum/$Maximum	Frequency (per year)	Special Features
International Multifoods, Box 2942, Minneapolis, MN 55402	IMC	0.75	0	0	10/1000m	12	
Kellogg, 235 Porter, Battle Creek, MI 49016	K	0.75	0	0	25/25000y	12	SSO
Lance, Box 32368, Charlotte, NC 28232	LNCE	0.70	0	0	10/1000m	12	
McCormick, 11350 McCormick, Hunt Valley, MD 21031	MCCRK	0.90	0	0	25/3000q	4	SSO OI
Nabisco, Nabisco Brands Plaza, Parsippany, NY 07054	NB	0.65	0	0	25/3000q	12	3-D OI
PepsiCo, Purchase, NY 10577	PEP	0.80	0	0	10/60000y	12	
Philip Morris, 120 Park Ave., New York, NY 10017	MO	0.85	0	0	10/60000y	12	
Pillsbury, 200 S. 6th, Minneapolis, MN 55402	PSY	0.75	0	0	10/1000m	12	
Pioneer Hi-Bred, 400 Locust, Des Moines, IA 50309	PHYB	0.80	0	0	25/1000m	12	5-D OI
Procter & Gamble, Box 599, Cincinnati, OH 45201	PG	0.70	0	Y	10/60000y	12	
Quaker Oats, Merchandise Mart Plaza, Chicago, IL 60654	OAT	0.70	0	0	10/30000y	12	5-D SSO OI
Ralston Purina, Checkerboard Sq., St. Louis, MO 63164	RAL	0.75	0	0	10/60000y	12	SSO
Reynolds (RJ), Reynolds Blvd., Winston-Salem, NC 27102	RJR	0.90	0	0	10/60000y	12	
Savannah Foods, Box 339, Savannah, GA 31402	SVAN	0.45	0	0	10/3000q	4	
Smucker (JM), Strawberry Lane, Orrville, OH 44667	SJM	0.85	0	0	50/3000q	12	
Staley Continental, 2200 Eldorado, Decatur, IL 62525	STA	1.30	0	0	25/1000m	16	
US Tobacco, 100 W. Putnam, Greenwich, CT 06830	UBO	0.80	0	0	10/1000m	12	
Universal Foods, Box 737, Milwaukee, WI 53201	UFC	0.60	0	0	25/1000m	12	5-D OI
Universal Leaf Tobacco, Box 25099, Richmond, VA 23260	UVV	0.80	0	0	10/1000m	12	
Vulcan Materials, Box 7497, Birmingham, AL 35253	VMC	0.55	5-3.00	Y	10/3000q	4	OI
Wrigley (WM), 410 N. Michigan, Chicago, IL 60611	WWY	0.55	4-2.00	Y	10/500m	12	

B. *Consumer goods—nonfood*

	Ticker Symbol	Beta	Service Fee	Commission	$Minimum/$Maximum	Frequency	Special Features
Allegheny International, 2 Oliver Plaza, Pittsburgh, PA 15230	AG	1.35	0	0	25/2000m	12	5-D+VC PRF OI

Company	Ticker						
Anchor Hocking, 109 N. Broad St., Lancaster, OH 43132	ARH	0.65	0	0	25/5000q	12	
Anheuser-Busch, 1 Busch Pl., St. Louis, MO 63118	BUD	0.65	0	0	25/5000q	4	
Avon Products, 9 W. 57th St., New York, NY 10019	AVP	1.00	0	0	10/5000m	12	5-D+VC OI
Brown-Forman Distillers, Box 1080, Louisville, KY 40201	BFD.B	0.90	0	Y	50/3000q	12	
Brown Group, 8400 Maryland, St. Louis, MO 63105	BG	0.90	0	0	25/1000m	12	
Burlington, 3330 W. Friendly, Greensboro, NC 27410	BUR	1.00	4-2.50	Y	10/1500m	12	5-D OI
Champion Products, 3141 Monroe, Rochester, NY 14618	CH	1.15	0	0	10/unlim	12	5-D PRF SSO OI
Cheesebrough-Ponds, 33 Benedict, Greenwich, CT 06830	CBM	0.85	0	0	10/1000m	12	
Cluett Peabody, 510 5th Ave., New York, NY 10036	CLU	0.85	5-2.50	Y	10/1000m	8	PRF
Collins & Aikman, 210 Madison Ave., New York, NY 10016	CK	0.95	0	0	25/1000m	12	
Corning Glass Works, Houghton Pk., Corning, NY 14830	GLW	1.05	5-2.50	Y	10/1000m	12	
Craddock-Terry, 3100 Al Lankford, Lynchburg, VA 24506	CDCK	1.15	5-3.00	Y	25/1000m	12	
Dominion Textiles, 1950 Sherbrooke, Montreal, Quebec H3H1E7	DTX.TO	0.60	0	0	0/4000q	12	5-D OI
Gillette, Prudential Tower Bldg., Boston, MA 02199	GS	0.75	0	0	10/3000q	8	
Gulf & Western, 1 Gulf and Western, New York, NY 10023	GW	1.10	0	0	10/1000m	12	PRF OI
Heilman (G) Brewing, Box 459, LaCrosse, WI 54601	GHB	0.90	0	Y	25/1000m	12	
Insilco, 1000 Research Pky., Meriden, CT 06450	INR	1.15	0	0	10/5000m	12	5-D OI
Jostens, 5501 Norman Center, Minneapolis, MN 55437	JOS	0.70	0	0	10/1000m	12	
Kidde, Box 5555, Saddle Brook, NJ 07662	KDE	0.90	0	Y	10/3000q	12	PRF
La-Z-Boy, 1284 N. Telegraph, Monroe, MI 48161	LAZB	0.85	0	Y	10/1000m	12	
Levi Strauss, Box 7215, San Francisco, CA 94120	LVI	1.15	0	0	10/3000m	12	
Magic Chef, 740 King Edwards, Cleveland, TN 37311	MGC	1.35	0	0	25/1500m	12	SSO OI
Maytag, 403 W. 4th, Newton, IA 50208	MYG	0.90	0	0	25/5000m	12	5-D OI
Mohasco, 57 Lyon, Amsterdam, NY 12010	MOH	0.90	0	0	10/500m	8	5-D PRF OI
Oneida Ltd., Oneida, NY 13421	OCQ	1.00	0	0	30/5000q	4	5-D OI
Roper, Box 867, Kankakee, IL 60901	ROP	1.15	0	0	0/3000q	4	
Russell Corp., Alexander City, AL 35010	RML	0.95	0	0	10/3000q	4	5-D PRF OI
Scott Fetzer, 14600 Detroit, Lakewood, OH 44107	SFZ	0.75	0	0	10/5000q	4	
Seton Co., 849 Broadway, Newark, NJ 07104	SEL	1.05	5-2.50	Y	50/1000q	4	
Stanley Works, 195 Lake, New Britain, CT 06050	SWK	0.95	0	0	10/1000m	8	5-D BOND OI

Dividend Reinvestment Plans

	Ticker Symbol	Beta	Cost Service Fee	Cost Commission	Voluntary Cash $Minimum/ $Maximum	Frequency (per year)	Special Features
Stevens (JP), 1185 Avenue of the Americas, New York, NY 10036	STN	0.85	0	0	10/3000q	4	
Stride Rite, 5 Cambridge, Cambridge, MA 02142	SRR	0.90	5-2.50	Y	10/1000m	8	5-D+VC PRF OI
US Shoe, 1 Eastwood, Cincinnati, OH 45227	USR	1.30	5-2.50	Y	25/1000m	12	
VF Corp., 1047 N. Park, Wyomissing, PA 19610	VFC	0.95	5-2.50	Y	10/3000q	4	OI
Walker (H) Resources, Box 33, Toronto, Ontario M5X1A9	HWR	1.00	0	0	100/5000q	4	5-D PRF
West Point-Pepperell, 400 W. 10th, West Point, GA 31833	WPM	0.95	0	Y	10/3000q	12	
Whirlpool, Benton Harbor, MI 49022	WHR	1.00	0	0	10/3000q	4	5-D+VC OI

C. Drug, health care and supplies

	Ticker Symbol	Beta	Service Fee	Commission	$Minimum/ $Maximum	Frequency (per year)	Special Features
Abbott Labs, Abbott Pk., North Chicago, IL 60064	ABT	1.05	0	0	10/1000q	8	
American Home Products, 685 3rd Ave., New York, NY 10017	AHP	0.80	5-3.00	Y	10/500q	4	
American Hospital Supplies, 1 American Plaza, Evanston, IL 60201	AHS	1.15	5-2.50	0	25/1000m	12	5-D SSO OI
American Medical, 414 N. Camden, Beverly Hills, CA 90210	AMI	1.35	0	Y	10/5000m	12	PRF OI
Bard (CR), 731 Central, Murray Hill, NJ 07974	BCR	1.15	0	0	10/1000m	12	
Bausch & Lomb, 1 Lincoln First Sq., Rochester, NY 14604	BOL	0.90	0	0	25/60000y	12	
Baxter Travenol, 1 Baxter, Deerfield, IL 60015	BAX	1.05	0	0	25/1000m	12	SSO
Becton, Dickinson, Mack Centre, Paramus, NJ 07652	BDX	0.95	0	0	25/3000q	8	
Beverly Enterprises, Box 90130, Pasadena, CA 91109	BEV	1.45	0	0	none		
Bristol-Meyers, 345 Park Avenue, New York, NY 10154	BMY	0.90	0	0	10/3000q	8	5-D SSO OI
Hospital Corp. of America, 1 Park, Nashville, TN 37202	HCA	1.30	0	0	25/12500q	12	5-D+VC OI
Humana, Box 1438, Louisville, KY 40201	HUM	1.35	0	0	none		
Johnson & Johnson, New Brunswick, NJ 08933	JNJ	0.95	0	0	25/3000q	4	SSO

Lilly (Eli), 307 E. McCarty, Indianapolis, IN 46285	LLY	0.85	0	0	25/1000m	12	5-D+VC OI
Manhattan National, 111 W. 57th St., New York, NY 10019	MLC	1.00	0	0	10/3000y	4	5-D+VC OI
Marion Laboratories, Box 9627, Kansas City, MO 64134	MKC	1.10	0	0	0/3000q	4	5-D SSO OI
Merck, Box 2000, Rahway, NJ 07065	MRK	0.80	4-2.00	Y	25/1000m	12	SSO BOND
National Medical, Box 25980, Los Angeles, CA 90025	NME	1.45	0	0	10/1000m	12	5-D+VC PRF BOND
Omnicare, 1300 Fountain Square, Cincinnati, OH 45201	OCR	1.00	0	0	10/1000m	12	
Pfizer, 235 E. 42nd St., New York, NY 10017	PFE	0.95	0	0	10/1000m	12	5-D SSO OI
Richardson-Vicks, 10 Westport, Wilton, CT 06897	RVI	0.80	0	0	10/3000q	8	
Rorer Group, 500 Virginia, Ft. Washington, PA 19034	ROR	0.75	0	0	25/3000q	4	5-D SSO OI
Schering-Plough, Box 1000, Madison, NJ 07940	SGP	0.80	0	0	25/36000y	12	SSO
Searle (GD), Box 1045, Skokie, IL 60076	SRL	0.85	5-2.50	Y	10/1000m	8	5-D+VC BOND OI
SmithKline, Box 7929, Philadelphia, PA 19101	SKB	0.85	0	0	10/1000m	12	OI
Squibb, 40 W. 57th Street, New York, NY 10019	SQB	0.85	0	0	25/1000m	12	OI
Sterling Drug, 90 Park Ave., New York, NY 10016	STY	0.75	4-2.00	Y	10/1000m	12	5-D OI
Sybron, 1100 Midtown Tower, Rochester, NY 14604	SYB	0.75	0	0	10/1000m	12	PRF
Tambrands, 10 Delaware, Lake Success, NY 11042	TPAX	0.80	0	0	100/5000q	8	
Upjohn, 7000 Portage, Kalamazoo, MI 49001	UPJ	0.95	0	0	25/3000q	12	SSO OI
Warner-Lambert, 201 Taber, Morris Plains, NJ 07950	WLA	0.90	0	0	10/1000m	8	5-D+VC OI
Whittaker, 10880 Wilshire, Los Angeles, CA 90024	WKR	1.25	0	0	25/1000q	4	

D. *Wholesale and retail trade*

Allied Stores, 1114 Avenue of the Americas, New York, NY 10036	ALS	0.80	0	0	25/30000y	12	
Ames Dept., 2418 Main, Rocky Hill, CT 06067	ADD	0.95	0	0	100/1000m	12	
Associated Dry Goods, 417 5th Ave., New York, NY 10016	DG	1.00	0	0	10/1000q	12	
Carter Hawley Hale, 550 S. Flower, Los Angeles, CA 90071	CHH	0.85	0	0	25/3000q	4	5-D OI
Dayton Hudson, 777 Nicollet, Minneapolis, MN 55402	DH	1.05	0	0	30/1000q	4	
Eckerd (Jack), Box 4689, Clearwater, FL 33518	ECK	1.05	0	0	25/1000m	12	
Federated Dept., 7 W. 7th, Cincinnati, OH 45202	FDS	0.95	0	0	25/1000m	12	5-D SSO OI
Fleming Co., Box 26647, Oklahoma City, OK 73126	FLM	0.70	0	0	25/5000q	12	5-D SSO OI
General Nutrition, 921 Penn, Pittsburgh, PA 15222	GNC	1.15	0	0	20/1000m	12	
Gorden Jewelry, 820 Fannin, Houston, TX 77002	GOR	0.70	2.00	Y	25/1000m	12	

Dividend Reinvestment Plans

	Ticker Symbol	Beta	Cost Service Fee	Commission	Voluntary Cash $Minimum/ $Maximum	Frequency (per year)	Special Features
Godfrey, Box 298, Waukesha, WI 53187	GDFY	0.65	0	0	10/1000m	4	
Handleman, 1055 W. Maple, Clawson, MI 48017	HDL	1.00	0	0	10/3000m	12	
Hannaford Bros., Box 1000, Portland, ME 04104	HRD	0.75	0	0	10/3000q	8	
Hartmarx, 101 N. Wacker, Chicago, IL 60606	HMX	0.80	0	0	25/1000m	12	
Jorgensen (Earl M), 10700 Alameda, Lynwood, CA 90262	JOR	0.55	5-2.00	Y	25/1000m	12	5-D+VC OI
Kroger, 1014 Vine, Cincinnati, OH 45202	KR	0.80	0	0	20/60000y	12	OI
Limited, Box 16528, Columbus, OH 43216	LTD	1.40	0	0	30/6000q	8	PRF SSO
Lowe's, Box 1111, N. Wilksboro, NC 28656	LOW	1.25	0	0	10/1000m	8	
Lucky Stores, 6300 Clark, Dublin, CA 94566	LKS	0.85	5-2.50	Y	25/500m	12	
Macy (RH), 151 W. 34th St., New York, NY 10001	MZ	1.00	0	0	100/3000q	4	5-D SSO OI
Marsh Supermarkets, 501 Depot, Yorktown, IN 47396	MARS	0.60	0	0	50/2000q	unlim	PRF
McKesson, 1 Port, San Francisco, CA 94104	MCK	0.75	0	0	10/60000y	12	PRF
Munford, Box 7701 Station C, Atlanta, GA 30357	MFD	0.90	0	0	25/3000m	12	PRF
Penn Traffic, 319 Washington, Johnstown, PA 15907	PNF	0.95	0	0	10/1000q	12	OI
Penney (JC), 1301 Avenue of the Americas, New York, NY 10019	JCP	0.95	4-2.00	Y	10/1000m	12	5-D OI
Revco Drug, 1925 Enterprise, Twinsburg, OH 44087	RDS	1.05	0	0	10/1000m	12	5-D OI
Rite Aid, Box 3165, Harrisburg, PA 17105	RAD	1.10	0	0	25/5000m	12	
Safeway, 4th & Jackson, Oakland, CA 94660	SA	0.75	0	0	0/5000q	12	5-D OI
SCOA Industries, 33 N. High, Columbus, OH 43215	SOA	0.90	0	0	10/2000m	12	5-D OI
Sears Roebuck, Sears Tower, Chicago, IL 60684	S	1.05	0	0	25/3000m	12	OI
Shaklee, 444 Market, San Francisco, CA 94111	SHC	1.40	0	0	10/3000q	4	
Southland, Box 719, Dallas, TX 75221	SLC	0.90	0	0	25/5000q	12	5-D SSO OI
Stop & Shop, Box 369, Boston, MA 02101	SHP	1.00	5-2.50	Y	10/1000m	8	
Walgreen, 200 Wilmot, Deerfield, IL 60015	WAG	0.95	0	0	10/1000m	8	SSO
Weis Market, 1000 S. 2nd, Sunbury, PA 17801	WMK	0.55	0	0	10/3000q	4	5-D SSO OI

Wetterau, 8920 Pershall, Hazelwood, MO 63042	WETT	0.90	0	0	10/1000m	8
Winn-Dixie, Box B, Jacksonville, FL 32203	WIN	0.60	0	0	10/1000m	12
Woolworth (FW), 233 Broadway, New York, NY 10279	Z	0.85	0	0	20/60000y	12

III. Services

A. *Advertising, publishing*

Addison-Wesley, Jacob Way, Reading, MA 01867	ADSNB	1.10	5-2.50	Y	10/1000m	8	
CBS, 51. W. 52nd Street, New York, NY 10019	CBS	1.00	5-2.50	Y	25/1000m	12	
Dow Jones, 22 Cortlandt, New York, NY 10007	DJ	1.15	0	0	25/1000m	12	
Foote, Cone & Belding, 401 Michigan, Chicago, IL 60611	FCB	0.70	0	0	25/1000m	12	
Gannett, Lincoln Tower, Rochester, NY 14604	GCI	0.95	5-2.50	Y	10/5000m	12	SSO
Houghton Mifflin, 1 Beacon, Boston, MA 02108	HTN	0.80	0	0	25/3000q	12	
Interpublic Group, 1271 Avenue of the Americas, New York, NY 10020	IPG	0.70	4-2.50	Y	10/1000q	12	
MacMillan, 866 3rd Avenue, New York, NY 10022	MLL	0.85	4	2.50	25/5000m	12	
McGraw-Hill, 1221 Avenue of the Americas, New York, NY 10020	MHP	1.15	0	0	10/1000q	4	
Media General, Box 26991, Richmond, VA 23261	MEGA	0.75	0	0	10/2000m	4	
Taft Broadcasting, 1718 Young, Cincinnati, OH 45210	TFB	0.95	5-3.00	Y	25/1000m	12	
Time, Inc., Time & Life Bldg., New York, NY 10020	TL	1.35	0	0	25/1000m	12	SSO

B. *Business equipment and services*

Alco, 825 Duportrail, Valley Forge, PA 19482	ASN	0.75	0	Y	25/1000m	12	
American Business Products, 2690 Cumberland, Atlanta, GA 30339	ABP	0.80	0	0	10/1000m	12	
Banta (George), Curtis Reed Plaza, Menosha, WI 54952	BNTA	0.80	0	0	10/1000m	8	
Browning-Ferris, Box 3151, Houston, TX 77253	BFI	1.15	0	0	25/1000m	12	
Corroon & Black, Wall St. Plaza, New York, NY 10005	CBL	0.65	5-2.50	Y	10/5000q	4	
Donnelley (RR), 2223 Martin L. King, Chicago, IL 60616	DNY	1.00	0	0	10/60000y	12	SSO
Equifax, Box 4081, Atlanta, GA 30302	EFX	0.70	0	Y	10/1000q	12	

Dividend Reinvestment Plans

	Ticker Symbol	Beta	Cost Service Fee	Commission	Voluntary Cash $Minimum/$Maximum	Frequency (per year)	Special Features
Marsh & McLennan, 1221 Avenue of the Americas, New York, NY 10020	MMC	0.75	5-2.50	Y	10/3000q	4	
Moore Corp., Box 78, Toronto, Ontario M5X1G5	MCL	0.80	0	0	none		5-D OI
National Service. 1180 Peachtree N.E., Atlanta, GA 30309	NAS	0.65	5-2.50	Y	10/3000q	12	
Purolator, 255 Old New Brunswick, Piscataway, NJ 08854	PCC	1.10	0	0	25/3000q	4	
SCM, 117 Prospect, Stamford, CT 06901	SCM	0.85	0	0	25/1000m	12	
US Leasing International, Box 3985, San Francisco, CA 94119	USL	1.05	4-2.50	Y	25/1000q	4	
Waste Mgmt., 3003 Butterfield, Oak Brook, IL 60521	WMX	1.20	0	0	25/2000m	12	
Xerox, Box 1600. Stamford, CT 06904	XRX	1.05	5-2.50	Y	10/1000m	12	

C. Recreation, hotel

American Recreation Center, 2135 Butano, Sacramento, CA 95860	AMRC	0.85	0	0	10/500m	12	
AMF, 777 Westchester, White Plains, NY 10604	AMF	1.15	0	0	25/5000q	4	SSO OI
Brunswick, 1 Brunswick Plaza, Skokie, IL 60077	BC	1.15	0	0	10/1000m	12	
Disney (Walt), Box 10099, Burbank, CA 91510	DIS	0.95	0	0	20/unlim	12	SSO
Fox-Stanley Photo, 8750 Tesoro, San Antonio, TX 78286	FSP	0.80	0	0	25/2000q	12	5-D SSO OI
General Cine, Box 1000, Chestnut Hill, MA 02167	GCN	1.15	0	0	25/2500q	8	
Huffy, Box 1204, Dayton, OH 45401	HUF	0.80	0	0	10/1000m	4	
MCA, 100 Universal City Plaza, Universal City, CA 91608	MCA	0.90	0	0	10/1000m	12	
McDonalds, McDonalds Plaza, Oak Brook, IL 60521	MCD	0.95	0	0	20/1000m	12	SSO
Murray Ohio, Box 268. Brentwood, TN 37027	MYO	0.75	0	0	10/2500q	8	
Outboard Marine, 100 Sea-Horse, Waukegan, IL 60085	OM	0.90	5-3.00	Y	10/3000q	8	
Santa Anita, 285 W. Huntington, Arcadia, CA 91006	SAR	0.55	0	0	50/5000q	12	5-D OI
Talley Ind., 2702 N. 44th, Phoenix, AZ 85008	TAL	0.85	0	0	10/1000m	12	PRF

Warner Comm., 75 Rockefeller Plaza, New York, NY 10019	WCI	1.10	0	25/5000q	4	5-D SSO OI
Wendys, 4288 Dublin-Granville, Dublin, OH 43107	WEN	1.15	0	20/1000q	4	SSO OI

D. Transportation

CSX, Box 32222, Richmond, VA 23261	CSX	1.20	0	25/5000q	24	5-D+VC OI
Emery Air Freight, Old Danbury, Wilton, CT 06897	EAF	1.30	0	10/2500q	4	
Flexi-Van, 330 Madison Ave., New York, NY 10017	FLX	0.80	0	25/5000q	4	
GATX, 120 S. Riverside Plaza, Chicago, IL 60606	GMT	0.95	0	25/3000m	8	
IC Industries, 111 E. Wacker, Chicago, IL 60601	ICX	1.00	0	10/60000y	12	PRF SSO
IU International, 1500 Walnut, Philadelphia, PA 19102	IU	1.10	0	10/5000q	8	PRF SSO
Leaseway, 3700 Park East, Beachwood, OH 44122	LTC	0.90	0	0/12000y	unlim	
Norfolk Southern, Roanoke, VA 24042	NSC	0.95	5-2.50	Y	10/3000q	4	
Ryder System, Box 020816, Miami, FL 33102	RDR	1.10	0	10/3000q	4	
Santa Fe So. Pacific, 224 S. Michigan, Chicago, IL 60604	SFX	1.30	5-2.50	Y	10/1000m	8	
Soo Line, Box 530, Minneapolis, MN 55440	SOO	0.65	0	10/1500q	12	
Transcon Lines, Box 92220, Los Angeles, CA 90009	TCL	1.50	0	10/500m	12	
Transway International, 81 Main, White Plains, NY 10601	TNW	0.75	4-2.50	Y	10/500m	12	
Union Pacific, 345 Park Ave., New York, NY 10154	UNP	1.45	0	10/60000y	12	PRF SSO

IV. Capital goods and technology

A. Aerospace

AAR, 2100 Touhy, Elk Grove Village, IL 60007	AIR	1.00	0	10/3000q	4	
Cessna, 5800 E. Pawnee, Wichita, KS 67201	CEA	1.30	0	10/5000m	8	
Fairchild, 20301 Century, Germantown, MD 20874	FEN	1.10	0	10/2500q	4	PRF
Grumman, 1111 Stewart, Bethpage, NY 11714	GQ	1.00	0	10/1000m	12	
Hexcel, 650 California, San Francisco, CA 94108	HXL	1.05	0	25/1000m	12	5-D+VC OI
Kaman, Blue Hills, Bloomfield, CT 06002	KAMNA	1.00	0	25/1000q	4	
Martin Marietta, 6801 Rockledge, Bethesda, MD 20817	ML	1.35	0	50/100000y	12	SSO OI
Northrop, 1840 Century Park E., Los Angeles, CA 90067	NOC	1.15	0	100/1000m	12	
Raytheon, 141 Spring, Lexington, MA 02173	RTN	1.20	5-2.50	Y	10/5000q	8	

	Ticker Symbol	Beta	Cost Service Fee	Cost Commission	Voluntary Cash $Minimum/ $Maximum	Frequency (per year)	Special Features
Rockwell International, 600 Grant, Pittsburgh, PA 15219	ROK	1.20	0	0	10/1000m	8	
Sunstrand, Box 7003, Rockford, IL 61125	SNS	1.20	0	0	25/3000q	12	
Van Dusen Air, 2801 E. 78th, Minneapolis, MN 55420	VAND	0.95	0	0	25/1000m	12	

B. Automotive and transportation equipment

	Ticker Symbol	Beta	Service Fee	Commission	$Minimum/ $Maximum	Frequency (per year)	Special Features
Allen Group, 534 Broad Hollow, Melville, NY 11747	ALN	0.90	0	0	25/3000q	8	
Arvin Industries, 1531 13th, Columbus, IN 47201	ARV	0.80	5-2.50	Y	25/1000q	4	
Barnes, 123 Main, Bristol, CT 06010	B	0.95	0	0	10/unlim	8	
Borg-Warner, 200 Michigan, Chicago, IL 60604	BOR	1.10	0	0	10/6000q	8	
Carlisle Corp., 250 E. 5th, Cincinnati, OH 45202	CSL	1.20	0	0	10/3000q	12	
Champion Spark Plug, 900 Upton, Toledo, OH 43661	CHM	0.85	4-2.50	Y	10/3000q	12	
Dana, Box 1000, Toledo, OH 43697	DCN	0.95	0	0	10/1000m	4	
Dayco, Box 1004, Dayton, OH 45401	DAY	0.80	0	0	25/1000q	4	
Donaldson, Box 1299, Minneapolis, MN 55440	DCI	0.95	0	0	10/1000m	12	
Eagle-Picher, Box 779, Cincinnati, OH 45201	EPI	0.85	0	0	10/1000m	12	SSO
Eaton Corp., Eaton Center, Cleveland, OH 44114	ETN	1.05	0	0	10/60000y	12	5-D SSO OI
Firestone Tire, 1200 Firestone, Akron, OH 44317	FIR	1.00	0	0	10/1000m	12	
Ford Motor, The American Rd., Dearborn, MI 48121	F	1.15	2-2.00	Y	10/1000m	12	
Gencorp, 1 General, Akron, OH 44329	GY	0.95	0	0	10/1000m	8	
General Motors, 3044 W. Grand, Detroit, MI 48202	GM	1.00	0	0	25/5000q	12	SSO OI
Goodrich (BF), 500 S. Main, Akron, OH 44318	GR	1.20	0	0	25/1000m	12	
Goodyear Tire & Rubber, 1144 E. Market, Akron, OH 44316	GT	1.00	0	0	25/5000q	12	5-D SSO OI
Premier Industries, 4500 Euclid, Cleveland, OH 44103	PRE	0.80	4-2.50	Y	10/5000q	12	
Sealed Power, Box 299, Muskegon, MI 49443	SPW	1.05	0	0	25/10000q	12	

Simpson Industries, 32100 Telegraph, Birmingham, MI 48101	SMPS	0.85	0	Y	10/1000m	12	
Smith (AO), Box 584, Milwaukee, WI 53201	SMC.A	1.00	0	0	0/5000q	8	
Standard Products, 130 W. 110th, Cleveland, OH 44102	SPD	1.15	0	0	50/3000q	4	

C. *Building materials and construction*

American Aggregates, Garst & Ave. B, Greenville, OH 45331	AMAG	0.95	0	0	10/5000q	4	SSO
American Standard, 48 W. 40th St., New York, NY 10018	AST	1.15	5-2.50	Y	10/3000q	8	
Armstrong World, Liberty, Lancaster, PA 17604	ACK	1.05	0	0	50/3000q	4	
Bank Bldg., 1130 Hampton, St. Louis, MO 63139	BB	0.80	0	0	25/1000m	12	
Blount, 4520 Executive Park, Montgomery, AL 36116	BLTA	1.00	0	0	10/25000y	12	5-D OI
Boise Cascade, 1 Jefferson, Boise, ID 83728	BCC	1.20	5-2.50	Y	25/unlim	12	
Butler Manufacturing, Box 917, Kansas City, MO 64141	BTLR	0.65	0	Y	none		
CBI Industries, 800 Jorie, Oak Brook, IL 60521	CBH	0.90	0	0	25/3000m	10	SSO
Ceco, 1400 Kennsington, Oak Brook, IL 60521	CCP	0.90	5-3.00	Y	25/1000m	12	
Champion International, 1 Champion Plaza, Stamford, CT 06921	CHA	1.30	0	0	10/5000m	12	PRF
Dravo, 1 Oliver Plaza, Pittsburgh, PA 15222	DRV	0.80	0	0	10/3000q	4	5-D SSO OI
Fluor, 3333 Michelson, Irvine, CA 92730	FLR	1.45	0	0	25/5000q	4	
General Shale, 3211 N. Roan, Johnson City, TN 37601	GSHL	0.95	5-2.50	Y	25/1000m	12	SSO
Gifford-Hill, Box 47127, Dallas, TX 75247	GFH	0.95	0	0	25/5000q	4	
Grow Group, 200 Park Ave., New York, NY 10166	GRO	0.95	0	0	20/1000q	12	
Ideal Basic Industries, Box 8789, Denver, CO 80201	IDL	0.90	0	0	25/5000m	12	5-D SSO OI
Libby-Owens-Ford, 811 Madison, Toledo, OH 43695	LOF	0.80	0	0	10/1000m	8	
Lone Star Industries, Box 5050, Greenwich, CT 06836	LCE	0.95	0	0	25/1000m	12	
McDermott International, Box 61961, New Orleans, LA 70161	MDR	1.35	0	0	25/15000q	4	SSO PRF BOND OI
Morrison-Knudsen, Box 7808, Boise, ID 83729	MRN	1.20	0	0	25/1000q	4	
National Gypsum, 4100 InterFirst Tower, Dallas, TX 75270	NG	1.05	0	0	10/30000y	4	
Nucor, 4425 Randolf, Charlotte, NC 28211	NUE	1.15	0	0	10/1000m	12	
Owens-Corning, Fiberglass Tower, Toledo, OH 43659	OCF	1.25	0	0	10/3000q	8	
Pacific Lumber, Box 7406, San Francisco, CA 94120	PL	1.15	0	0	0/1000m	12	

Dividend Reinvestment Plans

	Ticker Symbol	Beta	Cost Service Fee	Cost Commission	Voluntary Cash $Minimum/$Maximum	Frequency (per year)	Special Features
PPG Industries, 1 PPG Pl., Pittsburgh, PA 15272	PPG	1.10	0	0	10/3000q	4	OI
Robertson (HH), 2 Gateway Center, Pittsburgh, PA 15222	RHH	1.00	0	0	25/1000m	12	
RPM Inc., Box 777, Medina, OH 44258	RPOW	0.95	0	0	20/2000m	12	
Sherwin Williams, Box 6027, Cleveland, OH 44101	SHW	1.15	0	0	10/1000M	8	PRF
Stone & Webster, 90 Broad, New York, NY 10004	SW	0.75	0	0	10/3000q	12	
USG Corp., 101 S. Wacker, Chicago, IL 60606	USG	0.95	0	0	10/5000m	8	
Walter (Jim), Box 22601, Tampa, FL 33622	JWC	1.10	4-2.00	Y	10/1000m	12	
Weyerhaeuser Co., Tacoma, WA 98477	WY	1.20	4-1.50	Y	25/1000q	4	

D. Computer, electronics, and precision instruments

	Ticker Symbol	Beta	Service Fee	Commission	$Minimum/$Maximum	Frequency (per year)	Special Features
AMP, Eisenhower Blvd., Harrisburg, PA 17105	AMP	1.20	0	0	10/2000m	12	
Auto Switch, 50-56 Hanover, Florham Park, NJ 07932	ASV	0.85	0	0	10/2500q	8	
Avnet, 767 5th Ave., New York, NY 10153	AVT	1.45	0	0	10/unlim	8	PRF
Barry Wright, 1 Newton, Newton Lower Falls, MA 02162	BAR	1.10	0	0	10/1000m	12	
Bell & Howell, 7100 McCormick, Chicago, IL 60645	BHW	1.10	0	0	10/3000m	12	
Conrac, 3 Landmark, Stamford, CT 06901	CAX	0.85	0	0	10/3000q	8	
Control Data, Box 0, Minneapolis, MN 55440	CDA	1.50	0	0	10/3000m	12	
Eastman Kodak, 342 State, Rochester, NY 14650	EK	0.85	0	0	10/5000m	52	
EG & G, 45 Williams, Wellesley, MA 02181	EGG	1.40	0	0	10/1000m	12	
E-Systems, Box 226030, Dallas, TX 75266	ESY	1.20	0	0	25/5000m	12	SSO
Foxboro, 38 Neponset, Foxboro, MA 02035	FOX	1.05	0	0	10/5000q	8	
General Signal, Box 10000, Stamford, CT 06904	GSX	1.05	0	0	25/1000m	24	
Harris, 1025 W. Nasa, Melbourne, FL 32919	HRS	1.15	0	0	10/5000q	4	
Honeywell, Honeywell Plaza, Minneapolis, MN 55408	HON	1.20	0	0	10/3000m	12	
IBM, 590 Madison Ave., New York, NY 10022	IBM	1.00	0	0	10/5000q	12	OI
Johnson Controls, Box 591, Milwaukee, WI 53201	JCI	0.85	0	0	10/1500m	12	SSO PRF OI

Kollmorgen, 66 Gate House, Stamford, CT 06902	KOL	1.40	0	O	25/1000m	12	
Millipore, 80 Ashby, Bedford, MA 01730	MILI	1.15	0	O	25/3000q	4	
Moore McCormack, 1 Landmark, Stamford, CT 06901	MMR	1.15	0	O	10/3000q	12	
Motorola, 1303 E. Algonquin, Schaumburg, IL 60196	MOT	1.25	0	Y	25/3000q	12	
National Data, 1 National Data Plaza, Atlanta, GA 30329	NDTA	1.15	0	Y	25/1000q	12	
NCR, 1700 S. Patterson, Dayton, OH 45479	NCR	1.30	4-2.50	O	10/5000q	12	
Nicolet Instrument, Box 4451, Madison, WI 53711	NIC	1.25	0	O	10/1000m	12	
Pall, 77 Crescent Beach, Glen Cove, NY 11542	PLL	1.15	0	O	25/1000m	12	
Penril, 5520 Randolf, Rockville, MD 20852	PNL	0.95	0	O	10/5000q	12	OI
Perkin-Elmer, Main St., Norwalk, CT 06856	PKN	1.35	0	O	none		
Polaroid, 549 Technology, Cambridge, MA 02139	PRD	1.05	0	Y	10/3000q	4	
Ranco, 555 Metro Place N., Dublin, OH 43017	RNI	0.75	5-3.00	Y	10/3000q	4	
RCA, 29 Broadway, New York, NY 10006	RCA	1.05	3-2.50	O	0/5000q	8	
Sperry, 1290 Avenue of the Americas, New York, NY 10104	SY	1.30	0	O	25/3000q	12	5-D SSO BOND OI
TRW, 23555 Euclid, Cleveland, OH 44117	TRW	1.05	0	Y	10/1000q	8	
Varian, Box 10800, Palo Alto, CA 94303	VAR	1.40	5-2.50	Y	10/1000m	12	
Zenith Radio, 1000 Milwaukee, Glenview, IL 60025	ZE	1.25	5-3.00	Y	25/1000m	12	

E. Machinery, equipment, and supplies

Acme-Cleveland, 30195 Chagrin, Cleveland, OH 44124	AMT	0.90	0	O	10/5000q	4	
Acme Electric, 260 N. Union, Olean, NY 14760	ACE	0.80	0	O	none		10-D OI
American Hoist, 63 S. Robert, St. Paul, MN 55107	AHO	1.05	5-2.50	Y	10/1000m	12	
Apache, Foshay Tower, Minneapolis, MN 55402	APA	1.20	0	O	10/50000y	12	
Aro Corp., 1 Aro Center, Byran, OH 43506	ARO	0.55	0	O	10/3000q	4	
Black & Decker, 701 E. Joppa, Towson, MD 21204	BDK	1.10	0	O	10/3000q	4	
Briggs & Stratton, Box 702, Milwaukee, WI 53201	BGG	0.70	0	O	25/5000q	12	
Brown & Sharpe, Precision Pk., N. Kingstown, RI 02852	BNS	0.80	0	O	25/1000m	12	
Burndy, Richards Ave., Norwalk, CT 06856	BDC	0.90	0	Y	10/1000m	8	
Caterpillar Tractor, 100 N.E. Adams, Peoria, IL 61629	CAT	1.05	4-2.00	Y	10/unlim	12	
Chicago Pneumatic Tool, 6 E. 44th St., New York, NY 10017	CGG	0.75	0	O	10/500q	12	
Cincinnati Milacron, 4701 Marburg, Cincinnati, OH 45209	CMZ	1.20	0	O	25/1000m	12	

Dividend Reinvestment Plans

	Ticker Symbol	Beta	Cost Service Fee	Cost Commission	Voluntary Cash $Minimum/$Maximum	Frequency (per year)	Special Features
Clark Equipment, Circle Drive, Buchaman, MI 49107	CKL	1.00	0	0	10/3000q	4	
Colt Industries, 430 Park Ave., New York, NY 10022	COT	0.95	0	0	10/1000m	12	
Combustion Engineering, Box 9308, Stamford, CT 06904	CSP	1.20	0	0	10/12000y	12	
Cooper Industries, First City Tower, Houston, TX 77002	CBE	1.25	5-2.50	Y	25/1000m	12	PRF
Cummins Engine, Box 3005, Columbus, IN 47202	CUM	1.05	0	0	10/6000q	12	
Deere & Co., Johr. Deere, Moline, IL 61265	DE	1.10	5-2.50	Y	10/9000q	8	
Easco, 201 N. Charles, Baltimore, MD 21201	ES	0.75	0	Y	25/5000q	4	
Emerson Electric, Box 4100, St. Louis, MO 63136	EMR	0.90	0	0	25/2500q	4	
Emhart, Box 2730, Hartford, CT 06101	EMH	0.90	0	0	50/5000q	12	
Ex-Cell-O, 2855 Coolidge, Troy, MI 48084	XLO	1.05	0	0	10/3000q	4	
Federal-Mogul, Box 1966, Detroit, MI 48235	FMO	0.80	0	0	10/1000m	12	
Federal Signal, 1415 W. 22nd, Oak Brook, IL 60521	FSS	0.85	0	0	25/3000q	8	
Figgie International, 4420 Sherwin, Willoughby, OH 44094	FIGI	0.95	0	0	10/5000q	12	
FMC, 200 E. Randolf, Chicago, IL 60601	FMC	0.95	0	0	10/1000m	8	PRF
Foster Wheeler, 110 S. Orange, Livingstone, NJ 07039	FWC	1.20	0	0	10/unlim	12	
General Electric, 3135 E. Turnpike, Fairfield, CT 06431	GE	1.00	0	0	10/10000m	12	SSO OI
Gleason, Box 22970, Rochester, NY 14692	GLE	0.85	5-2.50	Y	10/1000m	12	
Gould, Gould Center, Rolling Meadows, IL 60008	GLD	1.25	0	0	10/1000m	8	
Goulds Pumps, 240 Fall, Seneca Falls, NY 13148	GULD	0.80	5-2.50	Y	10/1000m	12	
Harvey Hubbell, Box 725, Orange, CT 06477	HUB	0.85	0	0	10/1000q	12	
Ingersoll-Rand, 200 Chestnut, Woodcliff Lake, NJ 07675	IR	1.00	0	0	10/3000q	8	PRF
ITT, 320 Park Ave., New York, NY 10022	ITT	1.05	0	0	10/3000q	8	
Joy Manufacturing, 301 Grant, Pittsburgh, PA 15219	JOY	1.00	0	0	25/1000m	4	
Kennametal, Box 231, Latrobe, PA 15650	KMT	1.10	0	0	25/3000q	4	5-D OI
Keystone International, Box 40010, Houston, TX 77240	KII	0.85	0	0	50/5000q	4	OI
Kuhlman, Box 288, Birmingham, MI 48012	KUH	0.80	0	0	10/3000q	12	

Company	Code					
Massey-Ferguson, 595 Bay, Toronto, Ontario M5G2C3	MSE	0.80	5-3.00	Y	25/3000q	12	PRF
Midland-Ross, 20600 Chagrin, Cleveland, OH 44122	MLR	0.85	0	0	20/1000m	12	
Milton Roy, Box 12169, St. Petersburg, FL 33733	MRC	0.95	0	0	10/3000q	4	SSO
National Mine Service, 4900 Grant, Pittsburgh, PA 15219	NMS	0.80	4-2.50	Y	25/1000m	12	
Norton, 1 New Bend, Worcester, MA 01606	NRT	1.00	0	0	10/5000q	12	5-D SSO OI
Peabody International, Box 10063, Stamford, CT 06904	PBD	1.00	0	0	25/1000m	12	
Ransburg, Box 88511, Indianapolis, IN 46208	RBG	1.05	0	0	25/500m	12	
Rexnord, 350 N. Sunny Slope, Brookfield, WI 53005	REX	0.75	0	0	10/1000m	8	
Signal, 11255 N. Torrey Pines, LaJolla, CA 92037	SGN	1.30	0	0	10/60000y	12	SSO PRF
Square D, 1415 S. Roselle, Palatine, IL 60067	SQD	1.00	5-2.50	Y	10/1000m	8	
Standex International, 6 Manor, Salem, NH 03079	SXI	0.70	0	0	50/2500q	4	
Textron, 40 Westminster, Providence, RI 02903	TXT	1.05	0	0	25/1000m	12	
Thomas & Betts, 920 Route 202, Raritan, NJ 08869	TNB	1.00	0	0	10/3000q	4	
Timken, 1835 Dueber S.W., Canton, OH 44706	TKR	0.75	0	0	none		5-D OI
Toro, 8111 Lyndale S., Bloomington, MN 55420	TTC	0.60	0	0	10/1000m	12	
Tracor, 6500 Tracor, Austin, TX 78721	TRR	1.50	0	0	30/5000q	12	5-D+VC OI
Twin Disc, 1328 Racine, Racine, WI 53403	TDI	0.50	0	0	10/2000m	8	
Van Dorn, Box 5110, Cleveland, OH 44101	VDC	0.60	0	0	50/3000q	unlim	
White Consolidated, 11770 Berea, Cleveland, OH 44111	WSW	1.00	5-2.50	Y	10/1000m	8	
Zurn Industries, 1 Zurn, Erie, PA 16512	ZRN	0.95	5-2.50	Y	10/3000q	4	

V. Materials

A. Chemical

Company	Code					
Air Products & Chemicals, Box 538, Allentown, PA 18105	APD	1.20	0	0	50/3000q	12	
American Cyanamid, Berdan Avenue, Wayne, NJ 07470	ACY	1.10	0	0	10/1000m	12	SSO
Cabot, 125 High, Boston, MA 02110	CBT	1.30	0	0	10/5000q	8	
Celanese, 1211 Avenue of the Americas, New York, NY 10036	CZ	0.90	0	0	10/1000q	12	
Chemed, 1200 DuBois Tower, Cincinnati, OH 45202	CHE	0.80	0	0	10/1000m	12	
Crompton & Knowles, 345 Park Ave., New York, NY 10154	CNK	0.75	0	0	30/3000q	4	

Dividend Reinvestment Plans

	Ticker Symbol	Beta	Cost Service Fee	Commission	Voluntary Cash $Minimum/$Maximum	Frequency (per year)	Special Features
Dexter, One Elm, Windsor Locks, CT 06096	DEX	0.80	0	0	25/3000q	12	
Dow Chemical, 2030 Dow Center, Midland, MI 48640	DOW	1.20	4-2.00	Y	10/10000q	12	
Dupont (E.I.), 1007 Market, Wilmington, DE 19898	DD	1.15	5-3.00	Y	10/1000m	12	PRF
Ethyl, 330 S. Fourth, Richmond, VA 23217	EY	0.90	0	0	25/1000q	12	PRF
Ferro, 1 Erieview, Cleveland, OH 44114	FOE	0.90	0	0	0/3000q	unlim	
First Mississippi, Box 1249, Jackson, MS 39205	FRM	1.45	0	0	25/3000m	12	
Freeport-McMoRan, 200 Park Ave., New York, NY 10166	FTX	1.40	0	0	10/1000m	12	
Fuller (H.B.), 2400 Kasota, St. Paul, MN 55108	FULL	0.90	0	0	10/1000q	12	
GAF, 140 W. 51st St., New York, NY 10020	GAF	1.00	0	0	10/25000y	8	PRF
Grace (W.R.), Grace Plaza, New York, NY 10036	GRA	1.05	0	0	50/60000y	12	SSO PRF OI
Hercules, Hercules Plaza, Wilmington, DE 19894	HPC	1.15	0	0	10/2000m	12	
International Minerals, 2315 Sanders, Northbrook, IL 60062	IGL	0.95	0	0	10/1000m	12	
Koppers, 601 Koppers Bldg., Pittsburgh, PA 15219	KOP	1.10	0	0	25/1000m	12	PRF
Loctite, 705 N. Mountain, Newington, CT 06111	LOC	1.00	0	0	25/1000m	12	
MacDermid, Box 671, Waterbury, CT 06720	MACD	0.95	0	0	50/unlim	4	SSO
Minnesota Mining, 3M Center, St. Paul, MN 55144	MMM	1.00	5-2.50	Y	10/3000q	12	
Monsanto, 800 N. Lindbergh, St. Louis, MO 63167	MTC	1.00	3-2.00	Y	10/3000q	12	
National Distillers, 99 Park Ave., New York, NY 10016	DR	0.75	0	0	10/3000m	12	OI
Oakite Products, 50 Valley, Berkeley Heights, NJ 07922	OKT	0.55	0	0	25/1000m	12	
Olin, Box 1355, Stamford, CT 06904	OLN	1.20	5-2.50	Y	10/1000m	8	
Pennwalt, Three Parkway, Philadelphia, PA 19102	PSM	0.80	4-2.50	Y	10/1000m	12	
Union Carbide, Old Ridgebury, Danbury, CT 06817	UK	1.10	0	0	25/50000y	12	SSO OI
Williams Companies, Box 2400, Tulsa, OK 74102	WMB	1.15	0	0	10/5000m	12	OI
Witco Chemical, 520 Madison, New York, NY 10022	WIT	0.90	0	0	10/3000q	4	

B. *Mining, refining*

Alcan Aluminum, 1188 Sherbrooke, Montreal, Quebec H3A3G2	AL	1.20	0	50/1500q	4	SSO OI
Aluminum of America, 1501 Alcoa Bldg., Pittsburgh, PA 15219	AA	1.05	0	25/1000m	12	
AMAX, Amax Center, Greenwich, CT 06836	AMX	1.30	0	25/5000q	12	5-D SSO OI
ASARCO, 120 Broadway, New York, NY 10271	AR	1.35	0	25/1000m	12	SSO
Brush Wellman, 1200 Hanna Bldg., Cleveland, OH 44115	BW	0.90	0	10/5000q	4	
Cleveland-Cliffs, Huntington Bldg., Cleveland, OH 44115	CLF	0.95	0	10/5000q	4	
Eastern Gas & Fuel, 1 Beacon, Boston, MA 02108	EFU	1.00	0	10/3000q	4	5-D OI
Engelhard, Menlo Park, Edison, NJ 08818	EC	0.95	5-2.50	10/3000q	4	
Handy & Harman, 850 Third Ave., New York, NY 10022	HNH	1.25	0	10/60000y	12	
Homestake Mining, 650 California, San Francisco, CA 94108	HM	1.30	4-1.50	25/1000q	4	
Inco Ltd., 1 New York Plaza, New York, NY 10004	N	1.25	0	30/5200q	4	5-D SSO OI
Newmont Mining, 200 Park Ave., New York, NY 10166	NEM	1.20	1.50	10/1000m	8	
Phelps Dodge, 300 Park Ave., New York, NY 10022	PD	1.45	0	10/2000q	4	
Reynolds Metals, 6601 Broad, Richmond, VA 23261	RLM	1.00	0	25/3000q	12	

C. *Iron and steel mills, metal fabricating*

Armco, 703 Curtis, Middletown, OH 45043	AS	0.95	0	25/5000q	4	OI
Bethlehem Steel, Bethlehem, PA 18016	BS	1.30	0	10/3000q	12	
Carpenter Tech. Box 662, Reading, PA 19603	CRS	0.95	0	10/3000q	4	
Copperweld, 2 Oliver Plaza, Pittsburgh, PA 15222	COS	0.85	0	10/3000q	4	
Cyclops, 650 Washington, Pittsburgh, PA 15228	CYL	0.90	0	50/3000q	4	
Eastern, 112 Bridge, Naugatuck, CT 06770	EML	1.15	0	25/3000q	4	SSO
Harsco, 350 Popular Church, Camp Hill, PA 17011	HSC	0.60	0	10/unlim	12	
Inland Steel, 30 W. Monroe, Chicago, IL 60603	IAD	0.95	0	25/10000m	16	
Interlake, 2015 Spring, Oak Brook, IL 60521	IK	0.60	0	25/5000q	4	5-D OI
Lukens, 50 S. 5th, Coatsville, PA 19320	LUC	0.90	0	50/3000q	12	SSO
National-Standard, 1618 Terminal, Niles, MI 49120	LUC	0.80	0	50/3000q	12	SSO
Quanex, 1900 W. Loop S., Houston, TX 77027	NX	1.30	0	10/1000m	12	

			Cost		Dividend Reinvestment Plans		
					Voluntary Cash		
	Ticker Symbol	Beta	Service Fee	Commission	$Minimum/ $Maximum	Frequency (per year)	Special Features
SIFCO, 970 E. 64th, Cleveland, OH 44103	SIF	1.20	0	0	0/3000q	unlim	
Triangle, Holmdel, NJ 07733	TRI	0.70	4-1.50	Y	10/1000m	4	
US Steel, 700 Grant, Pittsburgh, PA 15230	X	1.05	0	0	50/3000q	4	OI
Zero Corp., Box 509, Burbank, CA 91503	ZRO	1.05	0	Y	25/1000m	24	

D. Paper, forest products, packaging

American Can, Box 3600, Greenwich, CT 06836	AC	0.90	0	0	10/1000m	12	
Ball, 345 S. High, Muncie, IN 47302	BLL	0.65	0	0	25/3000q	4	5-D OI
Bemis, 800 Northstar, Minneapolis, MN 55402	BMS	0.75	0	0	25/1000m	12	PRF
Brockway, McCullough, Brockway, PA 15824	BRK	0.75	5-2.50	Y	10/3000q	12	
Chesapeake Corp., Box 311, West Point, VA 23181	CSK	0.95	0	0	10/5000q	12	
Clevepak, 2500 Westchester, Purchase, NY 10577	CLV	0.80	0	0	10/3000q	12	5-D+VC PRF OI
Crown Zellerback, 1 Bush, San Francisco, CA 94104	ZB	1.20	0	0	25/1000m	12	SSO
Dennison, 275 Wyman, Waltham, MA 02254	DSN	0.75	0	0	10/3000q	4	
Domtar, 395 de Maisonneave, Montreal, Quebec H3A1L6	DTC	0.85	0	0	50/4000q	4	5-D
Engraph, 2635 Century N.E., Atlanta, GA 30345	ENGH	0.90	0	0	25/5000q	4	OI
Federal Paper Board, Box 357, Montvale, NJ 07645	FBO	0.90	5-2.50	Y	10/3000q	4	PRF
Fort Howard Paper, Box 130, Green Bay, WI 54305	FHP	0.95	0	0	25/1000m	12	
Great Northern Nekoosa, Box 9309, Stamford, CT 06904	GNN	1.00	0	0	10/1000m	4	
Hammermill Paper, 1540 E. Lake, Erie, PA 16533	HML	0.85	0	0	10/5000m	8	
International Pape:, 77 W. 45th St., New York, NY 10036	IP	1.15	0	0	25/20000y	12	SSO OI
Kimberly-Clark, 401 N. Lake, Neenah, WI 54956	KMB	0.80	5-2.50	Y	10/3000q	8	
Mead, Courthouse Plaza, Dayton, OH 45463	MEA	1.05	0	0	25/5000q	12	PRF
Owens-Illinois, 1 Seagate, Toledo, OH 43666	OI	0.85	0	Y	10/5000q	12	
Papercraft, Papercraft Park, Pittsburgh, PA 15238	PCT	0.90	0	0	10/1000q	4	
Peerless Tube, 58-76 Locust, Bloomfield, NJ 07003	PLS	0.90	0	0	10/1000q	4	

Company	Ticker	Price	Div	Y/N	Shares/Value	Qty	Notes
Pentair, 1700 W. Hwy 36, St. Paul, MN 55113	PNTA	0.80	0	0	10/3000q	12	
Potlatch, Box 3591, San Francisco, CA 94119	PCH	1.10	0	0	25/1000m	12	
Rexham, Box 2528, Charlotte, NC 28211	RXH	0.90	0	0	10/1000m	8	
Scott Paper, 1 Scott, Philadelphia, PA 19113	SPP	1.00	5-2.50	Y	10/3000q	4	
Sonoco, N. 2nd, Hartsville, SC 29550	SONO	0.75	0	Y	10/500m	12	
Union Camp, 1600 Valley, Wayne, NJ 07470	UCC	1.05	0.	0	25/4000m	12	
Westvaco, 299 Park Ave., New York, NY 10171	W	1.00	0	0	0/5000q	12	SSO OI

E. *Petroleum, oilfield services*

Company	Ticker	Price	Div	Y/N	Shares/Value	Qty	Notes
Allied Corp., Park & Columbia, Morristown, NJ 07960	ALD	1.10	0	0	25/5000q	12	SSO OI
Amerada Hess, 1185 Avenue of the Americas, New York, NY 10036	AHC	1.55	0	0	50/5000q	12	
American Petrofina, Fina Plaza, Dallas, TX 75206	APIA	1.15	5-2.50	Y	10/1000m	12	
AMOCO, Box 5910-A, Chicago, IL 60680	SN	1.25	5-3.00	Y	10/3000m	12	
Ashland Oil, Box 12328, Lexington, KY 40582	ASH	1.15	0	0	10/5000q	8	5-D PRF OI
Atlantic Richfield, 515 S. Flower, Los Angeles, CA 90071	ARC	1.20	5-2.50	Y	10/1000m	12	PRF
Baker International, 500 City Pkwy., Orange, CA 92667	BKO	1.40	0	0	10/1000q	4	
Chevron, 225 Bush, San Francisco, CA 94104	CHV	1.15	4-2.50	Y	25/1000m	12	
Diamond Shamrock, 717 N. Harwood, Dallas, TX 75201	DIA	1.10	0	0	10/10000q	4	
Dresser Industries, Box 718, Dallas, TX 75221	DI	1.25	0	0	25/1000m	12	OI
Exxon, 1251 Avenue of the Americas, New York, NY 10020	XON	0.85	0	0	10/60000y	12	SSO OI
GEO International, 1 Landmark, Stamford, CT 06901	GX	1.40	0	0	25/1000m	12	
Hughes Tool, 6500 Texas Com. Twr., Houston, TX 77002	HT	1.50	5-3.00	Y	25/1000m	12	
Imperial Oil, 111 St. Clair, Toronto, Ontario M5W1K3	IMOA	1.00	0	0	50/5000q	4	5-D OI
Kaneb Services, 14141 Southwest, Sugarland, TX 77478	KAB	1.25	0	0	25/3000m	12	OI
Kerr-McGee, Kerr-McGee Ctr., Oklahoma City, OK 73125	KMG	1.15	5-2.50	Y	10/1000m	8	
MAPCO, 1800 S. Baltimore, Tulsa, OK 74119	MDA	0.95	0	0	10/3000q	12	
Mobil, 150 E. 42nd St., New York, NY 10017	MOB	1.15	0	0	10/3000m	12	
NL Ind., 230 Avenue of the Americas, New York, NY 10020	NL	1.50	0	0	20/2000m	8	
NOVA, Box 2535, Calgary, Alberta T2P2N6	NVA.A	0.90	0	0	50/5000q	4	5-D PRF OI
Occidental Petroleum, 10889 Wilshire, Los Angeles, CA 90024	OXY	1.05	5-3.00	Y	10/1000m	12	

… Dividend Reinvestment Plans

	Ticker Symbol	Beta	Service Fee	Commission	$Minimum/$Maximum	Frequency (per year)	Special Features
Pennzoil, Box 2967, Houston, TX 77252	PZL	1.20	0	0	40/6000q	4	
Phibro-Salomon, 1221 Avenue of the Americas, New York, NY 10020	PSB	2.00	0	0	10/3000q	4	
Phillips Petroleum, Phillips Building, Bartlesville, OK 74004	P	1.15	0	0	10/3000q	8	
Quaker State, Box 989, Oil City, PA 16301	KSF	1.15	0	0	10/3000q	12	
Reading & Bates, 2200 Mid-Continent, Tulsa, OK 74103	RB	1.65	0	0	10/5000m	12	
Shell Oil, Box 2463, Houston, TX 77001	SVO	1.10	0	0	50/3000q	4	
Smith International, Box 1860, Newport Beach, CA 92660	SII	1.30	0	Y	none		
Southland Royalty, 801 Cherry, Ft. Worth, TX 76102	SRO	0.95	5-2.50	Y	10/3000q	4	
Standard Oil Ohio, Midland Building, Cleveland, OH 44115	SOH	1.20	0	Y	20/5000q	12	
Sun, 1801 Market, Philadelphia, PA 19103	SUN	1.20	0	Y	0/10000q	12	PRF
Texaco, 2000 Westchester, White Plains, NY 10650	TX	0.90	0	Y	10/25000y	4	
Tidewater, 1440 Canal, New Orleans, LA 70112	TDW	1.40	5-2.50	Y	25/5000q	8	
Unocal, Box 3235, Los Angeles, CA 90051	UCL	1.30	5-2.00	Y	25/1000	12	

VI. Public Utilities

A. *Electric (East)*

	Ticker Symbol	Beta	Service Fee	Commission	$Minimum/$Maximum	Frequency (per year)	Special Features
Allegheny Power, 320 Park Ave., New York, NY 10022	APY	0.65	0	0	50/5000q	4	OI
Atlantic City Electric, Box 1334, Pleasantville, NJ 08232	ATE	0.50	0	Y-VC	0/20000y	12	SSO OI
Baltimore Gas & Electric, Box 1475, Baltimore, MD 21203	BGE	0.60	0	Y-VC	10/6000q	12	5-D SSO PRF OI
Boston Edison, 800 Boylston, Boston, MA 02199	BSE	0.50	0	0	0/5000q	4	
Central Hudson G&E, 284 South Ave., Poughkeepsie, NY 12602	CNH	0.60	0	0	10/3000q	4	OI

Central Maine Power, Edison, Augusta, ME 04336	CTP	0.55	0	10/20000y	12	5-D SSO PRF OI
Central Vermont PS, 77 Grove, Rutland, VT 05701	CV	0.45	0	25/5000q	4	5-D SSO PRF OI
Commonwealth, 675 Massachusetts, Cambridge, MA 02139	CES	0.65	0	10/5000q	12	OI
Consolidated Edison, 4 Irving Place, New York, NY 10003	ED	0.65	0	20/3000q	12	OI
Delmarva Power, Box 231, Wilmington, DE 19899	DEW	0.50	0	25/3000q	12	5-D PRF OI
Duquesne Light, 1 Oxford, Pittsburgh, PA 15279	DQV	0.50	0	10/5000q	8	5-D SSO OI
Eastern Utilities, Box 2333, Boston, MA 02107	EUA	0.60	0	0/5000q	12	5-D SSO PRF OI
Fitchburg G&E, 120 Royal, Canton, MA 02021	FGE	0.60	0	25/3000q	4	5-D OI
Green Mountain Power, Box 850, So. Burlington, VT 05402	GMP	0.70	0	10/2000q	4	5-D OI
Long Island Light, 250 Old County, Mineola, NY 11501	LIL	0.65	0	10/5000q	4	5-D SSO OI
New England Electric, Box 770, Westborough, MA 01581	NES	0.45	0	25/5000m	12	5-D OI
New York E&G, Box 287, Ithaca, NY 14851	NGE	0.55	0	10/5000q	12	SSO OI
Newport Electric, Box 4128, Middletown, RI 02840	NPT	0.65	0	10/2 mil. y	12	SSO OI
Niagara Mohawk Power, 300 Erie Blvd., Syracuse, NY 13202	NMK	0.65	0	25/30000y	12	SSO OI
Northeast Utilities, Box 270, Hartford, CT 06141	NU	0.55	0	0/100000y	12	PRF OI
Orange & Rockland Utilities, 1 Blue Hill, Pearl River, NY 10965	ORV	0.55	0	25/5000q	12	PRF
Pennsylvania P&L, 2 N. 9th, Allentown, PA 18101	PPL	0.60	0	0/15000q	12	PRF OI
Philadelphia Electric, Box 8699, Philadelphia, PA 19101	PE	0.55	0	25/50000y	4	
Potomac Electric, 1900 Pennsylvania, Washington, D.C. 20068	POM	0.55	1.35	Y	25/3000m	12
Public Service E&G, 80 Park, Newark, NJ 07101	PEG	0.60	0	25/20000y	12	5-D SSO PRF OI
Rochester G&E, 89 East, Rochester, NY 14649	RGS	0.50	0	10/5000m	12	SSO OI
TNP, 501 W. 6th, Ft. Worth, TX 76102	TNP	0.55	0	25/5000q	12	SSO OI
United Illuminating, Box 1564, New Haven, CT 06506	UIL	0.65	0	10/10000q	4	SSO OI

A. *Electric (Midwest)*

American Electric Power, Box 116631, Columbus, OH 43216	AEP	0.60	0	0/5000q	12	5-D SSO OI
CILCORP, 300 Liberty, Peoria, IL 61602	CER	0.55	0	25/5000q	12	PRF BOND OI

Dividend Reinvestment Plans

			Cost		Voluntary Cash		
	Ticker Symbol	Beta	Service Fee	Commission	$Minimum/ $Maximum	Frequency (per year)	Special Features
Central Illinois PS., 607 E. Adams, Springfield, IL 62701	CIP	0.55	0	0	none		PRF OI
Cincinnati G&E, Box 960, Cincinnati, OH 45201	CIN	0.60	0	0	25/40000y	4	SSO PRF OI
Cleveland Electric, Box 5000, Cleveland, OH 44101	CVX	0.55	0	0	10/40000y	4	SSO PRF OI
Commonwealth Edison, Box 767, Chicago, IL 60690	CWE	0.60	0	0	25/3000q	4	5-D SSO OI
Consumers Power, 212 W. Michigan, Jackson, MI 49201	CMS	0.80	0	0	25/40000y	12	PRF OI
Dayton P&L, Box 1247, Dayton, OH 45401	DPL	0.60	0	0	25/1000q	4	PRF OI
Detroit Edison, 2000 2nd, Detroit, MI 48226	DTE	0.65	0	0	20/5000m	12	5-D PRF OI
Duriron, Box 1145, Dayton, OH 45401	DURI	0.75	0	0	10/1000m	12	
Empire District Electric, 602 Joplin, Joplin, MO 64801	EDE	0.40	0	0	50/3000q	4	5-D PRF OI
Illinois Power, 500 S. 27th, Decatur, IL 62525	IPC	0.60	0	0	25/5000q	12	5-D PRF BOND OI
Interstate Power, 1000 Main, Dubuque, IA 52001	IPW	0.50	0	0	25/3000q	4	SSO OI
Iowa Electric L&P, Box 351, Cedar Rapids, IA 52406	IEL	0.55	0	0	25/5000m	12	5-D OI
Iowa-Illinois G&E, Box 4350, Davenport, IA 52808	IWG	0.50	0	0	25/5000q	4	5-D OI
Iowa Resources, Box 657, Des Moines, IA 50303	IOR	0.50	0	Y-VC	10/5000m	12	SSO OI
IPALCO, Box 1595B, Indianapolis, IN 46206	IPL	0.60	0	0	25/3000m	12	OI
Kansas City P&L, Box 679, Kansas City, MO 64141	KLT	0.60	0	0	25/1000q	4	5-D SSO PRF OI
Madison G&E, 100 N. Fairchild, Madison, WI 53701	MDSN	0.70	0	0	none		OI
Midwest Energy, Box 1348, Sioux City, IA 51102	MWE	0.50	0	0	10/10000q	12	PRF OI
Minnesota P&L, 30 W. Superior, Duluth, MN 55802	MPL	0.55	0	0	10/5000q	12	5-D OI
Missouri PS, Box 11739, Kansas City, MO 64138	MPV	0.50	0	0	100/5000q	12	OI
Northern Indiana PS, 5265 Hohman, Hammond, IN 46320	NI	0.65	0	0	25/5000q	4	5-D OI
Northern States, 414 Nicollet, Minneapolis, MN 55401	NSP	0.60	0	0	10/5000q	12	PRF OI
Ohio Edison, 76 S. Main, Akron, OH 44308	OEC	0.60	0	0	10/40000y	12	5-D OI
Otter Tail, 215 S. Cascade, Fergus Falls, MN 56537	OTTR	0.60	0	0	10/1000m	12	5-D 3-D VC PRF OI
St. Joseph L&P, 520 Francis, St. Joseph, MO 64502	SAJ	0.45	0	0	10/3000q	4	PRF OI
Southern Indiana G&E, Box 569, Evansville, IN 47741	SIG	0.60	0	0	25/5000m	12	OI

Toledo Edison, 300 Madison, Toledo, OH 43652	TED	0.50	0	10/5000q	4	5-D	
Union Electric, Box 149, St. Louis, MO 63166	UEP	0.55	0	10/5000m	12	SSO PRF	
Upper Peninsula Power, 616 Shelden, Houghton, MI 49931	UPEN	0.65	0	50/3000q	4	PRF OI	
Wisconsin Electric, Box 2046, Milwaukee, WI 53201	WPC	0.60	0	25/3000m	12	5-D SSO PRF OI	
Wisconsin P&L, Box 192, Madison, WI 53701	WPL	0.55	0	20/3000m	12		

A. *Electric (South)*

Carolina P&L, 411 Fayetteville, Raleigh, NC 27602	CPL	0.65	0	25/2000m	12	3-D+VC SSO PRF	
Central Louisiana Electric, 415 Main, Pineville, LA 71360	CNL	0.55	0	25/5000m	12	5-D SSO PRF OI	
Dominion Resources, Box 26532, Richmond, VA 23261	D	0.50	0	0/5000q	12	SSO OI	
Duke Power, Box 33189, Charlotte, NC 28242	DUK	0.50	0	25/3000q	12	SSO OI	
FPL, Box 029100, Miami, FL 33102	FPL	0.65	0	25/5000q	4	5-D SSO PRF OI	
Florida Progress, Box 33042, St. Petersburg, FL 33733	FPC	0.65	0	10/2000m	12	5-D SSO OI	
Kentucky Utilities, 1 Quality, Lexington, KY 40507	KV	0.50	0	20/10000q	4	SSO OI	
Louisville G&E, Box 32010, Louisville, KY 40232	LOU	0.55	0	25/5000q	12	5-D SSO PRF OI	
Middle South Utilities, Box 61005, New Orleans, LA 70161	MSU	0.80	0	25/5000q	12	5-D SSO PRF OI	
Savannah Electric, Box 968, Savannah, GA 31402	SAV	0.60	0	25/3000q	4	SSO OI	
SCANA, Box 764, Columbia, SC 29218	SCG	0.60	Y	25/3000q	4	SSO	
Southern, 64 Perimeter Center, Atlanta, GA 30346	SO	0.60	0	25/6000q	12	5-D OI	
TECO Energy, Box 111, Tampa, FL 33601	TE	0.65	0	30/6000q	4	5-D 3-DVC SSO OI	

A. *Electric (West)*

Arizona Public Service, 411 N. Central, Phoenix, AZ 85036	AZP	0.75	0	0/25000q	12	SSO PRF OI	
Black Hills P&L, 625 9th, Rapid City, SD 57709	BHP	0.45	0	25/5000q	4	5-D OI	
Cntrl & Southwest, 2121 San Jacinto, Dallas, TX 75222	CSR	0.60	0	10/5000q	12	SSO OI	
CP National, 120 Montgomery, San Francisco, CA 94104	CPN	0.65	0	25/1000q	4	5-D PRF OI	
El Paso Electric, Box 982, El Paso, TX 79960	ELPA	0.65	0	25/3000q	12	OI	
Gulf States Utilities, Box 2951, Beaumont, TX 77704	GSU	0.65	0	25/9000q	12	SSO PRF OI	
Hawaiian Electric, Box 730, Honolulu, HI 96808	HE	0.55	0	100/5000q	4	5-D OI	
Houston Industries, 611 Walker, Houston, TX 77002	HOU	0.65	0	50/6000q	12	OI	
Idaho Power, Box 70, Boise, ID 83707	IDA	0.60	0	25/1000m	12	SSO OI	
Kansas G&E, Box 208, Wichita, KS 67201	KGE	0.60	0	25/5000q	12	5-D SSO PRF OI	

215

Dividend Reinvestment Plans

	Ticker Symbol	Beta	Cost Service Fee	Cost Commission	Voluntary Cash $Minimum/$Maximum	Frequency (per year)	Special Features
Kansas P&L, Box 889, Topeka, KS 66601	KAN	0.60	0	0	25/3000q	4	5-D OI
MDU Resources, 400 N. 4th, Bismark, ND 58501	MDU	0.65	0	0	50/5000q	4	5-D SSO OI
Montana Power, 40 E. Broadway, Butte, MT 59701	MTP	0.65	0	0	10/2000m	12	5-D SSO PRF OI
Nevada Power, Box 230, Las Vegas, NV 89151	NVP	0.50	0	0	50/5000q	4	5-D PRF OI
Northwestern PS, 400 Northwestern Bldg., Huron, SD 57350	NWPS	0.65	0	0	10/5000q	4	5-D OI
Oklahoma G&E, Box 321, Oklahoma City, OK 73101	OGE	0.55	0	0	25/1000q	4	OI
Pacific G&E, 77 Beale, San Francisco, CA 94106	PCG	0.60	0	0	25/2500m	12	PRF OI
Pacificorp, 851 S.W. 6th, Portland, OR 97204	PPW	0.65	0	0	25/5000q	12	SSO OI
Portland General Electric, 121 S.W. Salmon, Portland, OR 97204	PGN	0.55	0	0	50/3000q	4	SSO OI
Public Service Colorado, Box 840, Denver, CO 80201	PSR	0.60	0	0	10/5000m	12	PRF
Public Service of NM, Alvarado Sq., Albuquerque, NM 87158	PNM	0.55	0	0	0/24000y	4	3-D SSO PRF OI
Puget Sound P&L, Puget Power Bldg., Bellevue, WA 98009	PSD	0.55	0	0	25/5000q	12	5-D OI
San Diego G&E, Box 1831, San Diego, CA 92112	SDO	0.55	0	0	25/5000q	12	3-D SSO OI
Sierra Pacific Resources, Box 30150, Reno, NV 89520	SRP	0.45	0	0	25/5000q	4	OI
Southern California Edison, Box 400, Rosemead, CA 91770	SCE	0.65	0	0	0/5000q	4	5-D OI
Southwestern Electric, Mercantile Bldg., Dallas, TX 75201	SWEL	0.65	0	0	25/3000q	12	5-D SSO OI
Southwestern PS, Box 1261, Amarillo, TX 79170	SPS	0.55	0	0	25/3000q	12	5-D SSO OI
Texas Utilities, 2001 Byran Tower, Dallas, TX 75201	TXU	0.65	0	0	25/3000q	4	5-D OI
TNP Enterprises, Box 2943, Fort Worth, TX 76113	TNP	0.55	0	0	25/5000q	12	SSO OI
Tucson Electric, Box 711, Tucson, AZ 85702	TEP	0.55	0	0	25/5000q	12	PRF OI
Utah P&L, Box 899, Salt Lake City, UT 84110	UTP	0.55	0	0	25/10000q	12	
Washington Water, Box 3727, Spokane, WA 99220	WWP	0.45	0	0	0/5000q	12	OI

B. *Gas*

Alagasco, 1918 1st Ave., Birmingham, AL 35295	AGA	0.45	0	25/5000q	12	SSO OI
Arkla, Box 21734, Shreveport, LA 71151	ALG	1.10	5-2.50	10/unlim	8	Y
Atlanta Gas Lt., Box 4569, Atlanta, GA 30302	AGLT	0.55	0	25/5000q	12	SSO OI
Bay State Gas, 120 Royall, Canton, MA 02021	BGC	0.50	0	25/5000q	4	5-D SSO OI
Berkshire Gas, 115 Cheshire, Pittsfield, MA 01201	BGAS	0.75	0	15/1500q	12	SSO OI
Brooklyn Union, 195 Montague, Brooklyn, NY 11201	BU	0.55	0	10/5000m	12	SSO PRF
Cascade National Gas, 222 Fairview, Seattle, WA 98109	CGC	0.45	0	25/3000q	4	SSO OI
Columbia Gas, 20 Manchanin, Wilmington, DE 19807	CG	0.75	0	10/5000q	8	OI
Connecticut Energy, 880 Broad, Bridgeport, CT 06609	CNE	0.45	0	25/3000q	4	SSO OI
Connecticut Natural Gas, Box 1500, Hartford, CT 06144	CTG	0.50	0	10/5000q	12	PRF OI
Consolidated Natural Gas, 4 Gateway, Pittsburgh, PA 15222	CNG	0.65	0	25/3000q	4	SSO OI
Diversified Energies, 201 S. 7th, Minneapolis, MN 55402	DEI	0.30	0	none		OI
Ensearch Corp., 300 S. St. Paul, Dallas, TX 75201	ENS	1.10	0	10/15000q	8	
Entex, Box 2628, Houston, TX 77001	ETX	1.05	0	25/1000m	12	OI
Equitable Resources, 420 Blvd. of Allies, Pittsburgh, PA 15219	EQT	0.80	0	10/3000q	8	OI
Florida Public Utilities, Drawer C.W., Palm Beach, FL 33402	FPUT	0.55	0	25/2000q	4	SSO OI
Houston Natural Gas, Box 1188, Houston, TX 77001	HNG	0.85	5-2.50	25/1000m	12	Y
Indiana Gas, 1630 N. Meridian, Indianapolis, IN 46202	IGC	0.50	0	25/3000q	4	OI
Intermountain Gas, Box 7608, Boise, ID 83707	IMMT	0.65	0	10/1500q	4	OI
Internorth, 2223 Dodge, Omaha, NE 68102	INI	1.05	0	10/5000q	4	OI
KN Energy, Box 15265, Lakewood, CO 80215	KNE	1.10	0	5/3000q	12	5-D PRF OI
Laclede Gas, 720 Olive, St. Louis, MO 63101	LG	0.60	0	none		
Louisiana General Service, Box 433, Harvey, LA 70059	LGS	0.65	5-2.50	10/1000m	8	Y
Michigan Energy, Box 729, Monroe, MI 48161	MCG	0.35	0	10/3000q	4	5-D OI
Midcon, Box 1207, Lombard, IL 60148	MCN	0.85	0	25/3000q	4	5-D OI
Mobile Gas, 2828 Dauphin, Mobile, AL 36606	MBLE	0.65	0	none		SSO OI
Natural Fuel Gas, 30 Rockefeller, New York, NY 10112	NFG	0.65	0	25/1000q	4	PRF
NICOR, Box 200, Naperville, IL 60540	GAS	0.70	0	25/5000m	4	SSO PRF OI

217

Dividend Reinvestment Plans

	Ticker Symbol	Beta	Cost Service Fee	Cost Commission	Voluntary Cash $Minimum/$Maximum	Frequency (per year)	Special Features
Northwest Natural Gas, 220 N.W. 2nd, Portland, OR 92709	NWNG	0.80	0	0	25/5000q	12	SSO OI
NUI, 1 Elizabethtown, Elizabeth, NJ 07207	NUI	0.55	0	0	10/3000q	12	5-D SSO OI
ONEOK, Box 871, Tulsa, OK 74102	OKE	0.75	0	0	25/5000q	12	5-D SSO PRF OI
Pacific Lighting, Box 60043, Los Angeles, CA 90060	PLT	0.65	0	0	10/5000q	12	SSO PRF OI
Panhandle Eastern, Box 1642, Houston, TX 77251	PEL	1.05	0	0	25/60000y	12	5-D SSO OI
Pennsylvania Ent., 39 Public, Wilkes-Barre, PA 18711	PENT	0.65	0	0	10/5000q	8	SSO OI
Peoples Energy, 122 S. Michigan, Chicago, IL 60603	PGL	0.65	0	0	25/3000q	4	
Piedmont Natural Gas, Box 33068, Charlotte, NC 28233	PNY	0.35	0	0	25/3000q	4	5-D+VC OI
Primark, 8251 Greensboro, McLean, VA 22102	PMK	0.65	0	0	10/25000y	12	PRF OI
Providence Energy, 100 Weybosset, Providence, RI 02903	PVY	0.75	0	0	25/5000q	12	OI
Public Service of North Carolina, Box 1398, Gastonia, NC 28053	PSNC	0.70	0	0	25/3000q	12	5-D PRF OI
S.E. Michigan Gas, 405 Water, Port Huron, MI 48060	SMGS	0.70	0	0	60/3000q	4	OI
Sonat, Box 2563, Birmingham, AL 35202	SNT	0.80	0	0	10/6000q	8	
South Jersey Industries, 1 South Jersey, Folsom, NJ 08037	SJI	0.50	0	0	25/20000y	4	5-D+VC SSO OI
Southern Union, Interfirst Twr., Dallas, TX 75270	SUG	0.95	0	0	10/3000q	4	
Southwest Gas, Box 15015, Las Vegas, NV 89114	SWX	0.40	0	0	10/20000y	12	OI
Southwestern Energy, Box 1408, Fayetteville, AK 72702	SWN	0.85	5-3.00	Y	25/1000m	12	
Tenneco, Box 2511, Houston, TX 77001	TGT	1.10	0	0	10/3000q	4	5-D SSO PRF OI
Texas Eastern, Box 2521, Houston, TX 77252	TET	1.00	0	0	10/3000q	8	SSO PRF OI
Trans Canada Pipelines, Box 54, Toronto, Ontario M5L1C2	TRP	0.80	0	0	50/3000q	4	5-D OI
UGI, Box 858, Valley Forge, PA 19482	UGI	0.75	0	0	25/3000q	12	5-D SSO PRF OI
United Cities, 1200 Parkway Twr., Nashville, TN 37219	UCIT	0.70	0	0	25/3000q	12	5-D PRF OI
United Energy, Box 1478, Houston, TX 77001	UER	1.15	5-2.50	Y	10/1000m	8	

Valley Resources, 1595 Mendes, Cumberland, RI 02864	VR	0.55	0	0	25/5000m	12	5-D SSO OI
Washington Energy, Box 1869, Seattle, WA 98111	WECO	0.80	0	0	25/3000q	4	5-D OI
Washington Gas Lt., 1100 H St., N.W., Washington, D.C. 20080	WGL	0.55	0	0	25/6000q	12	PRF OI
WICOR, Box 334, Milwaukee, WI 53201	WIC	0.70	0	0	25/3000q	4	PRF OI
Wisconsin Southern, 120 E. Sheridan, Lake Geneva, WI 53147	WISC	0.80	0	0	50/2000q	4	OI

C. Water

California Water, 1720 N. 1st, San Jose, CA 95112	CWTR	0.50	0	0	none		SSO OI
Elizabethtown Water, 1 Elizabethtown, Elizabeth, NJ 07200	EWAT	0.60	0	0	25/3000q	12	5-D OI
Hydraulic, 835 Main, Bridgeport, CT 06609	THC	0.55	0	0	10/5000q	12	3-D SSO PRF OI
Indianapolis Water, Box 1220, Indianapolis, IN 46206	IWTR	0.60	0	0	25/5000q	12	SSO OI
Middlesex Water, Box 1500, Iselin, NJ 08830	MSEX	0.55	0	0	25/3000q	12	
Philadelphia Sub., 762 Lancaster, Bryn Mawr, PA 19010	PSC	0.65	5-2.50	Y	10/3000q	12	
San Jose Water, Box 229, San Jose, CA 95196	SJW	0.55	0	0	none		SSO OI
Southern Calif. Water, 3625 W. 6th, Los Angeles, CA 90020	SWTR	0.50	0	0	none		SSO OI
United Water, 200 Old Hook, Harrington Park, NJ 07640	UWR	0.40	0	0	25/3000q	12	5-D+VC SSO OI

D. Telecommunication

ALLTEL, 100 Executive Pkwy., Hudson, OH 44236	AT	0.55	0	0	10/20000y	12	SSO PRF OI
AT&T, 550 Madison Ave., New York, NY 10022	T	1.00	0	0	0/3000q	12	5-D SSO OI
Ameritech, Box 2566, Jacksonville, FL 32232	AIT	0.85	0	0	0/3000q	12	5-D SSO OI
Bell Atlantic, 1600 Market, Philadelphia, PA 19103	BEL	0.90	0	0	0/500q	12	SSO OI
Bell Canada, Box 6074, Montreal, Quebec H3C3G4	BCE	0.65	0	0	0/20000y	12	5-D OI
BellSouth, 675 Peachtree N.E., Atlanta, GA 30375	BLS	0.90	0	0	0/3000q	12	5-D SSO OI
Centel Corp., 5725 N.E. River, Chicago, IL 60631	CNT	0.65	0	0	25/5000q	12	SSO OI
Century Telephone, Box 4065, Monroe, LA 71211	CTL	0.70	0	0	30/3000q	4	5-D OI
Cincinnati Bell, 201 E. 4th, Cincinnati, OH 45201	CSN	0.35	0	0	0/3000q	4	OI
COMSAT, 950 L'Enfant S.W., Washington, D.C. 20024	CQ	1.10	5-2.50	Y	25/1000q	4	

Dividend Reinvestment Plans

	Ticker Symbol	Beta	Cost Service Fee	Commission	Voluntary Cash $Minimum/ $Maximum	Frequency (per year)	Special Features
Continental Telephone, 245 Perimeter Center, Atlanta, GA 30346	CTC	0.75	0	0	10/3000q	4	SSO OI
GTE, 1776 Heritage, North Quincy, MA 02171	GTE	0.85	0	0	25/5000q	4	SSO OI
Lincoln Telephone, Box 81309, Lincoln, NB 68501	LTEC	1.15	0	0	100/3000q	4	5-D+VC OI
NYNEX Corp., Box 2566, Jacksonville, FL 32232	NYN	0.70	0	0	0/3000q	12	5-D SSO OI
Pacific Telephone, 140 New Montgomery, San Francisco, CA 94105	PAC	0.95	0	0	0/3000q	12	5-D SSO OI
Rochester Telephone, 100 Midtown, Rochester, NY 14646	RTC	0.65	0	0	10/1000m	12	
Southern N.E. Telephone, 300 George, New Haven, CT 06506	SNG	0.60	0	0	0/3000q	4	OI
Southwestern Bell, 1 Bell Ctr., St. Louis, MO 63101	SBC	1.15	0	0	0/3000q	12	5-D SSO OI
Telephone & Data, 79 W. Monroe, Chicago, IL 60603	TDS	1.20	0	Y	10/3000q	4	
US West, 7800 E. Orchard, Englewood, CA 98011	USW	0.65	0	0	0/3000q	12	5-D SSO OI
United Telephone, Box 11315, Kansas City, MO 64112	UT	0.85	0	0	10/3000q	12	OI
Western Union, 1 Lake, Upper Saddle River, NJ 07458	WU	1.15	4-2.50	Y	10/5000q	4	

220

appendix B

COMMISSION COST DATA FOR INDIVIDUAL DISCOUNT BROKERAGE FIRMS

Name, Address, Telephone[a]	Minimum Commission[b]	Typical Trade[c]	Large Trade[d]	Low-Priced Stock Trade[e]	States with Offices[f]
Allied Securities, 12955 Biscayne Blvd., North Miami, FL 33181 LOCAL (305)891-2700	$35	86	NA	NA	FL
Anderson (C.D.), 300 Montgomery St., San Francisco, CA 94104 NATL 800-822-2222 LOCAL (415)433-2120 STATE 800-822-2222	$30	112	137	80	CA
Argus Investment, 11617 W. Bluemond, Milwaukee, WI 53226 LOCAL (414)476-1420 STATE 800-242-0771	$30	104	142	NA	WI
Arnold Securities, 609 2nd Ave. S., Minneapolis, MN 55402 NATL 800-328-4076 LOCAL (612)339-7040 STATE 800-292-4135	$35	109	143	89	MN
Aufmann-Spore, 9333 N. Meridian, Indianapolis, IN 46260 LOCAL (317)848-1319	$25	126	NA	141	IN
Baker & Co., 1940 E. 6th, Cleveland, OH 44114 NATL 800-321-1640 LOCAL (216)696-0167 STATE 800-362-2008	$35	105	98	66	FL OH
Boyle Securities, 552 S. Washington, Naperville, IL 60540 LOCAL (312)369-6789	$25	83	113	114	IL
Brenner Steed, 6077 Primacy Pky, Memphis, TN 38119 NATL 800-238-7125 LOCAL (901)761-2950 STATE 800-238-7125	$25	104	143	96	FL TN
Brokers Exchange, 6941 N. Trenholm, Columbia, SC 29206 NATL 800-922-0960 LOCAL (803)738-0204	$35	146	164	87	SC
Brooks-Campbell, 1861 S.W. 1st, Portland, OR 97201 NATL 800-547-6337 LOCAL (503)222-3588 STATE 800-452-6774	$29	110	99	72	OR
Brown & Co., 7 Water St., Boston, MA 02109 NATL 800-225-6707 LOCAL (617)742-2600 STATE 800-392-6707	$21	61	66	91	FL MA
Bruno Stolz, 425 N. New Ballas, St. Louis, MO 63141 NATL 800-325-1332 LOCAL (314)569-3900 STATE 800-392-1378	$30	93	88	116	MO
Buetti, Cannon, 45 John St., New York, NY 10038 NATL 800-221-3575 LOCAL (212)513-1100	$35	60	63	85	NY
Bull and Bear, 11 Hanover Square, New York, NY 10005 NATL 800-262-5800 LOCAL (212)742-1300	$30	58	53	121	NY

Burke, Christensen, 120 S. LaSalle, Chicago, IL 60603 NATL 800-621-0392 LOCAL (312)346-8283 STATE 800-972-1633	$25	94	96	132	IL WI
Bush Brokerage, 199 W. Palmetto, Boca Raton, FL 33432 NATL 800-327-0170 LOCAL (305)391-0550	$35	111	105	135	FL
Cabe (W.T.), 1270 Avenue of the Americas, New York, NY 10020 NATL 800-223-6555 LOCAL (212)541-6690	$25	109	134	101	NY
Carnegie, 509 Madison Ave., New York, NY 10022 NATL 800-223-1988 LOCAL (212)750-9450	$35	83	75	106	CA IL NY
Chayka & Loeb, 600 Old Country Rd., Garden City, NY 11530 LOCAL (516)747-1400	$30	106	143	93	NY
Clayton, Polleys, 50 Federal, Boston, MA 02110 NATL 800-252-9765 LOCAL (617)357-5474 STATE 800-882-1452	$24	68	79	106	MA
Collins Brokerage, 134 S. LaSalle, Chicago, IL 60603 NATL 800-621-1441 LOCAL (312)372-1733 STATE 800-572-6032	$40	96	NA	80	IL
Commission Discount, 2455 E. Sunrise, Ft. Lauderdale, FL 33304 NATL 800-327-1280 LOCAL (305)566-5022 STATE 800-432-8822	$30	115	NA	NA	FL

[a] NATL is the nationwide toll-free WATS number; LOCAL is the local telephone number in the firm's headquarters city; STATE is the statewide toll-free WATS number.

[b] Minimum commission charge per order.

[c] Commission costs are stated as a percentage of the average for all discount brokers, with 100 = average. Thus 90 means the commission rate charged by the firm is about 10 percent below average; 115 means the firm is about 15 percent above average. The typical trade category includes trades of 100, 200, 300, and 500 shares of a $20 stock, 200, 300, and 400 shares of a $30 stock, 200 and 300 shares of a $40 stock, and 200 and 500 shares of a $50 stock. The average transaction size is $9500.

[d] NA indicates commission rates for these trades cannot be calculated from the commission rate schedule provided by the firm. You must call and ask for commission rate quotes for specific trades. The large trade category includes trades of 1000 and 1500 shares of a $50 stock, 2000 shares of a $40 stock, and 2000 shares of a $50 stock. The average transaction size is $76,000.

[e] For trades involving a very large number of shares of a low-priced stock, you generally must ask for a commission quote. The low priced stock category includes trades of 2000 shares of a $2 stock, 1000 shares of a $4 stock, 500 shares of an $8 stock, and 400 shares of a $10 stock. The average transaction size is $4000.

[f] If you wish to open an account with an out-of-state discount broker, call or write to see if they are registered to do business in your state. Often firms are registered even if they do not maintain an office in the state.

Name, Address, Telephone[a]	Minimum Commission[b]	Typical Trade[c]	Large Trade[d]	Low-Priced Stock Trade[e]	States with Offices[f]
Corna & Co., 490 City Park Ave., Columbus, OH 43215 LOCAL (614)461-9193	$30	105	142	89	OH
Daley & Co., 526 Superior N.E., Cleveland, OH 44114 NATL 800-321-2030 LOCAL (216)241-4500 STATE 800-362-9913	$30	138	143	100	AZ CA GA NY OH VA
Dis-Com Securities, 1725 E. Hallandale, Hallendale, FL 33009 NATL 800-327-1216 LOCAL (303)454-9800	$25	102	NA	98	FL
Discount Brokerage, 67 Wall St., New York, NY 10005 NATL 800-221-8210 LOCAL (212)943-7888	$35	76	77	87	CA FL NY
Downstate Discount Brokerage, 825 W. Bay, Largo, FL 33540 LOCAL (813)586-3541	$30	114	NA	NA	FL
Drake, 23 N. Pinckney, Madison, WI 53703 NATL 800-362-1002 LOCAL (608)257-7898	$30	103	128	106	WI
Eastern Capital, 8133 Leesburg Park, Vienna, VA 22180 LOCAL (703)448-1020	$40	132	121	102	GA FL MA RI NJ VA
Exchange Services, Box 7471, Richmond, VA 23221 LOCAL (804)798-1391	$21	93	78	93	VA
Fidelity Brokerage, 161 Devonshire, Boston, MA 02110 NATL 800-225-2097 LOCAL (617)423-0116 STATE 800-882-1269	$30	108	115	87	NATIONWIDE
Finn (John), 932 Dixie Terminal, Cincinnati, OH 45202 LOCAL (513)579-0066	$30	134	NA	NA	OH
First Heritage Co., 5 Hanover Square, New York, NY 10004 NATL 800-621-7011 LOCAL (212)668-1776	$35	64	63	85	CA IL NY
First Los Angeles, 6055 Ventura, Encino, CA 91436 LOCAL (213)907-7800 STATE 800-232-2444	$25	105	105	107	CA
First National Security, 119 S. 19th, Omaha, NE 68102 NATL 800-228-9065 LOCAL (402)345-7000 STATE 800-642-8284	$25	92	107	90	CA MO NE
Francis (Roland), 8893 La Mesa, La Mesa, CA 92041 LOCAL (619)464-2346	$38	104	107	105	CA

Firm	Price	Col1	Col2	States
Freeman Welwood, Joseph Vance Bldg., Seattle, WA 98101 NATL 800-426-1160 LOCAL (206)382-5353 STATE 800-542-7884	$29	110	NA	76	OR WA
Glicksman Securities, 11675 Wilshire, Los Angeles, CA 90025 LOCAL (213)826-0886	$40	117	NA	NA	CA
Haas Securities, 120 Broadway, New York, NY 10271 NATL 800-221-3588 LOCAL (212)233-1700	$25	98	86	63	IL NY TX
Heartland, 208 S. LaSalle, Chicago, IL 60604 NATL 800-621-0662 STATE 800-972-0580	$30	81	98	92	IL
Heitner Equities, 314 N. Broadway, St. Louis, MO 63102 NATL 800-325-7665 LOCAL (314)241-4400	$30	92	88	107	MO
Heritage Securities, 505 5th Ave., S. Naples, FL 33940 LOCAL (813)263-1110	$30	82	90	237	FL
Icahn & Co., 1370 Avenue of the Americas, New York, NY 10019 NATL 800-223-2188 LOCAL (212)957-6318	$45	98	84	93	FL IL NY
Individual's Securities, 349 E. Northfield, Livingston, NJ 07039 NATL 800-645-5000 LOCAL (201)533-0502 STATE 800-832-8585	$30	151	NA	NA	NJ NY PA
Kahn & Co., 112 Clark Tower, Memphis, TN 38137 NATL 800-238-5598 LOCAL (901)767-6730	$30	121	NA	NA	CA LA TN TX
Kall & Co., 510 W. 6th, Los Angeles, CA 90014 NATL 800-421-0067 LOCAL (213)626-4221 STATE 800-252-9011	$35	100	59	84	CA
Kasner Securities, 10 S. Adams, Sarasota, FL 33577 NATL 800-237-9631 LOCAL (813)388-2121 STATE 800-282-9420	$40	99	98	80	FL
Kass (Kenneth), 147 Columbia Tpk., Florham Park, NJ 07932 NATL 800-526-4472 LOCAL (201)966-1595	$30	108	NA	NA	CT NJ NY
Kennedy, Cabot, 9465 Wilshire, Beverly Hills, CA 90212 NATL 800-252-0090 LOCAL (213)550-0711 STATE 800-252-0090	$22	121	53	131	CA
Kramer Securities, PO Drawer 431456, Miami, FL 33143 LOCAL (305)667-9922	$25	96	105	NA	FL
Lafferty, 50 Broad St., New York, NY 10004 NATL 800-221-8601 LOCAL (212)269-6637 STATE 800-522-5653	$50	72	88	96	NY

225

Name, Address, Telephone[a]	Minimum Commission[b]	Typical Trade[c]	Large Trade[d]	Low-Priced Stock Trade[e]	States with Offices[f]
LaSalle Street, 175 W. Jackson, Chicago, IL 60604 NATL 800-621-5393 LOCAL (312)427-4242 STATE 800-572-5568	$25	78	80	107	IL OH WI
Marsh, Block, 132 Nassau St., New York, NY 10038 NATL 800-221-2255 LOCAL (212)349-7330	$25	114	NA	NA	NY
Marquette de Bary, 30 Broad St., New York, NY 10004 NATL 800-221-3305 LOCAL (212)425-5505	$20	104	98	NA	NY
Murphy (Barry), 125 High St., Boston, MA 02110 NATL 800-225-2494 LOCAL (617)426-1770	$25	98	102	NA	MA
NEL Equity Services, 501 Boylston, Boston, MA 02117 NATL 800-472-7227	$30	126	134	101	MA
Odd Lots Securities, 60 E. 42nd St., New York, NY 10017 NATL 800-221-2095 LOCAL (212)661-6755 STATE 800-442-5929	$30	65	89	75	FL NY
Olde Discount Brokers, 735 Griswold, Detroit, MI 48226 NATL 800-521-1111 LOCAL (313)961-6666 STATE 800-482-4000	$30	95	67	109	NATIONWIDE
Ovest Securities, 76 Beaver St., New York, NY 10005 NATL 800-221-5713 LOCAL (212)425-3003	$30	77	71	114	NY
Pace Securities, 225 Park Ave., New York, NY 10017 NATL 800-221-1650 LOCAL (212)490-6363	$35	65	NA	NA	NY
Pacific Brokerage, 8200 Wilshire, Beverly Hills, CA 90211 NATL 800-421-8395 LOCAL (213)653-8002 STATE 800-421-3214	$25	39	43	64	CA NY
Parker, Alexander, 342 Madison Ave., New York, NY 10173 NATL 800-221-4872 LOCAL (212)370-0610 STATE 800-522-5629	$35	106	NA	NA	NY
Parsons Securities, 50 W. Broad, Columbus, OH 43215 NATL 800-282-2756 LOCAL (614)224-0038	$25	138	NA	100	OH
Peck (Andrew), 32 Broadway, New York, NY 10004 NATL 800-221-5873 LOCAL (212)363-3770	$45	81	52	133	NY
Pennsylvania Group, 2 Bala Cynwyd Plaza, Bala Cynwyd, PA 19004 NATL 800-345-1200 LOCAL (215)667-7200 STATE 800-572-1477	$35	105	98	97	FL PA

Peremel & Co., 1 N. Charles, Baltimore, MD 21201 NATL 800-492-0416 LOCAL (301)539-7171	$40	108	146	96	MD
Price (T. Rowe), 100 E. Pratt, Baltimore, MD 21202 NATL 800-638-5660 LOCAL (301)547-2308	$30	107	126	93	MD
Quick & Reilly, 120 Wall St., New York, NY 10005 NATL 800-221-5220 LOCAL (212)943-8686 STATE 800-522-8712	$35	98	85	75	NATIONWIDE
Recom Securities, 200 Minn. Fed., Minneapolis, MN 55402 NATL 800-328-8600 LOCAL (612)339-5566 STATE 800-292-7923	$30	105	NA	97	MN
Remsynder (Dwayne), 7911 Herschel, La Jolla, CA 92037 LOCAL (714)459-0686	$30	122	92	87	CA
Ried & Gilmour, 155 Wolf Rd., Albany, NY 12205 LOCAL (518)458-7445	$25	154	NA	NA	NY
Robinson Securities, 1 N. LaSalle, Chicago, IL 60602 NATL 800-621-2840 LOCAL (312)346-7710	$22	104	137	81	IL
Rose & Co., Board of Trade Bldg., Chicago, IL 60604 NATL 800-621-3700 LOCAL (312)987-9400 STATE 800-572-3188	$25	93	93	112	CA DC IL MA NY PA TX
Royal/Grimm, 20 Exchange Place, New York, NY 10005 NATL 800-221-5195 LOCAL (212)943-7960	$30	70	58	91	NY
Russo Securities, 170 Broadway, New York, NY 10038 LOCAL (212)962-7482	$35	70	57	99	NY
St. Louis Discount, 35 N. Central, Clayton, MO 63105 LOCAL (314)721-7400	$25	93	88	116	MO
Schwab (Charles), One Second St., San Francisco, CA 94105 NATL 800-648-5300 LOCAL (415)546-1000 STATE 800-792-0988	$30	113	97	84	NATIONWIDE
Scottsdale Securities, 1630 S. Lindbergh, St. Louis, MO 63131 LOCAL (314)991-1950	$30	85	81	98	IL MO OH WI
Seaport Securities, 50 Broadway, New York, NY 10004 NATL 800-221-9894 LOCAL (212)482-8689	$35	52	70	141	MA NY
Seibert (JD), 1010 Provident Twr., Cincinnati, OH 45202 LOCAL (513)241-8888	$35	112	113	102	OH

Name, Address, Telephone[a]	Minimum Commission[b]	Typical Trade[c]	Large Trade[d]	Low-Priced Stock Trade[e]	States with Offices[f]
Shearman, Ralston, 100 Wall St., New York, NY 10005 NATL 800-221-4242 LOCAL (212)248-1160	$25	110	96	NA	NY
Shepard & Vrbarac, 9023 Forest Hill, Richmond, VA 23235 LOCAL (804)320-9023	$30	108	90	93	VA
Siebert (Muriel), 77 Water St., New York, NY 10005 NATL 800-221-5842 LOCAL (212)248-0605	$30	105	106	NA	NY
Springer Investments, 6060 N. College, Indianapolis, IN 46220 LOCAL (317)255-6673	$22	154	NA	NA	IN
Stock Mart, 11915 LaGrange, Los Angeles, CA 90025 LOCAL (213)820-3090	$30	105	95	96	CA
Stock & Trade, 770 Lexington Ave., New York, NY 10021 NATL 800-223-5116 LOCAL (212)308-7440	$35	108	NA	NA	NY
Stock Cross, 1 Washington Mall, Boston, MA 02108 NATL 800-225-6196 LOCAL (617)367-5700 STATE 800-392-6104	$25	69	70	156	MA
Texas Securities, 815 Throckmorton, Ft. Worth, TX 76102 NATL 800-433-5658 LOCAL (817)336-4601 STATE 800-772-5974	$25	112	95	108	TX
Thomas (Robert), 6090 Central, St. Petersburg, FL 33707 LOCAL (813)381-3800	$35	112	92	98	CA FL GA NY RI VA WI
Thurston, Shumaker, 1333 Circle Twr., Indianapolis, IN 46204 NATL 800-428-4670 LOCAL (317)638-9162 STATE 800-382-5043	$35	105	144	88	IN
Tradex Brokerage, 82 Beaver St., New York, NY 10005 NATL 800-221-7874 LOCAL (212)425-7800 STATE 800-522-3000	$25	85	67	101	NY TX
Traid Securities, 115 Broadway, New York, NY 10006 NATL 800-221-8440 LOCAL (212)349-8060	$45	106	143	89	NY
Tuttle Securities, 12 Mony Plaza, Syracuse, NY 13202 NATL 800-962-5489 LOCAL (315)422-2515	$30	132	114	129	NY
Ule (Max), 6 E. 43rd St., New York, NY 10017 NATL 800-223-6642 LOCAL (212)986-1660	$25	138	143	107	NY

Vanguard, Vanguard Financial Center, Valley Forge, PA 19496 NATL 800-523-7025 STATE 800-362-0530	$35	110	129	86	PA
Wall Street Discount, 100 Wall St., New York, NY 10005 NATL 800-221-7990 LOCAL (212)747-5013	$35	58	71	87	NY
Waterhouse Securities, 120 Wall St., New York, NY 10005 NATL 800-221-8392 LOCAL (212)344-9780 STATE 800-522-5585	$30	75	98	80	CA NY
Werlitz Securities, 76 Beaver St., New York, NY 10005 NATL 800-221-7795 LOCAL (212)227-7354 STATE 800-522-5658	$30	56	71	51	NY
Western Discount Securities, 1919 14th, Boulder, CO 80302 LOCAL (303)440-0210	$28	116	124	106	CO
White (Jack), Bank America Bldg., La Jolla, CA 92037 NATL 800-542-6188 LOCAL (714)455-5300	$30	143	140	108	CA
White (Thomas), 235 Montgomery, San Francisco, CA 94104 LOCAL (415)986-8500	$30	100	120	90	CA
Whitehall, 1001 Avenue of the Americas, New York, NY 10018 NATL 800-223-5023 LOCAL (212)719-5522	$50	72	88	176	NY
Wisconsin, 1024 E. State St., Milwaukee, WI 53202 NATL 800-242-9196 LOCAL (414)276-4030	$30	105	143	96	WI
York Securities, 44 Wall St., New York, NY 10005 NATL 800-221-3154 LOCAL (212)425-6400	$35	66	85	80	NY
Ziegler Thrift, 169 Northstar, Minneapolis, MN 55402 NATL 800-328-4854 LOCAL (612)333-4206	$25	105	143	96	MN

appendix C

SELECTED INTERNATIONAL MUTUAL FUNDS

Name, Address, Telephone	Principal Countries Represented in Portfolio (%)	Total Countries in Portfolio	Sales Charge[a]	Minimum Purchase[b] Initial	Minimum Purchase[b] Additional
Alliance International, 140 Broadway, New York, NY 10005 NATL 800-221-5672　　　　STATE 800-522-2323	Germany (21) Japan (18) Netherlands (18) Australia (7) Switzerland (7)	10	None	$1000	$1000
First Investors International, 120 Wall St., New York, NY 10005 NATL 800-431-2550　LOCAL (212)825-7900　STATE 800-942-1941	United States (24) Hong Kong (19) Australia (12) Mexico (11) Spain (11)	8	9.3%	200	50
Kemper International, 120 S. LaSalle, Chicago, IL 60603 NATL 800-621-1148　LOCAL (312)781-1121	Japan (32) United Kingdom (10) Netherlands (7) France (7) Switzerland (6)	14	9.3	1000	100
Keystone International, 99 High St., Boston, MA 02110 NATL 800-225-2618　LOCAL (617)338-3395	United States (40) Japan (22) United Kingdom (12) Germany (6) Netherlands (4)	11	None	250	0
Merrill Lynch Pacific, 633 Third Ave., New York, NY 10017 LOCAL (212)692-2939	Japan (56) Australia (18) Hong Kong (6) Singapore (2)	5	6.95	250	50
G.T. Pacific, 601 Montgomery St., San Francisco, CA 94111 NATL 800-824-1580　LOCAL (415)392-6181　STATE 800-824-8361	Japan (46) Hong Kong (17) Australia (13) Singapore (9)	4	None	500	100

Fund	Countries				
Putnam International, 1 Post Office Sq., Boston, MA 02109 LOCAL (617)692-1000	Japan (29), United States (28), Germany (16), Netherlands (6), Switzerland (3)	11	9.3	500	50
T. Rowe Price International, 100 Pratt St., Baltimore, MD 21202 NATL 800-638-5660 LOCAL (301)547-2308	Japan (54), Netherlands (8), United Kingdom (7), Germany (6), Australia (5)	11	None	1000	100
Scudder International, 175 Federal St., Boston, MA 02110 NATL 800-453-3305 LOCAL (617)426-8300	Japan (20), Netherlands (12), Germany (9), Canada (8), Switzerland (7)	16	None	1000	0
Templeton Foreign, 405 Central, St. Petersburg, FL 33731 LOCAL (813)823-8712	Canada (27), Australia (13), Netherlands (13), Mexico (7), Hong Kong (4)	10	9.3	500	25
Templeton World, 405 Central, St. Petersburg, FL 33731 LOCAL (813)823-8712	United States (69), Canada (8), Netherlands (5), Japan (2), Bermuda (2)	10	9.3	500	25

Note: Information is subject to change. Refer to a recent prospectus for up-to-date information.

[a] Maximum sales charge (see discussion in Chapter 7). Lower rates are available for large purchases.

[b] Lower minimums may be available for IRAs and other retirement programs. See prospectus for details.

Name, Address, Telephone	Principal Countries Represented in Portfolio (%)	Total Countries in Portfolio	Sales Charge[a]	Minimum Purchase[b] Initial	Additional
Transatlantic, 100 Wall St., New York, NY 10005 LOCAL (212)747-0440	Japan (22) United Kingdom (16) Germany (14) Netherlands (13) Hong Kong (8)	17	None	$5000	$1000
United International Growth, 2400 Pershing, Kansas City, MO 64141 LOCAL (816)283-4000	United States (22) Japan (20) Germany (11) Netherlands (11) Canada (7)	9	9.3%	500	25

INDEX

Abelson, Adam, 67
Account executives, *see* Stockbrokers
Advisory fees, 63–65, 130, 131, 164. *See also* Transaction costs
American Depository Receipts, 128

Bachelier, Louis, 29
Barron, C.W., 56
Barron's, 67, 73
Beat-the-market investment approach, 26–32
 Contrarian investment tactics, 44
  investment merits, 45
 fundamental analysis, 36
  investment merits, 36–38
 gambling *vs.* investing, 176
 information needed, 33
 inside information, use of, 30–31
 investment merits, 1, 79, 101
 supertraders, 25–26, 29, 33
 tax cost, 166
 technical analysis, 33–34
  investment merits, 34–36
Berle, Adolf, 16
Beta, 90–91
 accuracy as measurement of risk, 110–111
 different ways to measure, 126
 management of portfolio, 111–115
 portfolio, 108, 109
 sources of information on, 125–126
 stability, individual stocks *vs.* portfolio, 111
 S&P quality rankings as proxy measure of, 126
 weighted portfolio, 109–110
 see also Risk
Bid-ask spread, 149
Blume, Marshall, 116
Blyth Eastman Dillon, 57
Board of directors, 13
 ability to control managers, 15–16
 role in corporation, 13–14
 see also Principal-agent contract
Bonds:
 long term, 98, 102–103
  inflation risk, 102
  investment objectives, 98, 102
 short term, 98, 101–102
  investment objectives, 98, 102
Bondweek, 49
Bradley, E.S., 181
Brealey, R.A., 181, 182
Brokerage commissions, *see* Commissions, brokerage
Brokers, *see* Stockbrokers
Bucket shops, 56
Buy-and-hold investment approach, 31–32
 active *vs.* passive, 45–46

235

INDEX

Buy-and-hold investment approach (*Continued*)
  compared to beat-the-market approach, 11–12, 27–29, 41–42, 45
  compared to returns for corporate insiders, 31
  tax shelter effect, 166–167
  see also Efficient market hypothesis; Portfolio management; Total investment portfolio planning (TIPP)

Capital gains, *see* Tax shelters
Chartist, *see* Technical analysis
Commissions, brokerage, 148–156
  comparison between discount brokers, 151–156
  full service brokers, 149
  mutual funds, 137–138, 140–141
  New York Stock Exchange, minimum, 148–149
  see also Transaction costs
Contrarian investment tactics, 44
  investment merits, 45
  see also Beat-the-market investment approach
Cootner, Paul H., 29
Corporate executives, *see* Managers, corporate
Corporation, defined as network of contracts, 13–14
Council on Environmental Quality, 20
Crawford, Arch, 66

Dean Witter, 57, 67, 130
Debt, *see* Bonds
DeLouise, Joseph, 65–66
Designated Order Turnaround system (DOT), 150
Discount brokers, 148–156
  commission rates, 151–156
    cost for individual firms, 221–229
    compared to full service brokers, 130–131, 150, 152
    by transaction size, 152
    variability between firms, 131, 151, 153–156
  quality, compared to full service brokers, 150–151
  selecting broker, 151–156
  services provided, 150–151
  title transfer, 149–150
  see also Stockbrokers
Diversification, *see* Portfolio management; Total investment portfolio planning (TIPP); Unsystematic risk

Dividend reinvestment plans, 130–136
  advantages, 132–133
  as alternative to mutual funds, 130
  major features, 131, 132
  Merrill Lynch Sharebuilder Plan, 147
  to qualify for use, 131
  specific provisions, 133–136, 185–220
  tax features, 136, 146
  transaction costs, 132
  use, to achieve TIPP portfolio management, 132–133
Dividends, 14, 81. *See also* Dividend reinvestment plans
Dodd, P., 181
Dow, Charles, 55
Dow-Jones Industrial Average, 43, 47

Earnings, corporate, 19–22
  as compensation for risk, 14
  difficulties in forecasting, 37–38
  and economic conditions, 19–22
  past trends and future prospects, 19–23
  reinvested, and expected dividends, 14
  stock prices reflect future of, 42
Economic conditions, 19–23
  and common stock earnings, 19–22
  past trends and future prospects, 19–23
  and returns on human capital, 22–23
  stagflation, 20
Efficient market hypothesis, 25–47
  defined, as fair game, 32
  effect of inside information, 30–31
  efforts to discredit, 54
  errors in estimating future returns, 92
  evidence to support, 26–30
  financial planning under, 46–48
  information needed to beat market, 33
  use, with TIPP principles of finance, 80
  see also Buy-and-hold investment approach; Portfolio management; Total investment portfolio planning (TIPP)
Equity, *see* Stock, common

Financial leverage, *see* Leverage
Financial management, *see* Portfolio management
Financial risk, *see* Leverage; Risk
Financial World, 28, 41
Forecasting, *see* Beat-the-market investment approach; Earnings, corporate; Efficient market hypothesis
Foreign stocks, 127–128
  international mutual funds, 128, 231–234

INDEX

Fraud, on Wall Street, 72–75
   misleading advertising, 73–75
   swindlers, 72–73
Friedman, Milton, 72
Friedman, Rose, 72
Friend, Irwin, 116
Full service brokers, see Stockbrokers
Fundamental analysis, 36
   investment merits, 36–38
   see also Beat-the-market investment approach

Garbade, K.D., 181
Gold, investment merits, 4
Granville, Joe, 66, 67, 68
Great Stock Market Crash, 114, 115
Greed-fear cycle, 40–42, 91, 113, 177
   during Stock Market Crash of 1929, 114–115
   effect of leverage, 113–115
   how to avoid, 78, 80–81, 94–95
   impact on investment decisions, 41–42
   in technical analysis, 34

Haney, Richard, 93
Haugen, Robert, 126
Hitschler, Anthony, 37
Holding period return, 81, 84, 85, 87, 90
Hulbert Financial Digest, 70
Human capital, importance in investment management, 12, 22–23, 177
Hutton, E.F., 57, 67

Ibbotson, R.G., 182
Index mutual fund, 142–143
   beta of, 142
   compared to conventional mutual fund, 142–143
   compared to TIPP-diversified portfolio, 143–146
   leverage with, 147–148
   Vanguard Index Trust, 142
   see also Mutual funds; No-load mutual funds
Individual retirement accounts (IRAs), 167–170
   liquidity risk, 169–170
   with mutual funds, 139
   as "safe" tax shelter, 168
   tax deferral feature, 160–161, 167–168
   TIPP rules for selecting, 169
   transaction costs, 169
   withdrawal penalty, 169–170
Inside information, 30
   corporate insiders, 30, 31
   problems with using, 30–31
   use, to select stocks, 30–31
   see also Beat-the-market investment approach
Institutional Investor, 28, 29
Internal Revenue Service (IRS), 159, 164–165
International investing, see Foreign stocks
Investment advice industry, 49–75
   early history, 55–56
   evaluating investment performance of, 50–55
      assimilating information, 53–55
      sources of information on, 51–53
   promotional practices, 53, 72–74
   tactics, 1–2
   value of service, 7, 50–51
   see also Investment advisors; Investment newsletters; Mutual funds; No-load mutual funds; Stockbrokers
Investment advisors, 63–65
   fee-only service, 63–64
   fee-plus-commission service, 64–65
   as marketing device, 65
   tax specialists, 158, 159
   see also Investment advice industry
Investment counselors, see Investment advisors
Investment management, see Portfolio management
Investment newsletters, 65–72
   reasons for success, 66–67
   tactics used in forecasting, 69–72
   see also Investment advice industry

Kahn, Herman, 20
Keogh plans, 170–171
   defined contribution *vs.* defined benefit plans, 170
   with mutual funds, 139
   tax deferred feature, 160–161
Kimpton, M.H., 181

Leverage, 111–115
   effect on greed-fear cycle, 113–115
   to manage portfolio risk, 111–112
   stocks, with tax-free municipal bonds, 167
   with tax shelters, 163, 165
   use with index mutual fund, 147–148
Livermore, Jesse, 67, 68
Lloyd, William, 93
Lorie, J.H., 181

McDonald, John G., 138
Managers, corporate, 13–19
   incentives to maximize profits, 16–19, 46

Managers, corporate (*Continued*)
  market control of, 15–16
  role in corporation, 13, 14
  see also Principal-agent contract
Margin call, 39, 113, 114
Margin loan, 112, 113, 114, 115
Market efficiency, *see* Efficient market hypothesis
Market risk, *see* Systematic risk
Markowitz, H.M., 182
Meadows, Donella H., 20
Means, Gardiner, 16
Media General Financial Weekly, 125, 126
Merrill Lynch, 56, 57, 62, 67, 73, 130
Merrill Lynch Sharebuilder Plan, 147
Money market securities, 96–101
  default risk, 96–97
  inflation risk with, 97, 102
  investment objectives, 100–101
  investment return, compared to rate of inflation, 100
  portfolio mismanagement risk, 97–98
Municipal bonds, 171–174
  after-tax yield, compared to taxable securities, 171–172
  effect of marginal tax brackets on after-tax yield, 171–172
  investment merits, 172–173
  mutual funds, 173–174
  tax reduction feature, 161–162
  as tax shelters, 171
  TIPP rules for selecting, 173
  unit investment trust, 174
Mutual funds, 136–147
  basic investment goals, 136–137
  commission cost for load funds, 138
  costs and benefits, 137, 143–146
  custodial services for retirement plans, 144, 146, 168
  international, 128, 231–234
  investment objectives, 138–139
  investor services, 144
  load *vs.* no-load, 137–138
  to obtain diversification, 130
  portfolio turnover rate, 140–141
  see also Index mutual fund; Investment advice industry; No-load mutual funds
Myers, S., 182

New York Stock Exchange, 148, 149, 150
New York Stock Exchange Index, 27, 73
New York Times, 68, 72
No-load mutual funds, 137–143

  alternative to dividend reinvestment plans, 137
  benefits, 138–139
  commission cost ratio, 140–141
  compared to load mutual funds, 137–138
  compared to TIPP-diversified portfolio:
    costs, 144–146
    investment merits, 143–144
    investor services, 144
  expense ratio, 139–140
    by size of fund, 140
  foreign stock, investing with, 146–147
  investment objectives, 138–139
  and portfolio risk, 139
  tax costs, 141–142
  taxes, 141–142
  transaction costs, 139–143
  Your Guide to Mutual Funds, 138
  see also Index mutual fund; Investment advice industry; Mutual funds

Official Summary of Security Transactions and Holdings, 31
Options market, 18, 56, 176
Organization of Petroleum Exporting Countries (OPEC), 20–21

Payout ratio, tax shelter effect, 167
Portfolio beta, measurement of, 108–110
Portfolio diversification, *see* Portfolio management
Portfolio management, 77–81
  basic strategy, 12
  of both human and financial capital, 22–23
  buy-and-hold investment approach, 31–32
  diversification, 46, 87–91, 108
    cost of, 7
    with foreign stocks, 127–128
    by industry, 116–119
    lack of by typical investor, 116
    rules for using industry classification, 119
  efficient market hypothesis, 25–47
  efficient portfolio, 87, 90, 108, 116
    how to develop and maintain, 107–128
  five-year review, 122, 123
  foreign stocks for diversification, 127–128
  leverage, to manage portfolio risk, 111–112, 147–148, 167
  managing portfolio risk, 87–90
    leverage, 111–112
    minimizing costs, 95–98
    personal, compared to no-load mutual funds, 143–146

INDEX

portfolio worksheet, 107
    use for diversification, 119–122
    return-risk tradeoffs, 86–87
    risk management, defined, 78
    stock selection rules, 124–125
    systematic risk in, 89, 108
    time diversification, 91–95
    total investment portfolio planning (TIPP), 86–98
    unsystematic risk in, 89–90
    see also Portfolio worksheet; Risk; Total investment portfolio planning (TIPP)
Portfolio worksheet, 107
    basic objectives, 107
    use for diversification, 119–122
    see also Portfolio management
Principal-agent contract, 13–14
    advantage to stockholders, 14–15, 45–46
    corporation, defined as network of contracts, 13–14
    costs of alternative control systems, 18–19
    enforced by markets, 16–18
    golden parachutes and greenmail, 18
    indirect market controls, 16–18
    between investors and financial analysts, 50–51
    stockholders' lack of direct control, 15–16
    between stockholders and managers, 14
    use, with TIPP principles of finance, 80
Profits, *see* Earnings, corporate
Prudential-Bache, 57, 67

Random walk, 35–36, 54. *See also* Efficient market hypothesis
Real Estate, 3
    effect of tax shelters on investment returns, 157
    investment merits, 3
    portfolio diversification, 3
    tax shelters in, 160, 163
        real estate investment trusts (REITs), 164
Registered representatives, *see* Stockbrokers
Risk, 81–82
    defined, as variability of returns, 81–82
    effect of diversification on, 87–89
    and expected rates of return, 83–86
    foreign exchange, 127
    and holding period return, 84–85
    measured by beta, 91
    measured by S&P quality rankings, 126
    measured by variance of possible returns, 88
    portfolio, 87–89, 108–110

    proportional to returns, 29
    systematic, 89, 108, 118
        measuring, 90–91
        in tax shelters, 164–165
    unsystematic, 89–90, 108
    see also Beta; Leverage
Risk management, 78, 85
Rukeyser, Louis, 1

Schwed, Fred, 61, 72
Securities, *see* Bonds; Index mutual fund; Money market securities; Municipal bonds; Mutual funds; No-load mutual funds; Stock, common
Securities and Exchange Commission (SEC), 30, 31, 66, 67, 74, 149
Securities Investors Protection Corporation (SIPC), 150
Security Owners Stock Guide, 125, 126
Share, *see* Stock, common
Sharpe, W.F., 181–182
Shearson/American Express, 57
Short selling, 38
Simon, Julian L., 20
Simplified Employee Pension plan (SEP IRA), 171
Sinquefield, R.A., 182
Smith Barney, 57
Solnick, Bruno, 127
Standard and Poor's 500 (S&P 500), 27, 28, 142
Stock, common, 11–14
    and average real rate of return in financial planning, 178–179
    earnings:
        as compensation for risk, 14
        reinvested, and expected dividends, 14
    foreign, for portfolio diversification, 127–128
        international mutual funds, 231–234
    holding period return, 81, 84, 85, 87, 90
    inflation protection, 103–104
    investment merits, 5–9
    investment objectives, 96–105
        blue chip stocks, 99, 104–105
        growth stocks, 99, 105
        maximum growth stocks, 99, 105
    investment vehicle, convenience, 5
    legal definition of, 13
    price:
        determination of, 6
        as financial information, 6–8
    prices and expected dividends, 14
    return-risk tradeoff, 81–87

Stock, common (*Continued*)
  returns, compared to debt, 103
  selection techniques, 124–125
  speculation, 175–176
  tax shelters with, 166–167
    effect of payout ratio, 167
  use in financial planning, 8–9
  see also Risk; Stock prices
Stockbrokers, 55–63
  commercial banks and thrift institutions, 149
    commission costs, 152, 153
  comparative value sales approach, 59, 61–62
  conflict of interest, 56–58
  full service brokers, 55, 60–63, 130–131
    compared to discount brokers, 130–131, 150, 151, 152, 153, 155
  as investment advisors, 55–63, 65
  investment timing sales approach, 59–60
  pressure to generate trading volume, 60–62
  sales tactics, 62–63
  title transfer, 149–150
    bundled with advisory services, 149
    role of broker and dealer, 149–150
  use of newsletters and research reports, 56–58
    bias towards short-term trading, 57
  see also Discount brokers; Investment advice industry
Stockholders, 13–14
  as owner-managers, 19
  role in corporation, 14
  see also Principal-agent contract
Stock market, determining value of information, 6, 33
Stock options, 18, 56, 176
Stock prices, 35–36, 42–46
  effect of time diversification on, 92–94
  fluctuations, 42–46, 92
  random walk, 35–36, 54
  reflecting future corporate profits, 6, 33, 42
  see also Efficient market hypothesis
Stock Reports, 125, 126
Stone, James, 32
Systematic risk, 89, 108, 118
  measurement of, 90–91, 108–110

Tangible assets, investment merits, 3–4
Taxes, *see* Tax shelters; Tax system; Transaction costs
Tax-exempt bonds, *see* Municipal bonds
Tax shelters, 157–174
  with common stocks, 166–167
    payout ratio, effect on, 167

  custodial services, 168
  general framework of, 160–163
  municipal bonds, 161–162, 171–174
  real estate, 160
    real estate investment trusts (REITs), 164
  retirement programs, 167–171
    individual retirement accounts (IRAs), 168–170
    Keogh and other plans, 170–171
  risk, 164–166
  tax-advantaged investments, 163–166
    leverage with, 163, 165
    limited partnership form, 163
    returns competed away by market, 163–164
  tax deferral type, 160–161
  tax reduction type, 161–163
  TIPP rules for effective tax planning, 159–160
  transaction costs of, 160, 164
  Uniform Gift to Minors Act, 166
  see also Municipal bonds
Tax system, 157–163
  complexity of, 157, 159
  effect:
    on investment decisions, 159
    on productivity, 158
    on taxpayer compliance, 158–159
  tax preferences, 157
  unintended results, 157–158
Technical analysis, 33–34, 60
  greed-fear cycle with, 34
  investment merits, 34–36
  see also Beat-the-market investment approach
Tinic, S.M., 182
Title transfer, 149–150
  bundled with advisory services, 149
  clearinghouse function, 150–151
  role of broker and dealer, 149–150
  see also Discount brokers
Total investment portfolio planning (TIPP), 77–105
  amount of unsystematic risk, 116, 143–144
  to avoid greed-fear cycle, 115
  effect on income and savings, 176–178
  and efficient market hypothesis, 80
  four components of, 86–98
  and principal-agent relationship, 80
  rules for effective tax planning, 159–160
  stability of portfolio beta, 111
  see also Buy-and-hold investment approach; Efficient market hypothesis; Portfolio management

INDEX

Towles, R.J., 181
Transaction costs, 78, 95–96, 116
  advisory fees, 63–65, 130–131, 164
  bid-ask spread, 149
  commissions:
    and advisory fees, 129–155
    brokerage, 148–156
  discount brokers, 148–156
  of dividend reinvestment plans, 132
  mutual funds, 136–147
  of rebalancing portfolio, 111
  rules for minimizing, 129–130
  stockbrokers, 55–63
  taxes, 157–174
  of tax-exempt bond funds, 173–174
  in tax shelters, 160, 164
  of typical no-load mutual fund, 139–143

Uniform Gift to Minors Act, 166

Unique risk, *see* Unsystematic risk
Unit investment trust, 174
University of Pennsylvania endowment fund, 69–70
Unsystematic risk, 89–90, 108
  portfolio diversification to eliminate, 87–89, 115–123
  in tax shelters, 165

Value Line Investment Survey, 125, 126
Vanguard Index Trust, 142
Veblen, Thorstein, 16

Wall Street, defined, 11
Wall Street Journal, 55, 68, 72
Weinstein, Stan, 66
West, R.R., 182

Your Guide to Mutual Funds, 138